The Sephardic Jews
of Spain and Portugal

The Sephardic Jews of Spain and Portugal

Survival of an Imperiled Culture in the Fifteenth and Sixteenth Centuries

DOLORES SLOAN
FOREWORD BY JONATHAN KIRSCH

McFarland & Company, Inc., Publishers
Jefferson, North Carolina, and London

LIBRARY OF CONGRESS CATALOGUING-IN-PUBLICATION DATA

Sloan, Dolores J.
  The Sephardic Jews of Spain and Portugal : survival of an imperiled culture in the fifteenth and sixteenth centuries / Dolores Sloan ; foreword by Jonathan Kirsch.
    p.   cm.
  Includes bibliographical references and index.

  ISBN 978-0-7864-3817-4
  softcover : 50# alkaline paper ∞

  1. Jews — Spain — History —15th century. 2. Jews — Spain — History —16th century. 3. Jews — Portugal — History — 15th century. 4. Jews — Portugal — History —16th century. 5. Sephardim — History — 15th century. 6. Sephardim — History — 16th century. 7. Spain — Ethnic relations. 8. Portugal — Ethnic relations. I. Title.
  DS135.S7S58   2009
  305.892'404609031—dc22   2008047026

British Library cataloguing data are available

©2009 Dolores J. Sloan. All rights reserved

No part of this book may be reproduced or transmitted in any form or by any means, electronic or mechanical, including photocopying or recording, or by any information storage and retrieval system, without permission in writing from the publisher.

On the cover: Santa María la Blanca, Toledo, Spain, ©2009 Tourist Office of Spain.

Manufactured in the United States of America

McFarland & Company, Inc., Publishers
  Box 611, Jefferson, North Carolina 28640
    www.mcfarlandpub.com

To Lisa, David, Victoria, Jimmy and Kim,
because history keeps memory alive.

To Everett and Tess,
because you write that history now.

To Dennis, because.

To the Sephardim and all those through time
who have been denied the openness of identity,

and to all who claim it now.

Acknowledgments

To everything there is a season, and for the beginning of this work it was the autumn of 1996 in New Mexico. Early encouragement from Randy Forrester and Gerard Martínez of the New Mexico Arts Division and from Priscilla Maurer, Betsy Robinson, JoAnn Duncan and Yolanda Dunaway was followed through the years by colleagues from PEN New Mexico, especially Ron Christ, Nancy Fay, and Barbara Riley.

In Los Angeles, Trudi Alexy took me under her wing and saw that I met her agent, Julie Popkin, who eventually would become mine. She also directed me to Arthur Benveniste, who was to open the richness of his Sephardic world to me. Trudi's books and presentations brought insight into the world of the crypto Jew, enriching us with the generosity of a free spirit and the passion of a storyteller.

The fluid prose and perceptive research of Jonathan Kirsch grace the Foreword of this volume. He prepared it, coincidentally, having just sent his own work on the Inquisition off to his publisher. I am also grateful to Jonathan for his guidance with publication matters, but foremost, for the warmth and quality of his friendship.

Raymond P. Scheindlin is most appreciated for permission to reprint his translation of Judah Abravanel's mournful poem and for the insightful e-mail that deepened understanding of the time and events. Anita Novinsky alerted me to her 1967 *Commentary* article about Belmonte, Portugal, which includes a prayer now gracing a page in this volume, and to selections from her epic studies on Brazil's crypto Jews. Peter Cole helped secure permission to quote from his sensitive translations of the poetry of Muslim and Christian Spain. Dirk Hansen's skills as cartographer resulted in most effective maps, while David Hirsch and Jon Hargis opened the door to UCLA's map resources.

The Society for Crypto-Judaic Studies became a rich storehouse of resource material on those Sephardic Jews who came to the New World centuries ago to escape the Inquisition. I was exposed to remarkable scholarship as editor of SCJS's publication, *HaLapid*, and participated at the Society's annual conferences. Particularly helpful has been the research of Stanley Hordes and Abraham Lavender. SCJS colleagues and friends who have enriched my work with their research, photographs and, in some cases, personal stories, include Kathleen Alcalá, Judy Frankel, Randy Baca Hensel, Mona Hernandez, Cary Herz, Sonya Loya, Roger Martínez, Louise Pitta Polsky, Gloria Trujillo and Genie Milgrom.

More rich resources came from Sephardic Synagogue Tifereth Israel of Los Angeles and the Sephardic Singles *Havurah* that had its beginnings there. Members passed along stories and legends of fabled ancestors, putting flesh and blood on the bones of my research. I am especially grateful to Ruby Hanan and Esther Eshkenazi-Gunther, whose efforts have brought me before audiences to speak on the subject, as have Eric Gordon of the Workman's Circle and Evelyn Hoffman, representing several Southern California area organizations.

Numerous professionals of all backgrounds have enriched the process. Kathleen Teltsch reviewed the completed manuscript, contributing her knowledge and skill as the first *New York Times* writer to report on many of the more contemporary events covered in the book. She also provided resource materials from her archives, but most treasured of all, the support of a warm friendship. Bernadette Gabay Dyer, Linda Janakos, Abraham Lavender, Jutta Schamp, and Emily Taitz — writers and scholars all — reviewed the manuscript as well, offering trenchant consultation at different stages of progress. Jutta made herself available whenever needed to preview a section and offer feedback. Kathleen Alcalá brought counsel on publication matters and insights from her own experience as author. Lisa Sloan Strom was irreplaceable — proofreading end notes and helping with the minutiae of images, captions and permissions.

Not enough can be said about the readiness of Art Benveniste to resolve computer challenges, advise on graphics and image reproduction and review the glossary. Kathleen LeMieux also put her experience at our disposal, making it possible to access sources needed in Spain, and cheerfully reviewing letters written painstakingly in Spanish.

Mary Kranz and Marjorie Acevedo, of the Doheny Library at Mount St. Mary's College, guided me to sources for hard-to-find quotations and images. Jim Kendall utilized his background in online research to uncover sources for maps. Rabbi Carrie Benveniste helped with occasional translation from Hebrew and Michele Green helped with translation from Portuguese. An indefatigable Gad Nassi kept books, articles and e-mail streaming across continents from Tel Aviv, since first contacted a decade past about his fine publication on Doña Gracia Nasi. Babette Sparr believed in this work from the beginning and contributed knowledgeable support in getting the manuscript read.

Others who have smoothed the pathway of the work are members of the Biographers Group and the PEN Fiction Writers Group. Thanks also to Dan Khoury for his ability to rescue images, turning a virtual sow's ear into a silk purse, and to Patricia Alpizar for her encouragement and help with translation.

The research coincided providentially with the flowering of cyberspace in the past two decades, the Internet now a resident in one's home and both tool and toy for cross-border interaction. It was a fortunate day when I found www.saudades-sefarad.org, about the descendants of Portuguese Jews, and its inspirational host, Rufina Bernardetti Silva Mausenbaum, who invited me to speak on a 2002 conference tour of Portugal's Jewish past. I also discovered www.sephardim.com, award-winning Web site on Sephardic names, whose host, Harry Stein, and wife Daisy made available the photo of the Abravanel coat of arms, Daisy's illustrious legacy. There is not a day when I do not pick up some useful information from a posting or e-mail by a *prima* or *primo* from the *saudades-sefarad, anousim* or *apellidos sefarditos* forums.

I celebrate the collegiality and support for each other's projects from my colleagues at Mount St. Mary's College, particularly Professors Elizabeth Sturgeon, Joan Johnson and Tom Walla and Sister Carol Brong.

Through the years, I was privileged to hear the stories of many from the villages of northern New Mexico, sometimes told in confidence. Their trust and courage made much of this possible. To Ana Pacheco, for her efforts to preserve the history of this rich heritage in *La Herencia* and her valued friendship, ¡*gracias!*

Now and always, appreciation for my family, without whom nothing would have any meaning: Dennis New; Lisa Sloan Strom, David and Everett Strom; Victoria Sloan; and Jimmy Sloan, Kim Fox and Tess Monet Sloan — very present along the journey. And to my first muses, parents Pearl and Bob Malis, and grandmothers Ida Malis and Rose Brandt — your encouragement kept the garden watered from earliest days.

Table of Contents

Acknowledgments vii
Foreword by Jonathan Kirsch 1
Preface: Of Storytelling and History 5

ONE. On the Eve of Expulsion: Visiting Sephardic Homes
in 1492 13

TWO. Isaac Abravanel: *¡Basta mi nombre que es Abravanel!*
It is enough to know my name is Abravanel! 26

THREE. Abraham Zacuto: From Discovery by the Stars to a
Crater on the Moon 53

FOUR. Luís de Santángel: Spain's Disraeli and *Converso* Bridge
to the New World 74

FIVE. Doña Gracia Nasi: "Piety of Miriam, strength of Judith" . . 101

SIX. "Thou preparest a table before me": Jewish Life in Cities,
Towns, Countryside 127

SEVEN. "In the presence of my enemies": Work, Usury,
Clothing and Entertainment 146

EIGHT. Resilience and Recovery: Turkey and Brazil, Two
Diaspora Communities 161

NINE. Endurance, Persistence and Identity: Insights from
the Sephardic Experience 180

Appendix: Judah Abravanel to His Son 201

Chapter Notes 209
Bibliographical Sources 219
Comments on Sources 225
Glossary 229
Index 233

Let scripture be your garden
and the Arabs' books your paradise grove...

*—Dunash ben Labrat,
mid–tenth century**

---

*Peter Cole, trans., ed. & intro. *The Dream of the Poem.* ©2007 by Princeton University Press. Reprinted by permission of Princeton University Press.

Foreword
by Jonathan Kirsch

Spain has imprinted itself on our collective imagination as the imperial power that opened the New World for exploration and settlement, a fact of history that is still celebrated as a national holiday in the United States, all to the delight of Italian-Americans and the despair of Native Americans. Christopher Columbus may have been born in Genoa, but his voyages of discovery were sponsored by *Los Reyes Católicos*, Fernando of Aragón and Isabel of Castilla. Long after the decline and fall of the Spanish empire, its fingerprints can be detected in the languages, folkways and politics of both North and South America.

But there are other reasons to ponder the history of Spain, which was sometimes glorious, sometimes tragic, and often both at once. At the opening of the third millennium, an era in which some observers regard the encounter between the Judeo-Christian West and the Islamic world as an apocalyptic "clash of civilizations," it is appropriate to recall that Spain was the only place in the West where Christians, Muslims and Jews lived in harmony and prosperity, a phenomenon known in Spanish usage as *la convivencia*—the Coexistence. So it was that one monarch in medieval Castilla proudly called himself "the king of three religions," and when a Spanish village was afflicted by drought, the clergy of all three faiths were invited to gather in the public square to pray for rain.

But it is also true that *la convivencia* came to a decisive end after seven centuries in the same year that Columbus and his toybox fleet sailed for China and ended up in the Caribbean. The kingdom of Granada, the last stronghold of Islamic sovereignty on the Iberian Peninsula, was finally conquered in 1492. And, in the same year, the grand inquisitor of the Spanish Inquisition — the notorious Tomás de Torquemada — prevailed on the Catholic Monarchs to issue a decree of expulsion that offered the Jewish community in

Spain a cruel and fateful choice — to convert to Catholicism or leave Spain forever. The same fate soon befell the Jews of Portugal. Thus began the Iberian version of the diaspora, a saga that is explored so richly and so compellingly by Dolores Sloan in the pages that follow.

The ugly facts of the Jewish expulsion are almost wholly overlooked nowadays. Somewhat better known is the heartbreaking dilemma of the Jews who consented to convert to Christianity in order to stay in their Spanish or Portuguese homes and then discovered that the Inquisition was determined to search out even the earnest converts and put them to the flames as "secret Jews." Not until the twentieth century would the world see an atrocity of the same Kafkaesque logic — the arrest, torture and execution of men, women and children whose only crime was the Jewish blood in their veins. Indeed, the Spanish laws of *limpieza de sangre*—"purity of blood"— anticipated the Nuremberg Laws of Nazi Germany by five hundred years.

As the reader will soon discover, the Jews of Sefarad — the Hebrew word for Spain — succeeded in creating a rich civilization of their own under *la convivencia*. Poetry and philosophy, often written in Arabic rather than Hebrew, flourished under the more benign Islamic rulers in Spain. The lingua franca of Spanish Jewry was a melodious blend of Hebrew and Spanish known as Ladino, and their music carried the notes and rhythms of both Iberia and the Maghreb. The foods they ate, the clothing they wore, even the way they prayed were rich and unique in ways that set them apart from their fellow Jews elsewhere in Europe.

Memories of Sefarad have always inspired a certain reverence and even exaltation among Jews around the world. The epoch that Fernando and Isabel sought to write out of Spanish history was regarded as a Golden Age, and rightfully so. Sephardic blood was regarded as a mark of distinction, even a kind of nobility. Indeed, some Jewish families commissioned genealogical studies — and some still do — in the hope that they would produce evidence to link them to the glorious days of the distant past. Benjamin Disraeli, one of many examples, appears to have invented some of the details of his own cherished Sephardic roots, an episode that demonstrates the allure of the dreams of Sefarad.

Concealed behind the scrim of memory and fantasy, however, are the hard facts of history. The plight of the Jews of Spain and Portugal in the fifteenth and sixteenth centuries is an episode that merits our attention not merely because of its exotic setting and surprising events, but because it says so much about the world in which we live today. To be sure, the parallels between the Spanish expulsion and the Holocaust are so striking that Cecil Roth, writing about the Spanish Inquisition in 1937, felt obliged to warn his readers that his book was not merely a parody of current events. But there are other resonances to be found here — the Jewish men and women whose lives are described here were caught in a no-man's-land between contending religions and cultures and political structures, the same grim landscape that exists all over the globe today.

Above all, the author allows us to see the human face of history. She gives names and biographies to the gifted and courageous but largely forgotten men and women whose lives were put at risk by the ambitions of kings and inquisitors. She retrieves the records of their accomplishments in arts and letters, commerce and diplomacy, science and theology. She shows the strategies for survival that enabled them to save their own lives and to preserve the rich legacy that they bestowed on the Jewish civilization. And Sloan does all of these things with a sure grasp of the intimate politics of human affairs, a scholar's command of the data and the powerful voice of a storyteller.

Jonathan Kirsch is the author of 11 books, including *The Grand Inquisitor's Manual: A History of Terror in the Name of God* (HarperOne, 2008). He is an adjunct professor at New York University, a guest commentator and broadcaster for KPCC-FM and KCRW-FM in Southern California, a book reviewer for the *Los Angeles Times*, and an attorney specializing in intellectual property law.

Are there words enough in all of song
    to praise the pen? Who else could bear
the burden of bringing back the past
and preserving it then as though with myrrh?

It has no ear with which it might hear,
    or mouth with which to offer answers;
and yet the pen, in a single stroke,
at once does both — observes and remembers.

> —*Shem Tov Ardutiel (Santob de Carrión),*
> *late thirteenth century, after 1345**

---

*Peter Cole, trans., ed. & intro. *The Dream of the Poem.* ©2007 by Princeton University Press. Reprinted by permission of Princeton University Press.

Preface: Of Storytelling and History

They watched the Romans come and go, saw the Vandals and Visigoths slay and slaughter. They melded their talents and skills with the conquering Muslims — like them, children of Abraham, father to both religions — who used them well and taught them much. They served loyally the reconquering Christian sires of Aragón and Valencia and Catalunya, yes, and Castilla. Their maps charted the way to victory for the galleons, cogs and caravels built in the shipyards of Barcelona. Their applications of math and astronomy created and improved the instruments of Portuguese and Spanish navigators and explorers. Their understanding of negotiation and world affairs found them sought after by monarchs for delicate diplomacy. Their ships brought sweets and spices to the tables of the titled and wealthy. Their artisans and craftsmen, musicians and poets created objects and words to adorn and appreciate. And their men of medicine ministered to royalty and commoner alike. Their sweat sweetened the soil of Sefarad.

The stream of Jewish life in Spain coursed for two millennia throughout the land they named after the prophet Obadiah's reference in the bible to "the captivity of Jerusalem that is in Sefarad." Still, they were to be outsiders always, thriving or surviving at the pleasure or displeasure of the host people, who changed with the waves of conquest and reconquest through the centuries.

Storytelling is both practical and magical. It is the ancient and revered handmaiden of the oral tradition, passing along history and mythology and communal values from one generation to another.

I have always held in awe those who tell the stories of the past. I first experienced this tradition in the northern villages and pueblos of New Mexico when my work for colleges and arts agencies took me there in the 1990s. I learned how *los viejitos*, the old ones, in traditional Hispanic homes and Native American elders in pueblos and reservations, have passed along tales, myths and legends on long, cold winter nights, as several generations sit warming themselves by the fire. The storyteller is as familiar a figure in the pottery from the Indian pueblos of northern New Mexico as is the *santero*, the artist of sacred subjects, who recounts legends and spiritual images through the various genres of Spanish colonial art. I remember with pleasure that delightful afternoon in the village of Mora, listening while venerable residents shared and debated infinite varieties of *La Llorona*, the legend of the crying woman, who must wander eternally looking for present day children to replace her own, whom she had put to death for reasons still argued over. Many a parent has secured a child's compliance by threatening a visit from the ghostly woman to steal away the defiant youngster. And I remember well the tales of my grandmother and her sisters, some solemn, some humorous, about the people of their ancestral village, the wise and the foolish, who became symbols of types of behavior by virtue of their legendary acts.[1]

And so, I gladly — yet humbly — take on the role of storyteller alongside that of researcher of Sephardic history, passing along to present generations selections from the millennia-old records and memories of a people with whom my own personal genealogical search indicates the potential of common ancestry. I wish to help increase the awareness of the Sephardim of medieval Iberia and the culture they shared for close to 2,000 years before their expulsion from Spain in 1492 and forced conversion in Portugal in 1497. Their achievements had enriched both the lands they left behind and those they were to settle in next. Study reveals their accomplishments: in science, medicine, philosophy, the arts, economy and government, as well as the not-so-noble acts that went along with membership in the human race. This was a people easy to romanticize, and the researcher must always be alert to the temptation to let the shining illumination of their greatness cover the shadows in the lives of very real people. This was — is — a people who continue to recreate sense and order in response to repeated disruption of their lives by unpredictable and violent acts. Their survival to this day is testament to their ability to maintain sacred practices and nurture sacred memories.

How and why did this volume evolve? The muse for the book first appeared during a trip to Spain in the summer of 1996, but probably had its roots in a series of life experiences beginning when I was eight years old. My interest in things Spanish began with a present of *The Little Spanish Dancer* by Madeline Brandeis. The book interlaces tales of a girl who dances flamenco with the history of medieval and renaissance Spain. In a chapter on Christopher Columbus, I had read that "Perhaps Columbus was a Jew who changed his religion and nationality.... This could well have been because at that time the Jews in Spain were being tortured and sent away from their country."[2]

This curious statement did not catch the attention of the eight-year-old reader. Decades, even scores of years, had passed before it stood out. I was more caught up in identifying with the fictional Pilar, her magic castanets, and how she attracted the greatest dancing master in all of Sevilla. Interest in Columbus, besides the reality of a school holiday, was to be postponed until I moved to New Mexico in 1990, and learned about the *conversos,* converted ones, or crypto Jews of the southwest. It was then that I began to look into why and how the Sephardim, as Jews had called themselves in the Muslim and Spanish Kingdoms, had left their homeland of at least twenty centuries.

In northern New Mexico, I worked with and became close to descendants of early settlers from Spain, who had come through *el Paso del Norte* via the Camino Real, along the Rio Grande, some with Juan de Oñate as early as 1598. The river was then called *el río bravo.* Wonderful word, *bravo,* translating as fierce, savage, wild, as well as brave, excellent and magnificent.[3] It took people of a similar ilk to penetrate the untamed northern frontiers of New Spain, to dare to plant crops in the hard soil during the short growing season, to risk the Apache and Comanche raids on intruder settlers. These were folks with nothing to lose and everything to gain from putting untamed space between them and the Holy Office, the Inquisition and its terror that had followed émigrés from Spain to the New World. I learned from Hispanic friends how the popularity of Old Testament first names in their families' villages pointed to the Jewish ancestry among many early settlers and their descendants, as Catholics traditionally name children after saints. I heard about the secret lighting of candles to this very day in some families on Friday night and the veneration of a saint called Esther around Easter, thinking they were simply passing on family customs, unaware of the association with Judaism.

Before leaving on my first trip to Spain in 1996, I researched briefly the history of the Jews in Spain, enough to know that Toledo and the cities of Andalucía had synagogues and other Sephardic structures, artifacts and monuments, preserved and accessible. And so, I traveled from Madrid to Salamanca, Toledo, Córdoba, Sevilla, Ronda, Granada and Barcelona. My pre-trip studies were superficial enough to shield me from knowing that the ashes of *conversos,* burned at the stake for secretly observing Judaism, had once drifted over the lovely plazas where I was dining on *paella* and *gazpacho* and enjoying performances of music and dance.

My reading had referred to Luís de Santángel, and how this *converso* finance minister and trusted courtier of the Catholic monarchs had made funding possible for Columbus' journey. Then I came upon a large metal sculpture honoring him in a museum, commemorating his crucial role in the voyage of discovery. Later, in Granada, there was Santángel's name again, carved at the base of the Columbus monument, paying tribute to him and others who had supported the navigator.

My limited overview of Judaica in medieval Spain included the Maimonides monument and the nearby medieval synagogue in Córdoba and the narrow streets with Sephardic names in the former Jewish district of Sevilla. I visited Toledo's *El Tránsito* synagogue and museum and was made aware, in several cities, of privately owned buildings that had once been Jewish houses of worship. A friendly Spanish woman, with whom I chatted while walking the windy streets of Granada's Albaicín, pointed out what appeared to be the imprint of a *mezuzah*, the traditional miniature scroll of the first five books of the bible, still etched on a doorway in the old Jewish quarter.

I returned from the trip, impressed with what I had learned about the depth to which Sephardic culture had been a part of both Muslim and Christian Spain, and determined to memorialize the richness of that culture and the heights reached by Sephardic individuals. I wanted to learn more about the contributions they had made despite the ever present reality of persecution and death, and pass that knowledge on. Awareness of their achievements would be enlightening, I believed, to present-day Jews and non–Jews alike. And, so, this book.

Raised by American-born parents with immigrant grandparents from the Austro-Hungarian Empire and Poland, I had not yet learned of the considerable presence and culture of the Jews of Spain. I did not realize that the place of origin for three of my grandparents had been part of Poland in the fifteenth and sixteenth centuries, and that the rulers had been hospitable to Jews after the expulsion and to *conversos* in the years that followed. This might explain, I realized, why my mother told me of the family legend that their ancestors came from Spain.

How many descendants of Sephardim are aware of their ancestors' glory? How many Jews and non–Jews know of its poetry, literature, music and dance? About the scientific contributions by Jewish mathematicians, cartographers, astronomers and physicians, such as Abraham Zacuto, Joseph Vicinho and the Cresques family? Of the significant roles Sephardic Jews played in advising kings and queens, with titles such as Royal Counselor (Abraham Seneor), Royal Treasurer (Gabriel Sánchez), Chancellor of the Royal Household (Luís de Santángel), Finance Adviser (Isaac Abravanel)? What about the banking families, so called because in addition to spices, gems and textiles, their vessels carried letters of credit and financial instruments, who furthered economic development throughout the known world? Doña Gracia Nasi belonged to one of those families and shepherded her enterprises and enormous wealth with wisdom and generosity in a patriarchal world.

Furthermore, how many know that the Jews were indeed an integral part of the Iberian Peninsula, probably since the destruction of the Temple in Jerusalem in the second century BCE? They were not relative newcomers to the soil of what is now Spain and Portugal, but long term inhabitants, with close to 2,000 years of life on Spanish soil.[4]

In all cultures, adults and children alike delight in stories of those who brave danger for their beliefs and principles. Every people needs to hear its own stories, for no one is exempt from the challenge to define, sometimes defend, one's cultural inheritance.[5]

This book focuses on nine individuals who became known and respected in Sephardic life during the era bridging the middle ages and the early modern period: Isaac Abravanel, Luís de Santángel, Abraham Zacuto, Doña Gracia Nasi, Amatus Lusitanus, Samuel Usque, Saadiah Longo, Moses Almosnino and Moses Hamon. However, great men and women are everywhere, in all social and economic classes, as they were in medieval Spain and Portugal and the diaspora. Although the literature is sparse, there were, doubtless, unsung individuals, Jew and Gentile, whose acts before and after expulsion and persecution merit acknowledgment. For example, we know about Don Isaac Abravanel inspiring and encouraging Jews in those fearsome pre-exile days, and Doña Gracia, safe in the Ottoman Empire after a long exile, urging on an economic boycott of Ancona for the burning of twenty-four Jews. There were also acts of courage and daring by Old Christians to protect Sephardic neighbors and colleagues. The Venetian printer Daniel Bomberg was one of these, active in an underground railroad network helping endangered Jews escape from Portugal.[6] These deeds, alas, go largely unreported in written or oral tradition, but they likely existed, because the present day experience of the Holocaust manifests everywhere righteous non–Jews who took life-threatening risks to save lives.[7]

My research convinces me that Judaism will not vanish as a faith, nor will Jews vanish as an ethnic people. The phenomenon of Jewish communities in Portugal and China, along with others in Africa and India, shows how the Law of Moses survives, although its rituals and practices may be transformed through the centuries from lack of contact with the mainstream and the life and death need for secrecy. We find this also in Spanish and New World sites, such as Mexico, Brazil, the American Southwest and New England. The identity with the greater whole appears to remain through time on some level of racial memory, until something retrieves it and brings it to recognition.[8]

I have attempted in this work to separate fact from hypothesis with documentation. Still, sparse records have made it necessary sometimes to "fill in" the blanks between what is documented with what, reasonably, could have taken place, given what is known of a person's character, personality and history, and of the lifestyles of those of comparable socioeconomic origins. I have let the reader know what is documented and what is conjectured.

Proper names have been spelled as they appear in Spanish-speaking countries and, when relevant, in Portuguese-speaking ones. For example, "Fernando and Isabel" appears rather than "Ferdinand and Isabella" and "Sevilla" rather than "Seville." Where eminent historians have disagreed, I have selected the choices of most recent scholars. Examples are "Zacuto" rather than "Zacut" and "Abravenel" rather than "Abarbanel" and other variations.

I write for those, Jew and non–Jew alike, who want to know more about this remarkable people. When most of Europe and the Christian world were just waking up in the darkness, the bright sun of the Sephardim illumined life in Iberia and the post-expulsion diaspora. It is testimony to the intelligence and resilience of men and women whose adventures and adversities, loves and losses, combined with intellectual and spiritual gifts to create a Golden Age, with benefits extending beyond their own experiences to us all. May we learn from their feats and their failings.

In the end there left, without strength, three hundred thousand people on foot, from the youngest to the oldest, all at one time, from all the provinces of the king, to wherever they were able to go. Their King went before them, God at their helm. Some went to Portugal and Navarre, which are close, but all they found were troubles and darkness, looting, starvation and pestilence. Some traveled through the perilous ocean, and here, too, God's hand was against them, and many were seized and sold as slaves, while many others drowned in the sea.... In the end, all suffered....

—*Isaac Abravanel**

---

*Isaac Abravanel. "Introduction to the Former Prophets." In David Raphael, ed., *The Expulsion 1492 Chronicles* (North Hollywood, CA: Carmi House, 1992), page 53.

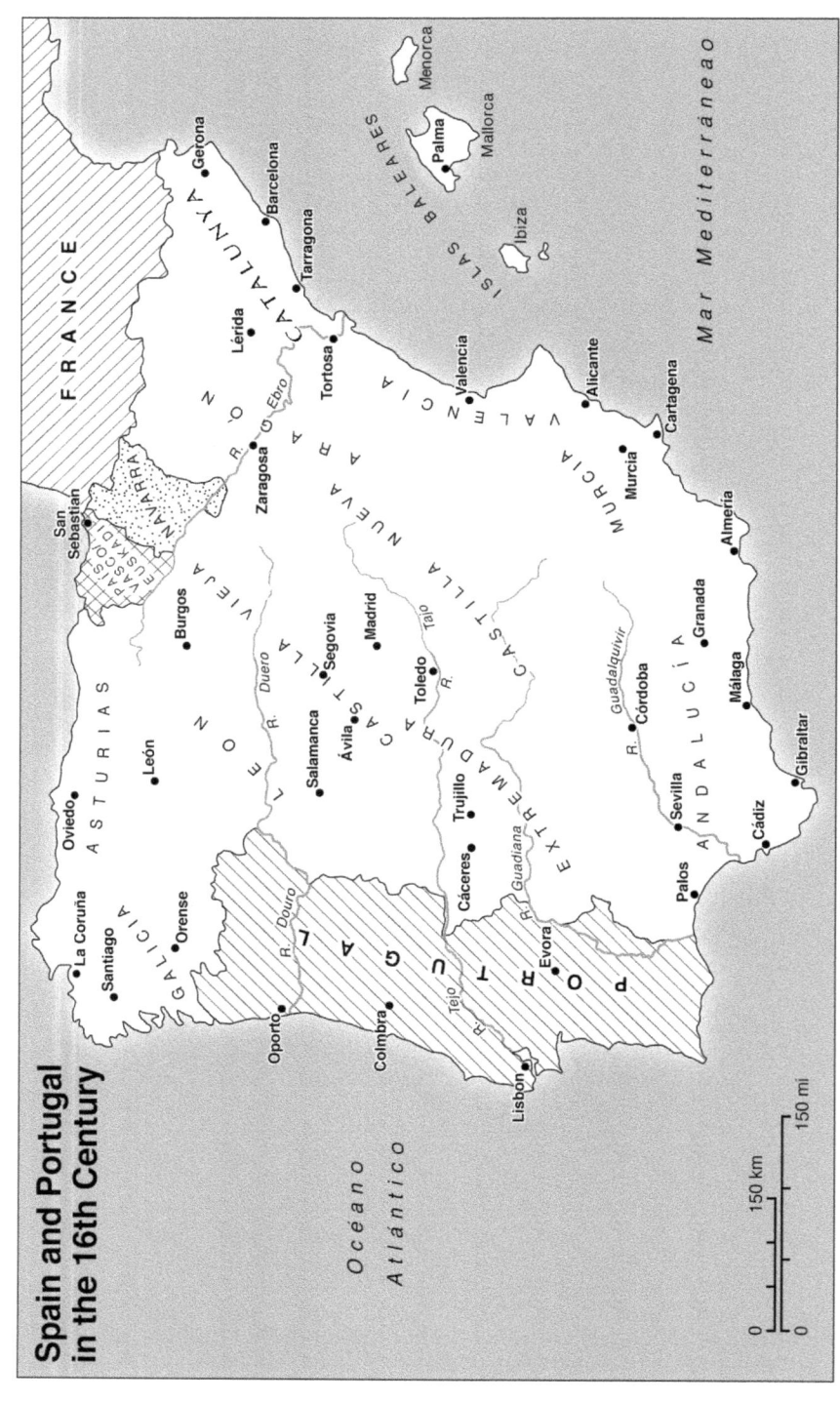

ONE

On the Eve of Expulsion: Visiting Sephardic Homes in 1492

Travelers to Spain in midsummer are well acquainted with the prevailing custom of late evening dinners and even later bedtimes, the streets alive with people well into the pre-dawn hours. Except for those whose work or circumstances require it, the streets are relatively empty in the long afternoons and early evenings, as those who can, wait indoors for the promise of coolness when the sun at last allows the baked earth to rest.

The midsummer heat of July could not have been much different in 1492 in Sefarad, as the Jews called Spain. Before the summer of the expulsion, one could take the heat in stride, knowing that in the time of one moon, it would begin to cool, and life would go on in ways Jewish people expected after 1,500 years or more on Iberian soil. That July, however, there was no such expectation in the *calls* and *juderías*—as Jewish quarters were called, depending on region and dialect. That summer was different because 100,000 to 200,000 Jews were preparing to leave home and country forever within a few days, crowding the high roads on the way to border crossings and seaports.[1]

A mass migration, which had already begun, would soon reach its zenith, shaking the foundations of the land and changing the meaning of home for hundreds of thousands of people. It was surprising that so many were still following the Law of Moses after one hundred years of increasing persecution and violence intended to force conversion to Christianity. Indeed, the Alhambra Decree, issued by *Los Reyes Católicos*, Fernando and Isabel, that year on March 31, accused the Jews of enticing thousands of New Christians, who had abandoned their faith at the baptismal founts, to return to Jewish practices. It expelled forever, from the recently unified Spain, those who were still observing their ancestral religion, requiring them to leave by August 3. During the summer of 1492, they would have to walk away from homes and lands, businesses and trades, synagogues and communities; abandon millennia-old cemeteries where *los antepasados*, the ancestors, lay buried. There were kinsmen, friends, rabbis, teachers, neighbors they would never see again. Families would be separated in the chaos of crossing borders, boarding ships or making their way past often hostile onlookers to embarkation points.

Observers recorded what they saw and heard. The Dominican priest Andrés Bernáldez, whose writings show anything but sympathy for non–Catholics, described the heavy price of exile for departing Jews.

> And in everything, they had miserable misfortunes. Indeed, the Christians took their many estates, rich houses and landed properties for a small amount of money.... They exchanged a house for an ass, and a vineyard for a small piece of cloth or linen, because they could not take out either gold or silver.[2]

It was no surprise that the difficulties experienced were even greater for the less prosperous and the poor, for nothing came without cost. Countless thousands did not have the funds needed for sea passage if one's family were to reach the Italian States, the Lowlands and even relatively near North Africa. And to settle in the Ottoman Empire, one had to face an arduous overland

The Jewish presence in Spain goes back perhaps two millennia. This ancient tombstone can be viewed in Toledo's Sephardic Museum, adjacent to the fourteenth century *Tránsito* Synagogue. Toledo was regarded as an important center of Hebraic scholarship in the Middle Ages. (Tourist Office of Spain in Los Angeles.)

journey through the Levant or across the Balkans, in addition to sea travel. Many thousands had no choice but to cross relatively nearby borders into Portugal and Navarra. Unlike well-to-do coreligionists, most could not pay the bribes to smuggle out forbidden gold, silver or currency.

In addition to selling what they could to New and Old Christians, there was food to prepare for the journey, clothing to be selected and packed. It was an intense, weeding out process, picking the very few keepsakes for packing. How did people decide what to take along and what to abandon as they left for an uncertain future in new lands?

It is a daunting challenge, in this early part of the twenty-first century, to convey a true sense of the impact that the expulsion of the Jews in 1492 had on Spain, the land where their roots reached two millennia deep, and on the society they were leaving. It is challenging because our own age dwarfs the numbers affected with its much higher figures and updated, grand-scale horrors. Yet our purpose here is not to focus on persecution and homelessness, although they are certainly a significant part of the picture, as are resilience and survival. It is to tell about a people and their Golden Age of accomplishments, noteworthy in the Europe of the time, and certainly unique for a population of Jews, compared with their brethren to the north and east. The Sephardic Jews of Spain and Portugal distinguished themselves over a period of 800 years or more with significant contributions to the sciences and medicine, to statecraft and political economy, to finance and commerce, to philosophy and the arts, and to the important skills enhancing the quality of day-to-day life. History records the legacy of their achievements, the benefits still being reaped.

We have chosen to begin with the portraits of four individuals, well-known in their time, then move on to the many thousands more of Spain's Sephardic population who were not so prominent. What does the record tell of their days before August 3, 1492, the deadline for departure, which ironically fell that year on the same day as Tish Ba'av, the solemn day when observant Jews mourn the destruction of the temple in Jerusalem?

As the family of Isaac Abravanel prepared to leave their home in Guadalajara for Valencia, where they would board a ship for the Italian peninsula, the distinguished statesman awaited an important visitor, representing the king. Luís de Santángel, chancellor of the royal household, or *escribano de ración*, of Aragón, trusted courtier of Fernando and Isabel, had been dispatched to deliver a very large sum of money to the monarchs' chief financial adviser.[3] Isaac Abravanel and Luís de Santángel had crossed paths often as highly-placed advisers to the Catholic Majesties of Spain. It is doubtful that they were friends or confidants. While both were statesmen and financiers to Fernando and Isabel, they could not have been more different in background and situation.

A devout Judaic scholar as well as courtier, Abravanel's writings on the bible were pored over by students of Judaism. He had become the acknowledged spokesman for professing Jews in Spain, having argued with king and queen to stop the edict of expulsion from going into effect. In contrast, Luís de Santángel was a *converso*, a man of commerce whose family had been converted from Judaism to Catholicism three-quarters of a century earlier, during a period of intense conversionary pressures. The baptism had taken place under the sponsorship of Bishop Santángel, hence the family's Christian name.

These two such remarkable — and different — men came together as Don Isaac prepared to leave the land. From their home in Guadalajara, fifty-six kilometers northeast of Madrid, the Abravanels planned to make the two-day journey to Valencia, their eastern port of departure, as the deadline of August 3 grew near.

Thus, this late July meeting brought one of the most powerful men in newly-unified Spain to the home of a soon-to-be-exiled statesman and biblical scholar. For the Abravanel family, this would be the third, but not final, flight from a country of residence. A century earlier, Don Isaac's grandfather, Samuel, chief accountant to the Court of Castilla, had fled to Portugal to be able to practice Judaism openly. He had converted to Christianity in the 1380s during severe conversionary pressures, but remained staunchly devoted to his ancestral faith. In his new country, he gained financial and political prominence once again.

Two generations later, his Portuguese-born grandson, Isaac, became a trusted official of King Alfonso's court, like father and grandfather before him, serving monarchs with their skills in diplomacy, economics and finance. After Alfonso's sudden death in 1481, however, everything changed for Don Isaac, who fell into disfavor with João, the new monarch. Accused of conspiring with royal enemies, he fled across the border into Spain, joined later by his family. His skills well known to the Spanish majesties, he was called upon soon after to serve as financial adviser. Ten years later, however, the Abravanels were preparing once again for an unsought departure and subsequent loss of wealth.

In contrast, the visitor that August morning, Luís de Santángel, was not directly affected by the expulsion order. His prosperous mercantile clan would enhance even more its great wealth and position of court influence, benefiting as New Christians, who were not subject to the economic and other restrictions on Jews — or to the edict of expulsion. Moreover, Fernando was known to be fond of Santángel, who had served him with loyalty and generosity. As

One. On the Eve of Expulsion

The marriage of Fernando and Isabel in 1469, bringing together their respective kingdoms, Aragón and Castilla, established them as *Los Reyes Católicos*, the Catholic Monarchs. They were determined to capture Granada, the remaining Muslim toehold on the Iberian Peninsula. (Padre Mariana, *La Historia de España,* Vol. VIII [Valencia: Benito Montfort, 1795]. In Generalitat Valenciana, ed. *Lluís de Santàngel y su época: un nuevo hombre, un mundo nuevo* [Valencia: 1992], 245.)

escribano mayor, he was close to the king's ear. As *contador mayor,* chief accountant, a position he also held, Santángel administered Aragón's treasury.[4] Wealth and prominence, however, could not protect all who bore his surname from the long arm of the Inquisition: his own mother had been imprisoned, then freed, and members of their family had been lost to the ever kindled flames before that.

As different as they were in temperament, personality, and religious path, Abravanel and Santángel had joined in the past for common causes. They had provided funds making possible the immanent journey of the Genoese navigator Christopher Columbus, who was then preparing his ships to sail from the port near Cádiz on August 3, the same deadline for Jews to leave Spanish soil. Both men had made badly needed loans for the Catholic Majesties' military efforts to take Granada from the Muslims. In fact, Don Isaac's loan to the Crown of 1,500,000 maravedis, along with funds from other Jews and New Christians, came at a crucial time in the siege, when finances were desperately needed for military supplies. It was this loan that brought the two men together that day. The king had sent Don Luís to repay the debt, and to grant permission for Abravanel to take a considerable amount of the funds out of the country with him.[5] This was quite an exception to the terms of the expulsion order, which severely limited exiles' exit money and possessions. It was even more remarkable, considering that Don Isaac had been the leading spokesman for practicing Jews, representing them vigorously and assertively before the Crown. All efforts to rescind the expulsion having failed, his was the strongest public voice urging coreligionists to defy conversion and leave the country.

There are some clues about their last recorded meeting that day, held against a backdrop of fast-moving historical events. The royal couple had pressured Abravanel to convert at the last minute, to follow the recent example of prominent courtier Abraham Seneor, who had joined Don Isaac in arguing before king and queen against the expulsion order. Conversionary efforts failed, despite Fernando's abortive efforts to have Abravanel's grandson kidnapped.[6] The king then made known that Abravanel and his family could remain without converting because of their value to crown and country. But Don Isaac had long made his path clear as outspoken and inspirational leader for Jews, committed to their covenant with God. The same defiance that he had demonstrated with the monarchs, when he and Seneor had failed to halt the expulsion, might also have been evident in his last meeting with Santángel.

The business of the day over, Santángel had yet to report to the Catholic monarchs on the success of his mission. At the time, they were holding court at Granada, wrested so recently from the Muslims after the surrender of Boabdil, their leader. There, they had taken up residence at the Alhambra, with its varied, yet orderly, lush vegetation and the ever present water, sparkling in fountains and acequias, the rectangular ditches connected to the river. We do not know his thoughts as his coach passed through Toledo, then the countryside of al-Andalus, on his way to the jewel of the vanquished Muslim empire, but given the inflammatory nature of the times, the security of his own family likely came to mind, given its history with the Inquisition. This was a serious concern of New Christians, who feared suspicion of heresy for the secret practice of Judaism. After all, it was the suspected religious backsliding of *conversos* that was specified in the edict as cause for the expulsion of those allegedly subverting former coreligionists.

Although her husband was doing the king's business with soon-to-be-exiled Jews, Doña Juana Santángel was sheltered from direct contact with

One. On the Eve of Expulsion

them as *dama de la casa*, lady of the house, of one of the wealthiest and most privileged New Christian men in the kingdom. If she knew of their grief and difficulties — of houses and lands, business inventories and livestock, going for a pittance because Old and New Christian buyers knew well the sellers' negative bargaining position — the knowledge would have had to come from gossiping servants and Old Christian service providers, not from relatives and *conversos*. For even within the privacy of salon and bedroom, no New Christians dared discuss among themselves the situation of departing Jews. A passing or eavesdropping servant might report comments perceived as sympathetic for the exiled ones to the Holy Office. There were even cases of New Christians informing on kinsmen for *judaizante*, the secret practice of Judaism, hoping the betrayal would protect their immediate families and interests.

The Santángels themselves were particularly vulnerable, as important relatives in Zaragoza had been burned at the stake in the past decade for alleged complicity in the assassination of the Grand Inquisitor of that city. Even with the fondness and respect of the king for Don Luís, their direct family had been severely threatened. Luís's mother, Brianda, was herself arrested and interrogated, her eventual release made possible, it was suspected, only by the Catholic Majesty's direct intervention. Even Don Luís, in such a high court position and a confidant of the king, had to wear the *sanbenito* in penance for a brief period after his mother's arrest. This yellow hooded cloak, with red crosses front and back, marked someone accused of heresy, who had confessed to his or her backslidings and pledged to be a faithful Christian. The penitent was obliged to wear the cloak in public for a given period of time.

We do not know the subjects that passed between Don Luís and his wife upon his return, but we can be sure that the family made certain to give visible evidence of their Catholic practice after his arrival. They were always under surveillance to assure their adherence to the church. Former Jews, they were resented by many Old Christians because of their wealth and influence at court. Doña Brianda's brush with the Inquisition showed how close the Holy Office could reach — even to the mother of someone most powerful — and the entire family had to be one in maintaining the appearance of devotion to the holy faith. Don Luís' uncle, convicted in Zaragoza of complicity in the plot against the murdered Inquisitor Arbués, had been burned at the stake, and an effigy of a kinsman who had fled abroad was consigned to fire along with the disinterred bones of another.

The Santángels mirrored the insecurities of all New Christians. Most *conversos* carried an enormous burden of guilt and fear this last decade of the fourteenth century. Indeed, this continued well into the early nineteenth century when the Inquisition finally came to a formal end. Even today, over 500 years later, there are titled and prominent Spanish families, Catholic clergy among their ranks, who live as if the terror still exists, hiding from the world outside any remnant of Jewish background and practices in their otherwise observant Christian families.[7]

As professing Jews prepared for the inevitable wrench of separation from Sefarad, there were heads of state, near and far, who anticipated that the unfolding expulsion drama would contribute to the weakening of Spain — a powerful national enemy. In Constantinople, Sultan Bayazid II of the Ottoman Empire questioned the wisdom of expelling so many of the country's most prosperous, productive and intelligent citizens.

"You call Ferdinand a wise king, he who impoverishes his country and enriches our own!" he is reported to have said, then declared welcome to the exiles.[8] In nearby Portugal, João II also opened his borders to Jews. Those who wished could enter after payment of a tax. A relatively few prosperous emigrants, thirty or so families, were permitted to establish permanent residence, while all others would be required to leave within eight months.

Bayazid and João had appraised the balance sheets of economics and politics, education and medicine, the arts and the sciences, and saw how the Jews had contributed to Spanish political power, military strength and scientific know-how. Now these skills and assets could be applied against the former beneficiaries. Wherever they settled, host countries would benefit from the Catholic Majesties' loss.

Future chapters will tell of the efforts Fernando made to influence his most valued advisers and their families to convert, as he did with the Abravanels. Nevertheless, significant numbers of Sephardim remained loyal to Judaism, and their absence would be felt deeply in the homeland they were about to leave. One such gifted individual was the renowned astronomer and astrologer, Abraham Ben Samuel Zacuto. Like Don Isaac in Guadalajara, the distinguished professor in Salamanca faced the impending challenge of upheaval, as he organized his papers and possessions for the journey. And, like the renowned statesman, Zacuto was respected for his knowledge of Judaica, having authored treatises on related subjects. A lone Jewish master at the great University of Salamanca, his patrons in the sciences had included Old Christian nobility and churchmen, such as Gonzalo de Vivero, Bishop of Salamanca, and Don Juan de Zúñiga, Grand Master of the Order of the Knights of Alcántara in nearby Gata.

It was Zacuto who developed the astronomical charts, an almanac of sorts, that Columbus would take with him on his voyage, about to set sail. Several New Christians, some hastily baptized just before the journey, were among ships' crews. They, too, had been trained in the use of Zacuto's navigational and astronomical tools. In fact, the almanac would save Columbus' life in the New World, when his accuracy in forecasting an eclipse would convince natives that a superior God protected the intruder they were about to do away with.[9] Ironically, the tools so well provided by Zacuto, the scientist, were to be put to their test and proven invaluable long months after Zacuto, the practicing Jew, had been forced to leave. The mantle of prominence as scientist and professor with powerful Old Christian patrons was not enough to exempt him, as professing Jew, from having to leave Spain. His family was, however, among the small number of prosperous and talented Sephardim invited by King João to settle in Portugal. His rabbi, the renowned *gaon* Isaac Aboab II, with whom he had studied since childhood, was among those who had negotiated with the king to arrange for this special dispensation. A royal welcome awaited him in Lisbon, where his expertise would be employed advising the king and training Portugal's navigators for voyages of exploration.

But, as it was for everyone, pulling up roots was most painful. It was here, in the gentle city of Salamanca, that his ancestors lay buried. Here was the great university that had hosted his early discoveries as student and rewarded them as master, the memories of childhood and family, the synagogue where he had prayed and celebrated with his community. Like all who would make the journey, he was concerned about the safety of his family and the unknown future.

As scientist, *Mestre*, or Master, Zacuto would want to maintain the flourishing network among fellow scientists and cartographers, as those who left would soon be scattered in different directions. Joseph Vicinho, his former student, was in Portugal, where he had developed some of the nautical instruments which would be used in the voyage of Vasco da Gama, along with Zacuto's tables and copper astrolabe. Vicinho had also translated the professor's celestial navigation almanac from Hebrew to Latin.[10] As court mathematician to King João, he had heralded the *mestre*'s anticipated arrival.

The past two centuries had seen significant progress in cartography, astronomy, mathematics, and medicine, due to the scholarly and scientific network in Iberia, Italy and the Lowlands. Earlier, the Muslims had encouraged their Jewish subjects in the study and applications of math and science. Palma, in Majorca, had become the center of mapmaking knowledge and production. There, the heralded Abraham Cresques was first among cartographers, with his son, Jehuda, continuing the tradition. As a New Christian, whose family converted during the massacres of 1391, Jehuda took the baptismal name Jaume Ribes, and relocated to Barcelona, where his work was much in demand in the city's ship building center. *Conversos* were forbidden to work with practicing Jews. Did Zacuto, on the eve of departure, worry that this would affect the pursuit of science?

As the astronomer readied for departure, the family of Joseph Nasi was likewise in preparation. Like the Zacutos, they were among the prosperous and skilled Jews offered permanent Portuguese residence. Don Joseph was a tax farmer in Briviesca, appointed by the king to collect revenues. These were highly coveted positions, making the occupants wealthy and then depended on for loans to royalty. The surname Nasi means "prince" in Hebrew and had been applied since the eleventh century to individuals who spoke for their *aljamas*, or Jewish communities, before the rulers. *Nasis* were known for both piety and Hebrew scholarship. As a *nasi*, we can assume that Don Joseph could be seen both at court and in the *yeshivas* or study centers where scholars gathered.

Exiles had to leave behind valuable libraries that could not accompany them into the diaspora, the place of settlement beyond the native land. Movable type and printing was a new technology, not yet a century old, so most of the abandoned books had been hand lettered by scribes. Works of Judaica would be considered illegal and, most likely, consigned to flame.

As Don Joseph and his family prepared for the border crossing, it could not be predicted that Portugal's King João was to die soon after their arrival in his country, and that scarcely three years later, his successor, Manoel, would order all Jews remaining in his land to be forcibly baptized as Catholics. At that time, the Nasi family would be known by the Christian names of de Luna and Miguez, and it is into this family that a daughter, Beatriz, would be born in 1510, eighteen years after the expulsion. She would grow up to marry Francisco Mendes, from the distinguished Benveniste family, and be revered in the next century as Doña Gracia Nasi, *La Señora*, a name as familiar in ruling European courts as in the humblest Jewish home.

The Benveniste family of her future husband-to-be was likewise prominent and respected among Spain's Sephardim. Although kinsmen of the Nasis, they could not be aware how intimately their lives would intertwine following Portuguese resettlement. In preparing to leave Spain, the Benveniste's two young sons, Semah and Meir, experienced the wrench of separation from friends and fellow students, as strong for the boys as for thousands of children similarly affected. Each could select only a few precious keepsakes from all his possessions to carry with him. What favorite toys or books were selected from among the many owned by children of wealth? Like most Jewish fathers of his class, it was probable that the Benveniste patriarch had familiarized his sons before the expulsion with a realistic and sobering orientation to what

A priest baptizes a Jewish couple, converted as a result of his preaching. The massacres of 1391 and increasing pressures to "convert or die" led thousands of Jews to convert to Catholicism, as did the expulsion decree one century later. (Retablo de San Marcos, attributed to Arnau Bassa, fourteenth century. In Generalitat Valenciana, ed. *Lluís de Santàngel y su época: un nuevo hombre, un mundo nuevo* [Valencia: 1992], 212.)

Jewish life would be like for them in the fifteenth-century environment of persecution and violence, although the possibility of exile may not have been considered. When forced to give up their faith five years later in Portugal, Semah was to be called Francisco and Meir, Diogo. They would amass great wealth heading the House of Mendes, trading and banking firm, and, as observed, Francisco would wed Beatriz de Luna, daughter of kinsman Don Joseph Nasi, who Roth writes would take the surname Miguez at his conversion.[11]

    Those of advanced years and in poor health faced arduous paths. Could they survive the physical journey and unknown obstacles? What lay ahead for the expelled ones? Even those with a clear destination and adequate means of getting there could not be sure. Unseaworthy vessels, piracy, last minute abuses on the way to exit points — these were potential terrors looming ahead. If prayer was palpable, the air over Sefarad would be shimmering with thousands of supplications for forgiveness, beseeching safe journey and resettlement.

    Some would surrender and convert to Christianity as the deadline approached — too weary or fearful to make the journey, too poor to provide for themselves and loved ones along the way, too discouraged by the specter of total loss. With others, attachment to Sefarad would win out over loyalty to a covenant with God, made in other times and places. After all, their ancestors had birthed, bred and been buried in the land for almost two millennia. Their paths led to the baptismal fount, choosing risk and reprisal of Inquisition over danger and loss of exodus.

    And what of the land that was ousting the Sephardim from its soil? Spain, newly unified following the Muslim defeat at Granada, had set in motion the beginning of its decline as a world power. The monarchs were expelling a people who had brought eminence to their kingdoms in science, math, medicine, education, economics, literature and art, and who had contributed to the vast geographical hegemony and military and commercial successes. The country was losing priceless economic resources, such as merchant and banking families, with vast riches in their coffers; astronomers, cartographers and navigational specialists, who had helped win wars and find new lands; artisans and craftsmen, whose skills had enhanced its people's comfort and pleasure. Enemies and competitors of the Iberian land would surely benefit from the influx of what Spain had cast out, intensifying the blows to Spanish power in the next two centuries, from the defeat of the Armada and the loss of trading advantages to the successes of navigation, commerce and empire by competitor nations.

One. On the Eve of Expulsion

In the following chapters, we will experience, one by one, the vivid, colorful lives and times of each of the individuals we have met thus far: Isaac Abravanel, Luís de Santángel, Abraham Zacuto and Gracia Nasi. These four exemplary individuals have been selected because they portray high points of achievement, which improved the quality of life in the lands they inhabited, the people who were their neighbors, and all Jews, everywhere. They represent diverse fields — government and finance, commerce and science, literature and art. Among them are religious and secular scholars and hard-headed men and women of business, along with humanitarians and philanthropists. Their lives are testimony to the achievements and culture of the golden age of Sefarad.

Their stories will be followed by accounts of the less prosperous and prominent Jews and their day-to-day lives in Iberia, as the tired fifteenth century gave way to the early modern period. How was lifestyle, occupation, social and economic status and religious and family life affected — first, by the relative harmony, or *convivencia*, of the Muslims, and then by the domination and oppression of the reconquering Christians? How did the tumult of repression and slaughter in the century before expulsion affect hopes, dreams and attitudes? What influence did exodus and diaspora have on Jewish self-image and world view?

Isaac Abravanel and Gracia Nasi passionately defended the eternality of Judaism, the former even in confrontation with monarchs. What can be learned on this subject as we study the experiences of the Sephardim, both professing Jews and *conversos*, and of the crypto Jews, those who observe elements of Jewish ancestry while publicly identified otherwise? What about the discovery of "lost" remnants of Jewry, tribes and peoples with Jewish pasts inferred from modern DNA studies? And how is the cultural/religious stew affected by today's manifestations of cultural identity among secular and nonobservant Jews? All this leads to the age-old question: what and who is a Jew, and what are the criteria for determining the answer?

From Sefarad in the Middle Ages to identity issues of today — this is the reader's journey through the centuries in the pages ahead.

~ TWO ~

Isaac Abravanel: *¡Basta mi nombre que es Abravanel!* It is enough to know my name is Abravanel!

Great men and women live twice — the years on the planet and the ones thereafter when their influence is still felt as much as, sometimes more than, it was when they walked among us. Sometimes this afterlife on earth lasts centuries.

Isaac ben Judah Abravanel was one of these rare beings. In his lifetime, rulers of four different nations sought his services, looking to the guidance of Don Isaac the statesman, negotiator, diplomat, financial adviser. Coreligionists saw him as their representative before royalty and their inspiration in the face of massacre, expulsion and resettlement. Scholars pored over Don Isaac's creative and prolific biblical interpretations for insight on the messiah and Jewish observance for centuries after his passing. His works influenced Jewish messianic thought throughout the Jewish diaspora.

He is, perhaps, best remembered for his tenacity in efforts to change the minds of Spain's monarchs who had issued the Alhambra Declaration, giving Jews three months to convert to the Catholic faith or leave the land by the deadline of August 3, 1492. When all efforts had failed, he confronted the mighty Queen Isabel as a peer, not a subject, predicting the heavy price her kingdom would pay with the loss of a population that had long served it well.[1]

Don Isaac was exiled thrice in his lifetime, each time regaining his family's fortune through his skills and the use of his talents by ruling monarchs. He combined his reputation for statesmanship with scholarship in Judaic history and biblical exegesis.

What were the wellsprings that nourished this combination of intellectual prowess, leadership skills and spiritual motivation? There was certainly a sense of destiny for Isaac, son of Judah Abravanel, treasurer to the brother of King João I of Portugal. Family legend traced the Abravanel lineage to direct descent from King David and pointed to centuries of public service, scholarship and distinction. Certainly, the belief in Davidian heritage and a sense of entitlement went a long way to place him in the courts of kings and the *yeshivas*, or schools, of scholars. His life story shows these at work through a long and fruitful life, beginning in Lisbon in 1437, where the boy Isaac was born into a family of wealth and privilege, with high expectations about his future. His father and grandfather occupied positions of responsibility and

This painting of the Abravanel family coat of arms hangs in the home of a twenty-first century descendant. The surname has come down through history in a variety of spellings, and is found in some form in many countries. (With permission from Daisy and Harry Stein.)

leadership in Portugal's royal court and he was raised to take his place alongside them.²

At the end of the fourteenth century, Isaac's great grandfather, Judah of Sevilla, served as royal keeper of the wardrobe, and his son, Samuel, followed him in the court of Henry II, becoming one of the wealthiest men in the kingdom of Castilla. It was a fruitful period for the family until 1378, when Sevilla began to be the center of anti–Jewish feeling. In 1391, Ferrán Martínez, a local priest, preached vigorously against what was called "the dead law of Moses" by those wanting Jews to convert. A mob entered the Jewish quarter of Sevilla soon after, killing 4,000 men, women and children who had refused baptism to change their faith. Historians are divided over when Samuel Abravanel, Isaac's grandfather, converted to Christianity with the name Juan Sánchez de Sevilla or his motives for doing so. Netanyahu cites Zacuto, Baer and Ayala, who make the case that he converted "in the last years of the eighties of the fourteenth century, at a time when hostility for the Jews in Sevilla was approaching the most critical and most explosive stage," and argues that "the records concerning his conversion are too meager to permit definite conclusions regarding the motives that led to it."³

Don Isaac's proud ancestor remained loyal to Judaism, however, enough to abandon his high position and wealth eventually and make his way to Portugal, where he could restore his Jewish identity and begin a corresponding rise in power and influence. His grandson never alluded to his grandfather's conversion in any of his writings. It was obviously a black period in the family history, perhaps one he wanted to forget. Following the escape from Sevilla, the family established itself in Lisbon. There, Isaac's father, Judah, was born. Growing into adulthood, Don Judah attained great prosperity, largely on the tide of opportunity that accompanied successful Portuguese navigation and the subsequent opening of commercial resources. He financed voyages of exploration, as well as wars of reconquest against Muslim rulers. In the very year of Isaac's birth, court ledgers recorded the king's repayment of a substantial loan to Don Judah, which had come from the treasurer's own substantial fortune.

And so, his son Isaac received an education both broad and thorough. He studied Talmud, becoming conversant in all areas of Judaic scholarship. Tutored in both Judaic and world philosophy, he was equally learned in the Greek thinker, Aristotle, as he was in the Sephardic philosopher, Maimonides. The influences of both secular and religious theorists were to become manifest in his writings later on. Besides his native tongue, he was fluent in Castillian, Hebrew and Latin.

He was tutored thoroughly in history as well, and was knowledgeable in statesmanship and world affairs, the curriculum for those born into privilege, for whom parents planned lives of influence and accomplishment. Young Isaac showed high intelligence and astute critical thinking in applying principles to issues, and was already writing papers on complex subjects when barely past his teens. He was not yet twenty when he wrote his first philosophical work, *The Forms of the Elements.* Here, he took the theory attributed to the Greek philosopher Aristotle that everything on earth is composed of the four elements — fire, water, air and earth — and explored their basic essences. The work is strangely secular when viewed later in the context of Don Isaac's life work, containing no reference to God or biblical citation. He quoted Aristotle's premise that everything nature does is for a purpose, and based his thinking on reason rather than religious thought. The young scholar's work demonstrated his grounding in the Arabic and Greek, as well as the Jewish, philosophers. He also evidenced background in two of the natural sciences of the day, astrology and medicine.

His second philosophical work, *Atereth Zekenim,* or *Crown of the Elders,* bridged the young man's movement from philosophy to religion and eventually to mysticism. Here, he dealt with the nature of God and prophesy, laying the foundations for his writings for the rest of his life. He lauded the wisdom of the biblical prophets, claiming it superior to the thinking of the philosophers. In a change of thought, he was critical of the very Aristotle quoted as an authority in his first work, *The Forms of the Elements.* The philosopher Maimonides, however, fared better than his Greek counterpart and other ideological colleagues and critics, remaining an intellectual and philosophical focal point throughout the writer's life. Abravanel was at the very heart of an ideological conflict that would obsess Jewish scholars for centuries to come: an ethos or belief based on logic and reason versus literal acceptance of the prophets' words as final and only guide to truth and behavior. In *Crown,* he took his place with the latter and stayed firmly planted there for the rest of his writing and teaching career.

For his next work, Don Isaac intended a commentary on the first five books of the Bible, the Pentateuch, heart of the Jewish Torah. He was put off from this task by responsibilities for the family's enterprises and his emerging career as public servant. This conflict, between biblical scholar and man of letters on one side and the prominent commercial leader and courtier on the other, was to repeat throughout his life. The former, his very *raison d'être,* would be shelved often by demands on him because of his economic and political status.

And so, like father and grandfather before him, he was destined for service to the Crown of Portugal. As planned, Don Judah introduced his son early into court affairs, and the influential position of the father smoothed the way for Isaac to be viewed as courtier material. Soon his own merits shone through, and he was appointed treasurer to King Alfonso V, with a place of respect among peers. The Abravanels were among the bankers of the day. Affluent Jews with personalities befitting courtiers were frequently appointed to positions by the Crown, through which they amassed fortunes. In return, they were expected to loan money when needed to the monarch of the day. Like his father, the son frequently made loans to support Portuguese military and other projects.

Don Isaac demonstrated early in his tenure that he would represent and defend his people. In 1471, he raised the necessary ransom for 250 Jews held as slaves by the king in Morocco. His coreligionists soon came to regard him as their national spokesman. His representations on their behalf, however, did not diminish the respect with which he was held by prominent Christians. The philosophical and well-read Alfonso V appreciated both the financial skills and rounded theological knowledge of the young Abravanel. Descended from a cultured family, the monarch's father, Duarte, and grandfather, João, were themselves writers. Alfonso valued the Abravanel scion who combined wizardry in finance with knowledge of Christian, Jewish, Greek and Roman philosophers. Indeed, the monarch rewarded his services in 1464 by exempting him from the requirements of dress and behavior imposed upon Jewish brethren. He did not have to wear the red, six-pointed star required on their clothes. He was permitted to travel throughout Portugal without the badge, and authorities were enjoined not to stop him on this account. Even earlier, in 1462, Alfonso had authorized him to live outside the *judería*, where Jews were required to reside, and granted him the privileges and freedoms of Christians, including the right to ride a mule, then prohibited to Jews.

The bequests from the king went even further. In 1480, Alfonso added to Abravanel's substantial wealth by confirming a gift of property outside Lisbon in Queluz, which he had received earlier from the Dukes of Braganza and Guimarães. Made in perpetuity by the dukes in appreciation for Abravanel's previous and anticipated services, the grant was made to him, his immediate family and heirs. It included "all its lands, pastures, waters, hills, springs, woods and with all the entries and exits and belongings, rents, rights and vegetable gardens...."[4]

Thus, the stage was set for the next act. A talented Isaac Abravanel, blending intellectual and spiritual skills with economic and political ones, had amassed a fortune and was well established in the Court of Dom Alfonso. At the same time, he was regarded by Jews as their national leader and representative. Now, however, he would be faced with a scenario that his wealth and achievements would be powerless to prevent.

Since early in his career, he had been associated with the fortunes of the powerful Dukes of Braganza. Some historians have traced his success in court to their support. This association was eventually to be his undoing when Alfonso died in 1481 and was succeeded by his son, João II. Jewish scribes have described Alfonso as a good king because of the relative liberty and privilege their people enjoyed during his reign.

The new king, however, was not pleased with his predecessor's generosity in sharing much of his power and the kingdom's lands with the feudal lords, especially with the House of Braganza, his most powerful rival. On assuming the throne, João determined to end the nobles' power, bring the national territory under his control and take back much of the land given to the lords. The Braganzas headed the list of those to be reined in. Shortly thereafter, the king claimed to have discovered a conspiracy by the dukes and their followers to kill him and take back their power. Fernando II, the king's brother-in-law and Duke of Braganza, was arrested and publicly beheaded in 1483. Soon after, Fernando's brother Diogo, Duke of Viseu, was stabbed and killed while in the king's presence.

Next, a few captives among those arrested for conspiring with the Braganzas claimed that Don Isaac and his son-in-law, Joseph, had been co-conspirators. Subsequently, Abravanel was summoned to appear at Evora before the king. He decided to comply, although anxious at the possibilities ahead, and stopped for the night in Arraiolos. There, he received a warning that the king was planning to put a death sentence on his head, linking him with the conspiracy. He changed course, headed north, crossed the river Tejo, and was soon over the border into Castilla.

Historians have pondered whether Isaac Abravanel was part of the conspiracy, or if his fall from favor offered an opportunity for the new king to purge from his court the influence of a Jewish courtier. Abravanel vigorously denied the charges against him. In his commentary on the book of Joshua, written early in his Castillian exile, he described how "The king was angry with me too, although I never did any injustice and no deceit was found in my mouth. Only because from time immemorial and from old good times I was an intimate friend of the persecuted noblemen and they asked my counsel...."[5]

Does the reference to asking counsel mean that he was consulted or at least informed of the alleged plot? Did Abravanel know of the conspiracy and, if so, should he have advised the king? There are arguments on both sides. Some writers claim that Isaac and his son-in-law, Joseph, must have known as they continued to make loans to the nobles, which were used in furtherance of the plot. Others point to his writings, where, although opposed to the divine right of kings, he stated that he did not support rebellion against rulers.[6]

Historian Elias Lipiner maintains that, yes, "in the fight between the

Crown and the nobility ... Abravanel sided with the nobility," but he chose this path because he believed it would be better for the Jews. Don Isaac had friendly relations with court nobles, which, Lipiner claims, "were maintained mainly for the purpose of interceding with the noblemen, or through them, in favour of the political status of the Jewish communities." Under existing conditions,

> ... the survival of the Jews depended basically on the favours obtained by means of mediation and intervention in the courts of the king and of the powerful lords of the kingdom. Therefore, it was more advantageous for the Jews to have the multiple power of the noblemen who surrounded Alfonso V, as well as the latter's traditional accessibility and good will, rather than having the power centralized in the hands of King João II, a harsh man who completely eliminated the influence of the noblemen.[7]

Enraged at the exile's escape, João confiscated Abravanel's properties and possessions. Meanwhile, the fugitive was safe in Castilla with his wife and children. He was forty-eight years old. He had lived almost one-half century of his life in a pleasant and fulfilling environment, appreciated and rewarded by his king, head of a successful commercial enterprise, patriarch and center of a thriving family, beneficiary of influential friendships. Although his responsibilities in court and commerce had generally prevented him from writing on biblical and Judaic themes, the intense desire of his heart, he had penned and published several treatises, which were well received by fellow scholars. He was the undisputed leader and spokesman for Portuguese Jewry, his family active in Jewish religious and secular affairs, with seats in the great synagogue in Lisbon. Now all that had ended, with flight in 1483 to an uncertain future. He was entering Spain, a country with a centuries-old record of increasingly severe persecution of Jews, its monarchs obsessed with the final push to rid their lands of Muslim occupation. In the quiet times that followed his settlement in Spain, he reflected sadly on good times that were no more.

He wrote wistfully of those days in his book of commentary on Joshua, which he completed only three months after stepping on Spanish soil.

> I lived peacefully as owner of my house, a house full of God's blessings in famous Lisbon.... The Lord commanded there the blessings in my barns, and all the earthly bliss.... My home became a place of meeting for the wise.... I was happy in the court of the king Dom Alfonso, a mighty king whose domain spread out and reached from sea to sea..., a king who trusted in the Lord, fearing God and departing from evil, seeking the good of the [Jewish] people.... Under his shadow I delighted to sit.[8]

And so, a new chapter commenced in the life and times of Isaac Abravanel, beginning the days in Spain with a concentrated literary effort. In less

Victorious, Fernando and Isabel lead their troops into Granada in 1492, bringing an end to the *Reconquista* and the Muslim ruling presence in Spain. (Tomás López Enguídanos. *Granada Rendida*. In Generalitat Valenciana, ed. *Lluís de Santàngel y su época: un nuevo hombre, un mundo nuevo* [Valencia: 1992], 245.)

than five months, he completed commentaries on Joshua, Judges and the Books of Samuel. The works embodied an interesting conflict. On one hand, he continued the anti-rationalist approach of his earlier *Crown of the Elders*, with even greater intensity. He was scathing in portraying the philosophers following Maimonides as knowing subverters of the foundations of Jewish faith. On the other hand, he showed intellectual open mindedness in referring to a broad spectrum of sources — Jewish, Christian, Greek and Roman — to arrive at his conclusions. He utilized what he saw as truths from each in forming his views. The sources included Thomas Aquinas, Augustine, Cicero and Seneca, as well as Pablo de Santa María, the contemporary New Christian churchman, who was Bishop of Burgos.

Written in the border town of Segura de la Orden, the commentaries were completed, providentially, the very month that he was summoned to an audience before Fernando and Isabel, *Los Reyes Católicos*, whose marriage had united the Kingdoms of Aragón and Castilla. It is not clear whether he requested the meeting or if his reputation preceded him as the effective former chief financial officer for the Portuguese crown. In this role, he had kept his king in funds and supplies in war and peace. Now he was particularly relevant to the Spanish rulers, who were deeply immersed in the military effort to wrest Granada from the Muslims and were in need of money and supplies.

Don Isaac's audience with the sovereigns took place in Tarazona, in Aragón. The meeting was fruitful for both sides. Fernando and Isabel seemed pleased with the counsel and support Isaac Abravanel could bring them and welcomed him as courtier. He responded to their satisfaction about his approach to court and military finance, and was received as a royal financial adviser. They had known of his presence on Spanish soil through their information network and had followed the Braganza case with more than passing interest, due to their support of the nobles. In addition, the monarchs had ignored a request from João for the extradition of the fugitive and his son-in-law. Now he was Don Isaac, financial adviser to the Catholic Majesties. Once again, his passion for biblical analysis and writing had to be interrupted as he entered their service. In his introduction to the commentary on the Book of Kings, completed decades later, he lamented the passage thus:

> I was about to start writing the commentary on the Book of Kings, when I was summoned to the court of the king of Spain, the most powerful of all the governors of the Earth, who ruled over the kingdoms of Castilla, Aragón, Catalunya, Sicily and other islands of the sea. And presenting myself to the courts of the king and the queen, I became their favourite for many days and stayed in their service for eight years.... In their courts and palaces I amassed all the wealth and honours that a person can acquire and enjoy. Consequently, however, my studies ceased and my work was interrupted, so that I could dedicate myself to foreign kings, whilst neglecting my own inheritance, the Kings of Judah and Israel and my commentaries to their books.[9]

And so, Isaac Abravanel moved his household to Toledo to serve as a tax farmer. As explained earlier, tax collecting positions were political plums, filled by royal appointment. They offered the only opportunity for Jews to enter public service, other avenues prohibited to them. The tax farmer was assured the opportunity to amass a large fortune from the generous commissions allowed him to carry out the work. He would then be expected to serve as banker of sorts, making large loans to replenish the royal treasury from the funds he had amassed through tax farming. This was the chance Don Isaac needed to recoup his lost prosperity.

Working under the leadership of Abraham Seneor, chief tax farmer of Aragón, he soon regained enough funds to make loans to royalty, earmarked for the Granada campaign. This was the last Muslim stronghold on the Iberian Peninsula, and the highest priority for capture by the Catholic Majesties.

It is worth noting that at the very time that Abravanel joined the service of Fernando and Isabel, the king was trying to convince, albeit unsuccessfully, a resistant Cortes of Aragón, a legislative body of nobles, to agree to his plan for expulsion of the Jews from his kingdom. They had already been expelled from Andalucía and were also soon to be exiled from Toledo. The Holy Inquisition had been in effect for three years, and had already struck terror into those converted to the Catholic faith. It had begun arresting individuals accused of *judaizante*, observing Judaism in secret, some of them members of the most powerful *converso* families. Even with these omens of serious trouble ahead, the king still managed to make it appear that the church, not the crown, was the initiator of anti–Jewish activity. That was due largely to the monarchs' policy to intercede as early as possible to stop outbreaks of violence against Jews when existing laws protected them. Enforcing law and order in their kingdoms would keep the balance of power among competing interests and prevent it from turning to conflict, so their reasoning went.[10]

It was the very division between Jew and *converso* that kept each of these from correctly interpreting early expulsionary and Inquisitional events as omens of increasing persecution for both groups. Practicing Jews appeared to have interpreted the Inquisition's efforts to quell heresy among converts as not directed at them and, further, perhaps God's punishment of errant brethren for betraying their ancestral religion. *Conversos*, on the other hand, appear to have viewed expulsion as affecting only those openly practicing Judaism, hoping that things might go easier for them once observant Jews would not be around to blame for New Christian backsliding.

It was ironic that Isaac Abravanel, former spokesman and leading protector of Portuguese Jewry, had entered the services of a monarchy designing, at that very time, the destruction of the Jewish presence in Spain. There is a manner of thinking indulged in by politicians, even those of the most altruistic stripe, to which he may have been prey — that one must first gain power in order to accomplish anything desirable. If Isaac Abravanel was to help his brethren, the reasoning went, he would first have to regain influence and wealth, for only from that position could he have any effect. This meant entering the services of royalty, whatever its nature, to gain its ears and be heard on Jewish issues.

Residing in Toledo, Don Isaac continued Judaic studies under Rabbi Isaac Aboab, who would be known as the last *gaon*, or most wise of rabbis, of Castilla. Later, he would move to Guadalajara to study at the rabbi's *yeshiva*, where his noteworthy fellow students would include Abraham Zacuto, the prominent astronomer, whom we will visit in Chapter Four.

For the time, however, his writing was laid aside, as he immersed himself in his work as tax farmer and financial adviser. His tax farming regions were far flung, from Atienza near Guadalajara in north central Spain; Riquena in Valencia and Villena in Alicante, both in the east; as well as several areas in the south. Soon he was able to make up a considerable portion of his lost fortune.

As the battles raged in Granada, the name Abravanel appeared in the Crown's account books as creditor, with large loans to the queen and the war treasury. Don Isaac and colleague, Abraham Seneor, were assigned to administer and supply the armies in the south. Their services were much appreciated, with Abravanel becoming the queen's personal financial adviser, as well as her commercial representative.

In addition to gaining the confidence of the royal couple, Don Isaac became part of a circle of influential business and court associates and friends, having applied the social skills and likeability that had stood him so well in the past. Relatively soon after his flight from Portugal, he was able to take his place among the courtiers and most powerful leaders in Spain — not bad, considering he was starting all over on foreign soil.

As well as he did, however, he never regained the equivalent in influence and fortune as in his native land. There, his counsel had been sought after and listened to on important political matters. In Spain, his advice was requested for financial matters only. Nevertheless, he had the opportunity to speak on behalf of fellow Jews, and did so occasionally. And he used his influence to persuade affluent Jews to make loans for the war effort.[11]

Don Isaac was outspoken in his support of Christopher Columbus, a seaman from Genoa who had petitioned the king and queen to support a westward voyage to the Indies. They had first met in Lisbon, when Abravanel was chief financial officer to the Portuguese Crown. Then, in 1487, they met again in Málaga. Convinced of the importance of the proposed voyage, Don Isaac joined with *converso* Luís de Santángel, whom we met in Chapter One, the influential chancellor of the royal household, and with other courtiers, Jew and New Christian, who also supported Columbus.[12]

Future prognosticators will make much of the presence of so many Jews and New Christians among the backers of the Genoese seaman. They will surmise that Columbus himself may have had Jewish roots. This will be attributed to symbols resembling Hebrew found in his writings; his written references to another king to whom he pays homage, perhaps the Hebrew God; and the overwhelming support he received from so many of the most prominent Jews and *conversos* of Aragón and Castilla. They will point to the presence on his ships of several New Christians. One, Juan de Torres, was converted just days before the voyage. He was selected for the voyage because of his knowledge of Hebrew and to be the first on shore to see if the natives spoke that language and were descendants of Israelites.

Research has not revealed any evidence to support suppositions that Columbus was a Jew or descendant of Jews, although the coincidences cited continue to feed the legend. This will receive more attention in Chapter Three, when we visit the world of Abravanel's co-supporter of Columbus, Luís de Santángel.

Still, one must ask, why the appeal to so many influentials of Jewish background? Certainly, the new opportunities for trade and prosperity would attract those with commercial connections. Another, more poignant theory put forth, is that supporters of Columbus reasoned that any new lands discovered might act as havens for Jews fleeing increasing persecution. This discussion will be revisited in Chapters Three and Four.[13]

Alas, Isaac Abravanel was not able to salute Columbus' ships, the Niña, the Pinta and the Santa Maria, as they sailed with their crews of Old and New Christians from the western port near Cádiz on August 3, 1492. His family was on a ship out of Valencia, in the east, heading for the Italian Peninsula. For months before, he had been immersed in frantic efforts to change the minds of Fernando and Isabel on the Alhambra Decree, which they had signed on March 31, mandating all professing Jews to leave Spain forever by the beginning of August.

With Abraham Seneor, Abravanel had been fighting the good fight to stop enactment of the edict. The decree and its severity had surprised even Don Isaac, a seasoned courtier. Even the venerable Don Abraham was caught off guard. Not that they had ignored the steady erosion of Jewish rights and protections. The timing shocked even the most hardened veteran of court machinations, exposing what future generations were to categorize as the true Machiavellian nature of the crown. Indeed, two decades after the edict's proclamation, the Italian statesman Niccolò Machiavelli was to write about the political behavior of royalty, particularly the emphasis on success rather than morality. It has been surmised that Fernando was his model.

The expulsion decree came on the heels of a successful military victory, spurred on in its final stages by generous loans and strategic support from Jewish and *converso* financial advisers and crown supporters. Al-Andaluz — and all of Spain — was free of Muslim ruling presence of 800 years, thanks in large part to these benefactors. And yet, even those Jews who helped make this possible were compelled to convert or leave by the end of July, along with fellow coreligionists. This included learned scientists and physicians, master silversmiths and carpenters, merchants and jurists, rich and poor — everyone, including Isaac Abravanel and Abraham Seneor.

Most shocking was the finality of the expulsion, telling observant Jews that they would never be able to return, and giving them very little time to prepare: three months to wrap up almost two millennia on the soil of Sefarad.

Heavy restrictions added to the rapacious measure and limited what could be carried out by the exiles, allowing crown, church and Old Christians to benefit from abandoned assets in land and personal possessions. Exiles were specifically prohibited from taking out gold and silver coins and minted money.

However ominous the new turn of events, protesting Jews and *converso* leaders had weathered other storms of restriction and destruction in the past.[14] They believed it possible to disuade Fernando, who up to then had been open always, in mind and pocketbook, to his best interest. During the time between signing and proclaiming the document, approximately one month, they had several audiences with the king. At the first, Abravanel and Seneor were joined by Don Abraham's influential son-in-law, Melamud. Also present was Alfonso de la Caballería, the prominent converso courtier. Fernando greeted the group in a friendly manner, and appeared to listen attentively to the points put forth. The supplicants called attention to the record of faithfulness of Jews as subjects, who had supported the reconquest, militarily and financially. They pointed to the important role they played in the land's economy and the disastrous affect they claimed expulsion would have on the kingdoms' wealth and resources. They further emphasized Jews' willingness to do even more financially, to demonstrate loyalty and patriotism. The last particularly appeared to get the king's attention. The audience ended with the monarch saying he would take what he had heard under consideration.

Two weeks later, Dons Isaac and Abraham sought another audience. This time, they were armed to prove the high degree of Jewish loyalty to the Crown, with Abravanel offering a gift of 30,000 ducats from his own fortune. The king appeared pleased and open to changing his mind, when Tomás de Torquemada, the Chief Inquisitor, was reported to have burst upon the scene with a dangling crucifix and a comparison of the offer to the thirty pieces of silver that betrayed Jesus.[15] The audience ended abruptly, and from that point on the king appeared in full support of the decree.

The two men then made their final intervention, this time with the queen. Their entreaties, stressing past Jewish support for crown causes and the serious effect expulsion would have on the country's economic and cultural life, came to naught. The queen placed responsibility directly on her husband and denied power in the matter. She assured them that it was Fernando, not she, who conceived of the expulsion, and further, that his inspiration came directly from God. "The Lord hath put this idea into the mind of the king," she was reported to have told them, followed by "The king's heart is in the hands of the Lord, as the rivers of water. He turns it whithersoever He Will."[16]

At that point, Abravanel, realizing that further efforts would be in vain, is said to have admonished the queen in a manner most remarkable, given her status as reigning monarch. In his chronicles, written in the first half of the next century, Elijah Capsali would record that Abravanel had written a letter to the queen "in which he chastised her mercilessly and showed no respect for her rank ... he had written that God would avenge the Jews from her and her household, and so on. He also reminded her that all those who had been bad to the Jews had ultimately perished."[17] Abravanel had dared to threaten and predict disaster, even God's wrath, for the king and queen at the zenith of their power — the king and queen who had united Spain, driven the Muslim conquerors from its soil, and were on the verge of launching a massive colonial empire.

The expulsion edict took affect very soon after, and Don Isaac assumed leadership, inspiring observant Jews to keep steadfast on the righteousness of their position and the need to stay committed to their faith through the trying days ahead. As with past persecutions designed to win conversion, the decree led many to the baptismal fount, avoiding the loss of lands and businesses and all but a few possessions and assets. The majority held firm, however, despite the trauma of tearing out millennia-old roots. Abravanel was everywhere, the acknowledged leader of his outcast people, encouraging, inspiring, reminding them of the covenant with God and their privilege in receiving Torah.

The king, for his part, faced the loss of Don Isaac's valued services, and wanted to stop his effort discouraging conversions. He assured Abravanel that he could remain in Spain without converting. Don Isaac turned this down and continued preparing his family and his people for departure.

The Abravanels' oldest son, Judah, had joined his father in Spain upon exile from Portugal. In his early thirties, he was a renowned physician in the service of the king. Fernando urged him to convert to keep his medical skills at court and when Judah refused, the king set in motion plans to kidnap his year-old son Isaac. The plot was discovered in time to send the child to Portugal. He was not to be reunited with his parents, who were never able to make contact with him. It was not known if he was one of the children forcefully taken from their guardians in 1493 and placed with Old Christian families or whether he was included with the unfortunate youths sent to the newly captured island of São Tomé, where many perished from neglect and hunger.[18]

Meanwhile, as the deadline for exile grew closer, Abraham Seneor joined the thousands leaving the ancestral faith, leading his family to baptism with the king, queen and Cardinal Mendoza as sponsors. Capsali reported that "...I have heard it rumored that Queen Isabel had sworn that if Don Abram Seneor did not convert, she would wipe out all the Jews...."[19]

An estimated 120,000 Jews from Castilla crossed the border into Portugal, 20,000 from Andalusía sailed from Málaga to North Africa and several thousand more from the north headed for Navarra.[20] Others traveled west to sail from Valencia for the Italian Peninsula. For some, the first haven was only a stopping place on the way to the ultimate destination of the Ottoman Empire, where the Sultan Bayazid is said to have questioned Fernando's wisdom at impoverishing his kingdom and enriching the Turkish ruler's.

Whatever the destination, the path was painful. Abravanel was to write later of the exodus:

> In the end there left, without strength, 300,000 people on foot, from the youngest to the oldest, all at one time, from all the provinces of the king, to wherever they were able to go. Their King went before them, God at their helm. Each pledged himself to God anew. Some went to Portugal and Navarra, which are close, but all they found were troubles and darkness, looting, starvation and pestilence. Some traveled through the perilous ocean, and here, too, God's hand was against them, and many were seized and sold as slaves, while many others drowned in the sea. Others again, were burned alive, as the ships on which they were traveling were engulfed by flames. In the end, all suffered: some by the sword and some by captivity and some by disease, until but a few remained of the many.[21]

Despite the severe constraints on what Jews could take out of the country, Don Isaac asked for and was permitted two thousand ducats in gold. Son-in-law Joseph received the same dispensation. In return, they gave the monarchs control of over one million maravedis in loans, with the right to collect on them.

In Chapter One, we recalled a meeting between Abravanel and Luís de Santángel, sent to repay a loan of 1,500,000 maravedis. Some of this was probably converted into movable bills of exchange, along with other assets. So while there were large losses, Don Isaac, his three sons — Joseph, Judah and Samuel — and their families did not leave Spain penniless as they had eight years before in Portugal.[22]

Don Isaac was fifty-six at the time of the departure. One wonders what thoughts were passing through his mind on the ship headed out of Valencia in late July for the Italian peninsula. It was to be the second major upheaval for his family. It is not known whether he knew of the welcome King Ferrante of Naples had offered to earlier exiles, compared to rejections by other Italian states. Perhaps his vessel, like those of previous convoys of exiles, stopped first at other ports, such as Genoa, where it was turned away, as were others. Regardless, the passengers were received into the kingdom of Naples.[23]

Naples' King Ferrante was kinsman to Spain's Fernando, as illegitimate son of Alfonso V, uncle of the Spanish monarch. Like most European rulers, he was under pressure from several sources, each determined to preserve and enhance their positions vis à vis royalty. One was the nobles, whose powers were eroding in the age of absolute monarchy. Another was the newer burgher class, demanding restrictions to limit Jewish competition in business and commerce. Then there was the church, eager to convert Jews and to keep *conversos* faithful. To defend and strengthen their position, rulers had to juggle their need for loans and services from Jews with the steady anti–Jewish bombardment. In countries where the leaders had unlimited control, however, they could afford to keep nobles, burghers and church at bay, while continuing to utilize the benefits accruing from a Jewish population. As an absolute ruler, then, Ferrante of Naples could afford to disregard pressures against Jews and make them welcome. Another example was the Duchy of Este in Ferrara and Padua, as we will see in Chapter Five.

In Naples, Don Isaac's reputation as statesman and financial wizard once again preceded him as it had when he crossed into Spain years before. Once again, he was invited into the court, where his expertise was utilized. He was also

The Abravanel family was celebrated for the qualities of its members. Impressed with the nobility and character of Isaac's daughter-in-law, Benvenida Abravanel, the Viceroy of Naples, Pedro de Toledo, appointed her tutor for his daughter, Leonora, or Eleonora. As Duchess of Tuscany in later years, the young woman continued to regard Doña Benvenida as a surrogate mother, and spoke on behalf of Jewish welfare when appealed to by her former tutor. Painter Agnolo Bronzino portrays Eleonora in elegant attire. (Agnolo Bronzino. Portrait [detail] of Eleonora de Toledo with her son, Giovanni [Florence: Uffizi], ca. 1544. Photo/Representation by Alinari/Art Resource, NY, ART 166666.)

able to take advantage of financial opportunities, and become wealthy again. Within two years, he and sons Samuel and Judah were among the most prominent individuals in the land.

Abravanel used this position to represent the Jewish people and speak on their behalf. He was particularly effective in keeping Ferrante's support for his Hebrew subjects, despite the common belief that the influx of Jews had brought the plague to Naples. The king was generous in setting up health centers to care for those infected, and in providing food for the needy, rather than exiling them.

It was a peaceful respite for Abravanel. He was able once again to resume his scholarship. Naples was the center of a humanist movement, with Aristotelians and neo–Platonists in lively, intellectual conflict. Looking back at his *Crown of the Elders*, written in Portugal when barely twenty, one could easily understand the neo–Platonist attraction for Don Isaac. He held the ideal as eternal and absolute as compared to the Rationalists' espousal of the transitory and imperfect senses. Son Judah, whose medical career flourished in Naples, was becoming known for his poetry and writings in philosophy. Called *Leone Ebreo*, the Hebrew Lion, he immersed himself in the debate between the Aristotelians and the neo–Platonists. His alignment with neo–Platonism undoubtedly influenced his father along those lines. This was to be Don Isaac's philosophic foundation when he would write *The Deeds of God* in 1496.[24]

Two years after his arrival in Naples, Abravanel finished his commentary on Kings. He presented a parallel between the ancient destruction of the Jewish nation and its people's exile with the present diaspora and exodus of his coreligiouists. He raised the spiritual questions common to both ages about the role of God in such disasters, and covered them in the next work, *Eternal Justice*. He wanted to show the enduring nature of the Jewish people, and hoped to do this later in a work called *The Days of the World*.

Soon, alas, he was forced to put aside pen and paper once again to become embroiled in a political situation facing Naples and its king. Barely eighteen months after Abravanel's arrival in the Italian state, Ferrante died and was succeeded by his son, Alfonso. The new ruler found himself facing a long-simmering situation which had given his father much concern, the imminent invasion by France, whose king, Charles VIII, had long wanted to capture Naples. In addition, there was the threat of revolt from elements of his population, including nobility and burghers. These unlikely partners had in common the desire to assert their power over the monarchy, and the kingdom's insecure position offered an opportunity to make their demands heard.

Alfonso knew his smaller military force could not prevail over a French invasion, and fearful of insurrection from within, he planned abdication and exile in Sicily. He headed for Mazzara in 1495, then under Neapolitan command. Don Isaac was by his side, requested by the king to accompany him.

One might wonder why Abravanel left his family to accompany a powerless former monarch into exile. He had been in Naples only two and one-half years, and had enjoyed peace, celebrity, increase of fortune and a supportive atmosphere for writing and study. One possible answer is the French king's hostility to Jews and the danger to Don Isaac were he to remain. But even this was small justification for leaving behind family and fortune. The probable explanation was his loyalty and gratitude to the royal family,

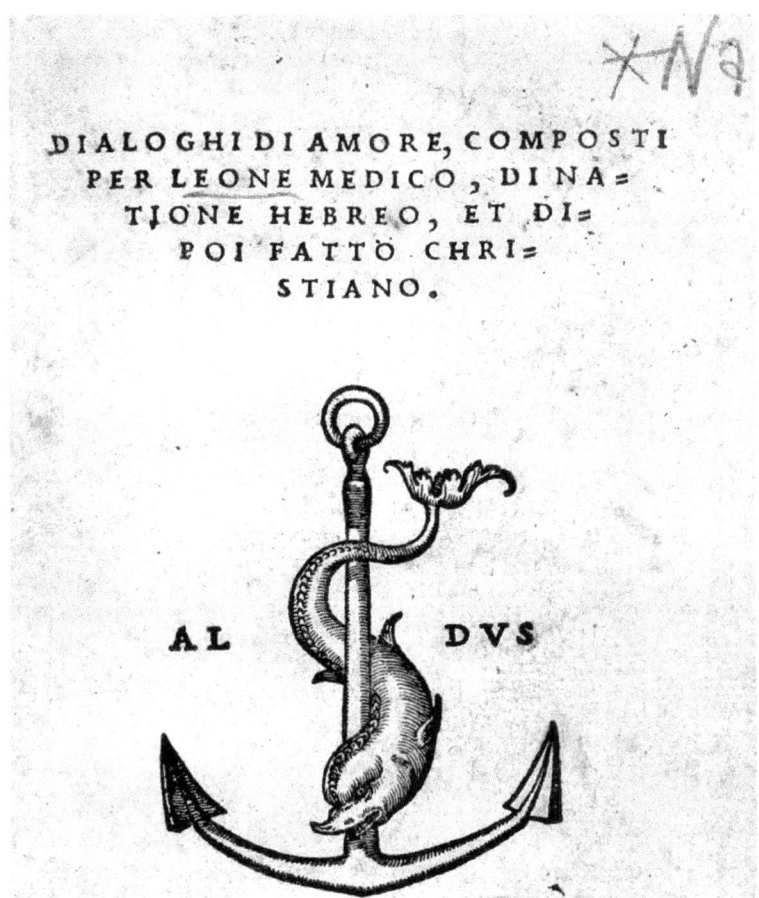

Isaac Abravanel's son, Judah (1437–1508), became known as Leone Ebreo, poet, philosopher and physician. His neo-Platonic work, *Dialoghi di Amore*, Dialogues of Love, was well received in the Renaissance of sixteenth-century Italian principalities such as Venice and Genoa, and is said to have influenced his father's thinking and writing. The title page of this 1545 edition reads "*Dialoghi di Amore,* composed by Doctor Leone, of the Hebrew nation, who later converted to Christianity." The claim of conversion has been questioned because of Abravanel's firm adherence to Judaism in his life and work and the supposition that the claim was added in the publication process, after the author's death. See Appendix for Judah's poem mourning the loss of his son. (Leone Hebreo. *Dialoghi di Amore* [Venice: 1545], title page, RB423:9, fol. 1r. Courtesy of the Library of the Jewish Theological Seminary.)

who had welcomed his ship and the caravans of homeless Jews, turned away at sea from other Italian ports, and sheltered them from a hostile population.

Indeed, soon after Charles' army entered the city, French forces backed local elements in an organized massacre and sacking of the Jewish community. Abravanel's home was among those broken into. His library and some manuscripts were lost, and as he wrote in his commentary on Deuteronomy, "My entire enormous wealth was stolen."[25]

At this time, son Judah left Naples to settle in Genoa, where he took up his medical career once again. Don Isaac was faced with the problem of safety for the rest of his family remaining behind. Yet he hesitated moving them with the continuing power shifts among France, Venice, the Vatican and Spain, all players in the drama.

In April of 1495, Abravanel joined Alfonso in Palermo, then went on with him to Messina. The monarch's son, Ferrante II, was allied with a Spanish force in an effort to oust the French from Naples. Alfonso had brief hopes of returning to the helm of his kingdom, but these ended when he realized that his son would not agree to give up the monarchy. He entered a monastery in Palermo, and Abravanel left Messina in June for Corfu, under Venetian rule, to explore the city republic as a more permanent, possible home for his family. Another choice for resettlement was the Ottoman Empire. Son Samuel had studied in Salonika in the past, and Jews had enjoyed the good will of the sultan.

Corfu was an eye-opening experience, with Don Isaac able to reconnect with scholars and rabbis. Jews were able to pause there and enjoy the freedom offered while planning their next step, usually emigration to the Ottoman Empire. While nourished by this intellectual and spiritual environment, Abravanel also became aware of the Jewish emigrés' despair, their neglect of the spiritual and pursuit of the material, all results of homelessness and suffering.

This stimulated his thinking on the age-old questions facing his people. At this point, he suspended his work on a commentary on Isaiah to take on a defense of the foundations of Jewish faith as an antidote to the abandonment of principle he saw everywhere. He began work on *Principles of Faith*, written to defend the foundations of Judaism represented by Maimonides. At the same time, he would present his views on belief which opposed those of the Rambam, who embodied the rationalist thinking of the time. Abravanel's principles were expressed within the text as his twenty-seven "objections" to the Rambam's thirteen. *Principles* would become Abravanel's most popular work. In it, he affirmed support for the fundamentals of Judaism, while rebutting, respectfully, Maimonides' interpretations. It is indeed this work, and his writings on messianism, completed later in his last years, that would be the most consulted and influential of Abravanel's for centuries. Some historians would blame it, with hindsight in the years ahead, for Jews rejecting the use of organized action to confront oppressors. Don Isaac counseled prayer and patience instead, to prepare for the messiah, who, it was believed, would rescue them.[26]

Corfu offered Don Isaac an opportunity to consider how aspects of life in a Muslim environment might affect his family should they migrate there. He realized that it would be more comfortable for them to find a new home within European culture. Venice, then, became his destination. Family members left behind in Naples would wait until the French were defeated so they could move freely and join the patriarch.

At the close of the fifteenth century, the Venetian Republic was approaching her zenith as a dominant sea power. Relative freedom was allowed to Jews living within her borders. In line with his thoughts of settling there, Abravanel went first to Monopoli in Sicily, also under Venetian control, arriving in late 1495 or early 1496. Once again, he had respite from political and social responsibilities and resumed his writing. He finished his commentary on Deuteronomy soon after his arrival, and entered a period of re-evaluation of personal, professional and spiritual issues.

When immersed in action, whether in work or family or community, one lives very much in the present. When activity ends, however, and there is time for contemplation, significant and sometimes disturbing issues arise that have been ignored in the former frenzy of movement. Thus it was with Don Isaac. He had surely witnessed horrors and experienced homelessness. His shrinking fortune was in peril. He had been separated from loved ones for over two years, and would remain so for at least five more, although he did receive visits while in Monopoli from son Judah, son-in-law Joseph and the latter's brother Jacob, who lived in nearby Bari.

It is in this period of transition that Abravanel wrote two pieces dealing with the ancient redemption of the Jews. He wanted to inspire the Jewish people living, as he was, without homeland, security and peace, and discovered that the analysis and retrospection accompanying the writing helped inspire him as well. A few months after arriving in Monopoli, he completed *Passover Sacrifice*, on the meaning of the biblical story of transition from slavery to freedom and the promise of one's land. Next, he worked on *Inheritance of the Fathers*, presenting the teachings of the sages as God-inspired, and as a heritage for Jews who observed their religion, even though it often meant suffering and hardship.

These works completed, he ruminated about why the suffering continued and when or whether it would end. These questions lay at the bedrock of any attempt to inspire the Jewish people, at home nowhere, safe nowhere.

He agreed that, yes, we suffer as a result of holding fast to the legacy of our beliefs, then asked if this suffering must continue forever. Was there to be no end? These questions led him to the age-old promise of salvation. And so, in July of 1495, he began the first of three works on the messiah.

It was natural for Don Isaac to focus on his people's traditional expectation of messianic salvation, given his personal witness and study. Homeless and persecuted and at the mercy of rulers, churchmen, the resentful middle classes and the mobs always ready for incitement, Jews everywhere yearned fervently for the messiah to save them. Don Isaac's works mirrored Jewish anguish and desperation throughout the diaspora and in the few scholarly outposts of the Holy Land. His three works, *Wells of Salvation, The Salvation of His Anointed* and *The Announcer of Salvation*, took almost three years to write and were finally completed in February, 1498. They were to influence Jewish thought for centuries into the future. *Wells* validated the messianic yearning and predicted the arrival of the promised one in 1503. The next two books provided documentation for this belief through analysis of biblical and other references.

He next penned *New Heavens*, relating astrologically the concept of creation to Maimonides' theories and in August, 1498, he completed the commentary on Isaiah, which he had begun in Corfu. This had indeed been a most prolific period for the philosopher and biblical sage.

The Italian war had been over since 1496, but Don Isaac elected to stay in Monopoli long after to finish the messianic trilogy. Then, in 1501, French forces, in league with Spain under a secret treaty, crossed the Alps and met in Naples, where they were victorious. During this period, Abravanel wrote *Deeds of God*, heavily influenced by son Judah's neo–Platonic thinking, which the latter had expressed in his work in progress, *Dialoghi d'Amore*, Dialogue of Love.

Soon, France and Spain were at war with each other over Naples, with Spain ultimately prevailing. Abravanel had been in Monopoli for the past seven years, immersed in a relatively peaceful and intellectually fruitful period of his life. His son Judah had become personal physician to Gonsalvo de Córdova, leader of the Spanish forces, who entered the war against France in support of Naples' Alfonso. Gonsalvo and Abravanel had been acquainted in Spain, where the former was among the more liberal noblemen, friendly toward the Jews. In 1503, Don Isaac finally departed Monopoli to join his son-in-law, Joseph, who had settled in Venice as an established and prominent physician. Soon the remnants of his family in Naples joined them, and they were reunited at last.

Abravanel had been separated from his family for eight years. During that time, there had been opportunities for him to join them, or at the very least, to arrange to meet them, although regarded as an enemy by both France and Spain, he would have risked capture were he to enter Naples or the territory of either nation. However, he appeared to have benefited from the isolation, first in Corfu, then in Monopoli, which afforded him ample time and space to write and contemplate.

Venice was to be the last country of residence for the aging Abravanel, now sixty-six years old. He arrived at a crossroads in the city's history. The Queen of the Sea, as the republic was called, was facing serious threats to her well-being. Chief among these was Portugal's dominance of the spice trade since Vasco da Gama's successful 1503 voyage had opened a new sub–African trade route to the Indian continent. Thanks to this, the Portuguese could carry spices directly to Europe by ship, reducing cost and increasing profit considerably. Venice had earlier controlled the spice trade until the advance of the Ottoman Empire absorbed the Greek outposts that served as her trading colonies. She had compensated for this by arranging with Egypt to utilize its sea route to India. Thus, she had stayed in command of the trade, although the costs were much higher. Now, however, the Portuguese had eliminated the competitive edge, and Venice realized that she had to negotiate with the new trade giant for a piece of the spice trade. She wanted to win the Portuguese over to an arrangement similar to the one with Egypt: an expensive monopoly, but a monopoly nevertheless, thus worth the cost. For without the trade revenues, Venice could not continue in a leadership position due to financial losses from military and economic activities.

A recent arrival in Venice, Isaac Abravanel soon found himself in the center of governmental activity. Once again, the scholar, writer and biblical philosopher gave way to the financial statesman. He soon appeared before the governing Council of Ten, *il Consiglio dei Dieci* with a plan that would serve as the basis for negotiations with the Portuguese.

The members of *Il Dieci* came away with a positive opinion of the newcomer. Undoubtedly, they knew about the high position in state finance he had held in Portugal and of his widely acknowledged financial services to Spain's Catholic Majesties. His plan was accepted, and because of his former service as treasurer to the Duke of Viseu, (a Braganza executed by João II when Don Isaac had fled to Spain), his son Joseph was dispatched to present the plan in Lisbon. Manoel, brother to the executed duke, was now king. Joseph was a good choice, then, as the ruler regarded him highly. Negotiations followed, with Portugal eventually rejecting the proposal. Her political economy dictated she not surrender her competitive edge to the Adriatic Venetian power, even for a tidy sum over a period of several years. We will see in Chapter Five how the Lisbon-based House of Mendes eventually headed by Doña Gracia Nasi, would come to corner the mercantile aspects of the spice trade thirty years later.

Despite the failure of negotiations, Venetian rulers continued to show their respect for Abravanel and ask his counsel from time to time. This was Abravanel's final effort as statesman. He moved again into his writing. Ahead lay almost five years of prolific literary activity. It was significant that this talented and remarkable individual, who had lived through so much turmoil, danger and crisis, would end his days in relative peace, doing what he enjoyed most. He produced several more works, finishing at last *Principles of Faith* and the messianic trilogy. *Principles'* introduction set forth the book's intention to help the average person navigate among the several circulating guide lists for Jewish belief and decide which to follow. Another purpose was to represent Maimonides and his principles, then under assault by critics such as Albo and Crescas. After taking apart their objections, however, Abravanel set forth twenty-eight of his own disagreements with the Rambam's principles and added on nine propositions. It is interesting how Don Isaac, exponent of the position that the sages' teachings are literal truth, began by defending Maimonides, the exponent of rationalism, from attacks by others before going on the offensive himself. It appeared to be a case of respect for his intellectual and spiritual peer, with whom he identified in the strong espousal of Judaic fundamentals, regardless of differences on how to effectuate them. Don Isaac's high regard for the Rambam was evident, even as he took on the latter's Thirteen Principles and replaced them with his own. One visualizes a meeting of the two in heaven, where the 200-year time gap between them is dissolved, and they can debate long into the celestial night, surrounded by scholars.

His political career at rest, immersed in his studies and writings, Don Isaac was forced to compensate for his increasing physical fragility. He described it in *Answers to Saul:* his eyesight and hands were increasingly weak and he needed assistance in putting words to paper. Nevertheless, he continued his literary and scholarly efforts to the end, which came in December of 1508, at the advanced age of seventy-one.

Isaac Abravanel was mourned by Jew and Christian alike. His body was buried in Padua, as Venetian laws prohibited interment of Jews within city boundaries. Nevertheless, the leaders of Venice paid special tribute as he was honored by the republic that sheltered him at the end of a long and tumultuous life, and to which he gave his last political service.

He left his heirs and his people a prodigious spiritual and literary inheritance. Even Christian scholars and clergy would study the works of the man who had translated Thomas Aquinas' *Quaestio de spiritualibus creaturis* and referred in his writings to the Latin analyses of Christian scholars.

For Jews, the voluminous collection of twenty works was to provide bulwarks against the erosion of their faith and ammunition in defending it against

Prolific writer and biblical exegete, Isaac Abravanel influenced Judaic thought centuries after his passing, particularly on messianism. His commentary in *Nevi'im Rishonim*, The First to Understand, was published in 1511, three years after his death in 1508. (Isaac Abravanel. *Nevi'im Rishonim* [Pesaro: 1511], 1693:1, fol. 1r. Courtesy of the Library of the Jewish Theological Seminary.)

Christian proselytizers. Scholars and laymen alike combed *Principles of Faith* and the messianic trilogy for beacons of hope to light their way through the dark reality of everyday Jewish life in the early modern period which followed.

He served six kings well, helping them to fill their coffers with funds for military efforts as well as the day-to-day expenses of running and ruling their realms. His counsel had been much sought after in political as well as financial matters. As a courtier, his natural talents had been boosted by the sense of mission, his lineage replete with service to monarchs and splendid records of success in doing so. He was the closest thing to a prince for a commoner, raised with a belief in his destiny, prepared for leadership, and set early on the path to multiple layers of high service. Propelling this had been his family's conviction of their descent from the royal house of Israel's King David, referred to by Don Isaac in his introduction to the commentary on Isaiah, and said by some to have girded him in the legendary rebuttal to Queen Isabel, when the expulsion decree was imminent.

Loewe asserts that "The great things about Abravanel were his sanity and dignity.... In his actions he was sober and deliberate. He never lost his head; he never exaggerated; he took long views; he had a calm and judicial outlook." This was particularly visible in the period just before the issuing of the Alhambra Decree, and until the expulsion, when Don Isaac took on the role of chief defender and inspiration for his fellow Sephardic Jews. Loewe calls him "a true *Shtadlan*," or defender: "Amid the overwhelming attacks of Church and Crown he was able to prepare a double defense, to organize the relief of the wanderers and to fit them out with literary weapons with which to meet their adversaries who sought to destroy their faith in their religion."[27]

In his seminal work, *Don Isaac Abravanel*, Netanyahu quotes praiseworthy descriptions by Don Isaac's coreligionists: "great eagle," "as wise as Daniel" and "a man of God." He adds that "in times of tragedy and disaster like those in which his Jewish contemporaries lived, nothing so fortifies a people's morale as does a great leader whom they can revere and follow."

At the same time, Netanyahu claims that Abravanel failed to grasp the political situation of Europe's Jews, homeless and outcast, destined to be scapegoats at a time of shifting power bases. He calls Don Isaac's mysticism a "veil," preventing him from applying the clarity and genius for which he was renown to his long view of Jewish needs and protections.[28]

Netanyahu bemoans the failure of Abravanel to grasp the possibility of *aliyah*, Jewish return to Palestine, "a realistic course, a plan of regaining the Promised Land by settlement and colonization.... Such advocacy might have changed the entire historic attitude of the Jews toward their national problem and kept their eyes fixed on earth, rather than upon heaven."[29]

Two. Isaac Abravanel

This judgment, made with hindsight, appears unduly harsh. Isaac Abravanel epitomized the thinking of the age that gave him birth. In the philosophic conflict within Judaism at that time, he argued for the primacy of the prophets' teachings, as expressed in the Torah and interpreted by the sages. The rationalism of Maimonides, which allowed for present day interpretation of the law and teachings, grew out of an earlier and less grim period in Sephardic Jewish history, often referred to as its golden age. Although wealthy and allied with friends of Judaism in his great battles, Don Isaac remained a solitary leader once forced to leave Portugal, where his power base had been strong. He never regained the same highly influential position. This must be weighed when comparing his approach to protecting Jews from persecution with that of Gracia and Joseph Nasi, one-half century later, as will be seen in Chapter Five. Scion of the powerful House of Mendes, comparable to the Rothschilds of their day, Joseph had become the Duke of Naxos of the Ottoman Empire, and, with his redoubtable aunt, Gracia, was an influential of great wealth and resources. In addition, the Nasis were *judaizing* New Christians, who had been separated from formal Judaism until well into their adult years, and had practiced an unofficial version of their religion in secret. It was natural that their approach to Judaism would be more relativistic, relying on pragmatism and survival rather than ancient guidelines by prophets long gone.

Three times an exile, with loss of a power base each time, Abravanel's world view was governed by the lifelong Judaic teachings he carried with him. His was the perspective of the powerless and rootless, armed through history with only the Torah and the promise of God. It would lie to the Nasis, one-half century later, to use tools like economic boycott and Holy Land settlement to attempt rescue of endangered Jews.

Abravanel recreated the Sephardic Passover *Haggadah* to keep tradition alive in the diaspora. On this holiday, Jews observe their freedom from slavery in Egypt, and the forty-year passage in the desert to the Promised Land. In the *Haggadah,* which is read aloud at the *seder,* or ritual dinner shared with family and friends, there is a litany of gratitude praising God, repeated by all assembled. Singled out for thanksgiving are bringing the Jews out of Egypt to freedom and giving them the Torah and the Sabbath. After each recitation of a blessing, the group chants "*dayanu,*" translated as "it would have been sufficient," meaning that each act of God for the Jews stands alone as a great gift. We will borrow this format to recognize the awesomeness of Isaac Abravanel's gifts to his people.

> If he had merely argued before the King and Queen of Spain against expelling his people, it would have been sufficient.
> If he had argued and not advised the monarchs of the impermanence of their kingdom and the endurance of the Jews, it would have been sufficient.

If he had done these and not mobilized and inspired his people to resist conversion, it would have been sufficient.

If he had led observant Jews into their diaspora, and not accompanied the good King Alfonso into exile out of gratitude, it would have been sufficient.

And if he had done all these and not created a legacy of written works to inspire and educate his people and all readers, it would have been sufficient.

His descendants in the twenty-first century, five hundred years later, are legion. They live in many countries. The *Abravanel Family Newsletter*, published by an American descendant, Allan R. Abravanel of Portland, Oregon, includes articles on the diaspora and achievements of those in the family bloodline.

One issue features a story about the accomplishments and heritage of Moises Naim, Venezuelan government leader and political scientist, whose mother "is an Abravanel, whose family emigrated from Turkey to Italy, and then to Venezuela." Next is an article, originating in Budapest, about the athletic achievements in the United States of a nineteen-year-old with physical disabilities, bearing the name Abarbanel. Following that, is a letter from an Abarbanell from Klimovsk near Moscow, who is a Russian broadcasting leader and theater director. He traces the first Abarbanell in Russia to "an officer of Napoleon's army in 1812." The issue also contains a photo of Eli Abravanel, professional soccer player from Israel.

Another article covers Scholar Jonathan Skolnik's research into "the fascination with the Sephardi Scholar and statesman" as "a unique German-Jewish phenomenon." In the hundred years that witnessed a progression from Emancipation to exile and extermination, Abravanel was used by German-Jewish writers to invoke various (and opposing) political positions, but the Abravanel of German-Jewish fiction was always a paragon of Bildung [learning] and moral fortitude." The article closes with the English translation of an inscription to family members that a German woman, Regine Marcus, wrote in 1938 in a copy of Abraham Heschel's 1937 novel, *Don Jizchak Abrabanel*.

> Your nobility should not look backwards, but forward! From whence you came does not make up your honor, but rather where you go! In these lines shall grandchildren become ancestors. And thus strives the descendant of the great scholar Abarbanell in her own education and that of her children.

The signature at the end of the inscription is "Berlin 1938, Regine Marcus, whose mother still bore the name Abarbanell." Alas, Marcus' name later appears in German World War Two records as a deportee from Berlin to the concentration camps.[30]

The masthead of each issue of *The Abravanel Family Newsletter* carries the ancestor's proud and defiant words: "Basta mi nombre que es Abravanel." It is enough that my name is Abravanel. No more need be said.

THREE

Abraham Zacuto: From Discovery by the Stars to a Crater on the Moon

The voyages of Christopher Columbus and Vasco da Gama are considered the most momentous of the Age of Discovery because of the significant land and sea frontiers that the navigators crossed and the significant effects these journeys had on subsequent events. Each voyage opened prosperous new trade routes and largely unknown lands to European exploration, exploitation and settlement, with subsequent substantial power shifts among the nations and major population movements on five continents.

While Columbus and da Gama merit the significance that has been placed on their journeys, there is one more name, however, that belongs among the eminences of navigational achievement. The almanac and astrolobe he developed were basic to the success of each of these journeys. Like the seamen, then, it can be said that Abraham ben Samuel Zacuto, astronomer and astrologer, contributed significantly to the opening of new riches, new routes and new lands in the fifteenth and sixteenth centuries.

His celestial tables and copper astrolabe, along with the significant developments throughout the fourteenth and fifteenth centuries by fellow Sephardic scientists, mathematicians and cartographers, made it possible for navigators to maintain course when the sun and the North Star were not visible. Zacuto's *Almanach Perpetuum*, or *Hajibbur Hagadol*, its original Hebrew title, was as much a consulted guide on da Gama's flagship as it had been on Columbus' ship; his improved astrolabe, a forerunner of the navigational sextant, enhanced the success of the Portuguese navigators.[1]

The life of Abraham Zacuto reveals much about the forces, both ancient and contemporary, that have propelled scientific energy and creativity through the ages and the journeys of those who would come upon unspoiled lands and resources to explore and exploit. The urge to venture beyond the known is unique to no one period in history; rather, the records of adventurous voyages and overland explorations have long been recorded in history, often becoming the stuff of sagas. One in particular is the noteworthy voyage of the year 1,000, when the Norse Leif Ericson made the first known European footfall in the Western Hemisphere.[2]

Four hundred years later, in the early fifteenth century, Portugal's Prince Henry, third son of João I, spearheaded successive voyages moving progressively south along the western coast of Africa, including the islands lying offshore. The list of navigators and their "discoveries" reads like a litany, beginning with Gonçalvo Zarco and Tristão Vaz Teixeira, who came upon Porto Santo and Madeira in 1419–20. They were followed fifteen years later by Gil Eanes, who in 1434 rounded Dobrou or Cape Bojador, and by Nuno Tristão, who came upon Cape Branco in 1441 and Senegal in 1446. Next was Diogo Gomes in 1460, who discovered the Cape Verde archipelago. That same year, Pedro de Sintra reached Cape Ledo in Sierra Leone, and the following year, Liberia. In the 1480s, the next king, João II, took up Henry's lead, sponsoring Diogo Cão, who reached the mouth of the River Zaire, rounded Cape Santa María, studied the Angola coast and came upon Namibia.

It was left for Bartholomeu Dias to round the Cape of Good Hope in 1488, setting the stage for da Gama's ultimate voyage a decade later to continue east to India and its spices by an as yet uncharted route.[3] This was to be the crown of the past century's explorations. If such a passage were to prove feasible, Portugal could dispense with the present overland trade route and the political and economic costs entailed, and trade directly for the Levantine spices, gems and other commodities.

In his search for new routes to greater riches, Prince Henry the Navigator and his successors had developed the caravel to carry their seaborne explorers. This was a light and fast moving vessel with lateen or triangular sails. In the early fifteenth century, Henry established the maritime academy at Sagres on the southwestern most tip of Portugal. There, he brought together prominent geographers, astronomers, astrologers and cartographers, most of them Sephardim. From them, the navigators learned about developments in course plotting and map reading and to work with wind systems and ocean currents, as well as to use new tools and equipment. As it will be seen, Zacuto was to be among this distinguished training staff a generation or more later in the century.[4]

Throughout the fourteenth and early fifteenth centuries, the great Sephardic cartographers of Mallorca had charted the warfare and trading seascapes for the galleons, cogs and caravels of the Christian kings, as they had before for Muslim vessels. Charles VI of France was so impressed by the

Three. Abraham Zacuto

Abraham Cresques, patriarch of the renowned Sephardic family of Mallorcan cartographers, prepared this atlas for the royal court, ca. 1373. Written in Catalán, it is considered perhaps the most significant atlas of the Middle Ages. The map included the first description of *el nocturlabio*, a medieval navigational instrument which determined the time of night by measuring the position of Ursa Major, or the Big Dipper, in relation to the North Star. Abraham's son, Jafudá or Jehuda, served at Sagres, Portugal's navigational academy, in the next century. Jafudá converted to Catholicism when the massacre of 1391 decimated the Sephardic population of Mallorca, moving to Barcelona and taking the name Jaume Ribes. (Generalitat Valenciana, ed. *Lluís de Santàngel y su época: un nuevo hombre, un mundo nuevo* [Valencia: 1992], 117.)

Catalán *Atlas* of *Mestre* Abraham Cresques of Mallorca that he ordered a special room prepared in his palace for its display. The *Atlas* was a gift to the French monarch by Prince Juan of Aragón, who had commissioned it in 1376. The Cresques family was perhaps the most well known of the school of cartographers, centered in the Balearic Islands since the mid–fourteenth century. Abraham Cresques had served as an adviser to Spanish and Portuguese rulers, and, later, his son, Yehuda, would join the prominent scientists and navigation specialists, training navigators and seamen at Sagres.[5]

Venice, "Queen of the Sea" on the Italian peninsula, was then at her zenith in the use of sea power for trade and conquest. She had been successful in negotiating the agreements and payments necessary for countries to the east to allow her traders to pass from the Mediterranean to the Levant and back, making her first in benefits from the spice trade. This was a hazardous and expensive path over land and water. It was also necessary to face the burgeoning Ottoman Empire, as it increased its competition with European ports.[6] A Portuguese route around Africa, headed directly to India, would eliminate payments to other powers through whose territory traders had to pass, reduce the diplomatic and other hazards implicit in the political economy of the day and make Portugal paramount over Venice and other national contenders for the lucrative eastern Mediterranean trade. Those were the stakes facing Portugal's King Manoel as he struggled in 1497 with whether and when to commission a captain and fleet for the sub–African voyage.

It has been seen that Manoel's predecessor, João II, had sponsored the significant preparatory explorations outlined above. In addition, Joseph Vecinho, his court mathematician and scientist, had headed a 1485 voyage to Guinea, during which he tried out the new *Almanach Perpetuum* by the Sephardic astronomer Abraham Zacuto. The tables had proven most effective, helping his navigator calculate the ship's position more accurately than ever.[7] Vecinho, also Jewish, had studied under *Mestre* Zacuto, former astronomy professor at the University of Salamanca.

Vecinho continued as navigation adviser to Manoel I, who had succeeded João upon his death in 1493. Zacuto was then court astronomer to Manoel, having first served under João upon his arrival in Portugal, following his expulsion from Spain in 1492. Along with the other explorers, Vecinho was helping lay the groundwork for the proposed voyage around the Cape of Good Hope to the Levantine. All that remained was for the king to give the green light to the journey.

Yet Manoel held back. There was much at risk in the politics of the day if the journey failed, given his dream to rule someday over a united Spain and Portugal. Vecinho understood the disquietude of the king, yet he knew that the success of such a journey would give Portugal unrivaled dominance over the lucrative spice and other trades. Perhaps it was he who advised Manoel to ask *Mestre* Abraham what the stars portended for this voyage. Manoel summoned his court astronomer, then, to a private audience, and asked his opinion of the voyage's viability. He told him that his reply would determine the future of the enterprise and swore him to secrecy.[8]

It was not the first time that monarchs had sought out Zacuto's counsel as they struggled with decisions regarding navigation. In the winter of 1486–1487, when Christopher Columbus first asked Fernando and Isabel, Spain's Catholic Majesties, to support his westward journey, the Salamanca professor was summoned to give his opinion on its probable success. He had responded in favor of the voyage.[9] Now, ten years later, he was facing a similar challenge and the responsibility that went with it. In his response to Manoel, he emphasized first, that, despite the apparent effects of planets and stars on human affairs, God alone determines their paths and all outcomes. Nevertheless, his study of the celestial balance had told him that all portents for the voyage were positive. He advised the king that, despite distance, seafaring risks, and the potential of encountering hostile populations, "your Highness will discover and subjugate a large part of India in a very short time."[10]

A pleased Manoel presented Zacuto with gifts and cautioned him once more to keep their interchange confidential. Subsequently, the navigator Vasco da Gama was made captain and preparations were begun for his voyage. History would validate Zacuto's predictions of success, and the monarch would come to be called Manoel the Fortunate.

Much of what we know of Zacuto's heritage comes from his historical and philosophical work, *Sefer Yohassin*, or *The Book of Lineage*. He writes of his ancestors coming to Spain from France in 1306, at the time of the French expulsion of the Jews, and settling in Castilla. In the introduction to a German edition of the work published in 1926, Abraham Haim Freimann describes both sides of Zacuto's family as "of noble descent," meaning descended from learned Jewish scholars, quoting the astronomer's words that they "never left the study of the torah since the days of old."[11]

The Zacutos had been in Spain for almost one hundred and fifty years when the future astronomer was born in 1452 in the old university city of Salamanca. He was named after his grandfather, Rabbi Abraham Zacuto, *El Viejo*. It had been a turbulent period of increasing persecution for Sephardim. Earlier chapters mention the conversion frenzy of 1391, when mobs, fired up by churchmen, slaughtered thousands of Jewish inhabitants and destroyed their residential areas in most cities of Christian Spain. Fearing for their lives, many Jews converted. Thousands more followed, well into the fifteenth century, after successive incidents of violence and increasingly restrictive laws

Vasco da Gama kneels before Manoel I, as Abraham Zacuto watches, holding a copy of *Almanach Perpetuum*, astronomical tables he has developed that will be put to use on the voyage to India around the Cape of Good Hope. See illustration on page 62. (J. H. Amshewitz. *Vasco da Gama Leaving Portugal*. Painting in William Cullen Library, University of the Witwatersrand, Johannesburg, South Africa.)

affected Jewish life and livelihood. In his *Yohassin*, which Zacuto would complete in later years, he wrote with pride that his ancestors had held firm to their religious faith, despite the continuing specter of terror and persecution. As we will see, his life story became a testament to that tradition.

Much of his boyhood was spent immersed in studies of Torah and Talmud. His tutors were his father, Samuel, and Isaac Canpanton, head of the Toledo *Yeshiva*, whom Joseph Caro called "one of the greatest scholars of his time."[12] He next took up studies with the revered Rabbi Isaac Aboab II of Castilla who was called *gaon*, or most revered learned one, by his colleagues. The rabbi's family had long been respected among Sephardic scholars, and his descendants were found later throughout the Mediterranean diaspora and in the Lowlands. Aboab was the founder of the *Yeshiva*, or Hebrew academy, in Guadalajara.

As we read in Chapter Two, many prominent scholars, among them Isaac Abravanel, came to live in or near Guadalajara so they could study with him.

The study of Torah and Talmud was to be a vital area of Zacuto's life and one with which he closely identified. He refers to himself as "*Rabi*" in his writings. Barely in his twenties, Abraham ben Samuel Zacuto was also called *Rabi* by Judaic scholars for his knowledge of Talmud. The young man's writings were already contributing to Hebrew thought and discourse. While mastery of both science and religion was not common in late medieval Europe, it was certainly not rare among Zacuto's Sephardic peers, who often demonstrated achievement in religious studies, as well as in their worldly professions.[13]

In the early 1470's, the young man became a student at Salamanca, oldest and most respected of Spanish universities, whose motto, *Omnium cientiorum princeps Salmantica docet*, declares that Salamanca is foremost in the teaching of all the sciences. Founded in the thirteenth century by Alfonso X of Castilla, who has been called *el sabio*, the wise one, the university was also the largest in Spain, with many influential graduates, and its "style" was adapted throughout Iberia. It fulfilled Alfonso's intentions as a center of research in the sciences, particularly astronomy and astrology,[14] which were considered related disciplines at that time.

Zacuto was in the right place at the right time. His talent and ability were recognized early by scholars and local eminences. Gonzalo de Vivero, Bishop of Salamanca, was one of these. Impressed by the gifted student, he used his influence to have him appointed to the vacant university chair in astronomy and astrology. Given the restrictions of the era, it is worth exploring the history of this churchman, who became the patron of a Jewish scholar and secured a professorial post for him at the most prestigious university in Spain.

Bishop from 1447 to 1480, Gonzalo de Vivero was indeed a late medieval-era model for the Renaissance man. Head of his religious order and counselor to kings, he represented monarchs on diplomatic missions and served notably in military campaigns of the *Reconquista*. Vivero was also known for his strong interest in science and letters. A book collector, his renowned library included rare works on agriculture, morals, law and medicine, as well as literature and the arts. There was even a translation from lighter reading, the popular French romance of the day, *Arbol de las Batallas*, by Honoré Bonnet.

As ruling prelate of the district, the noted university was under his jurisdiction.[15] Perhaps the gifted young Zacuto, still in his teens, first came to his attention as he observed the lively after-class sessions of classmates with their professors. In the universities of the late middle ages, professors were called readers as well as masters, because they first read their lessons in class, then met afterwards with students for questions. Since masters assumed the traditional position of leaning against the university's courtyard pillars during the ensuing dialogues, the interaction was called *asistir el poste*, or holding up the pillar with one's back. Interchanges *al poste* were lively and intense, with professors obligated to stay until all questions are answered. The significance of these sessions in the learning process is underscored in a letter from nobleman Enrique de Guzmán to his son. The father advises the young man, who is beginning university study, to take full advantage of the sessions.

> As one comes out of a class, it is necessary to go to the cloister and hear the questions put by his fellow scholars to the master at the pillar in order to get one's difficulties solved, and to understand the subject better, which will encourage him to study with care, so that he too can argue with the master.[16]

Vivero may have seen the young Zacuto in dialogue with his masters, and sought him out to learn about him, his knowledge and abilities. Soon, the bishop became Zacuto's patron. A respectful, yet warm relationship developed, with the two sharing frequent discussions on astronomy and related subjects. Not long after, the gifted protégé was appointed to the seat in astronomy and astrology.

It was the custom for professors to be selected at public meetings for vacant faculty seats. The electors were students, rather than peers, voting from among two or more candidates. The system was open to corruption, with many a tale of less affluent, hungry students accepting feasts and other favors in exchange for their votes.[17]

It is not known whether Vivero, as jurisdictional prelate, needed to utilize these means of persuasion, or if his word was sufficient to help his Jewish protégé to win the most prestigious academic post in the sciences in Spain. Researchers do not agree on the year of the appointment, but review of the literature points to the early 1470's, with the astronomer in his late teens or early twenties.

Bishop Vivero was well-informed and knew of the limitations imposed on sea journeys by the inability to maintain direction far from land without the stars. He realized that the young astronomer's knowledge could be put to work creating an almanac that would chart the positions of sun and moon throughout the year, thus facilitating sea captains in calculating distances from the equator and in setting and maintaining course latitudes.

Soon, Vivero encouraged Zacuto to prepare such an almanac. It began taking form in 1473, when the astronomer was twenty-one years old, and was completed in five years. It was written in Hebrew and Aramaic, and was titled *Hajibbur Hagadol*, The Great Essay. In 1481, Juan Selayo, the astronomer's colleague, was to translate the doctrinal exposition preceding the tables into Castillian Spanish.[18]

Hajibbur Hagadol brought fame to its author, and Zacuto became much sought after for opinions on navigation. The work crossed borders, eventually even continents. In the next decade, Joseph Vecinho translated ten pages and the tables from Hebrew/Aramaic into Latin, to be put to use as courtier to King João. He completed the translation, which he called *Almanach Perpetuum*, in 1485, while on a mission for João to Guinea to verify Zacuto's figures of latitudes at the altitude of the sun. Soon after, Vecinho also translated this abridged *Hajibbur Hagadol* into Castillian, supplementing Juan Selayo's version.[19]

As has been said, copies of the *Almanach* accompanied Columbus and da Gama on their voyages, empowering them to plot and maintain course effectively. In his diary, Columbus writes how he and his men were saved from death during his first voyage. Knowing from the *Almanach* of an approaching eclipse, he warned the leaders of a menacing tribe that his god would take away the moon. The natives retreated, seeing the eclipse as evidence of the intruders' most powerful deity.[20]

Hajibbur Hagadol was organized into nineteen chapters, following the Hebraic cyclical number and Maimonides' writings about *Rosh Hodesh*, the traditional new moon ritual. In the Introduction, Astronomer Zacuto assured himself as Talmudist Zacuto that the work was harmonious with Judaic teachings. He wrote that since the ancient Talmudists had presented no prohibitions against making known the movements of sun and moon, he could go ahead with the work.

> ... en verdad, cosa cuya revelación no vedaron nuestros maestros [the Talmudists] por ello todo mi empeño en fijar todos los movimientos aquéllos....

He also referred to Maimonides' writings, which encouraged knowledge of celestial stages for the observance of the new moon.[21]

In a lengthy acknowledgment section, Zacuto thanked *los sabios anteriores*,

wise ones of the past. His chief classical references were Ptolemy, second century Greek astronomer, mathematician and geographer, and Menaleus of Alexandria. He also recognized the Muslims Albulhosain, Alí Ibn Regal and Averroes. Christian King Alfonso X, *el sabio*, was acknowledged for *Libro del Saber de Astrología*, Book of Astrological Knowledge, which includes tables by Jewish scientists that had been requested by the monarch. In *Hajibbur Hagadol*, Zacuto recognized eleven Jewish scientists as primary sources, among them Rabbi Judá b. Axer, called *El Santo*, Abraham Ben Ezra, Maimonides and Jacob Poel.[22]

Sephardic Jews were able to come into prominence as scientists in the late medieval and early modern period, thanks largely to *convivencia*, the period in which they lived harmoniously for more than seven hundred years with their Muslim rulers. They were able to study astronomy, astrology, medicine and mathematics with Muslim scientists advanced in these subjects, who agreeably shared what they knew. Soon, there were gifted Sephardim in prominent positions in these fields.

Maimonides, to whom Zacuto referred in *Hajibbur*, was a case in point. The renowned philosopher and Talmudist, born Moses ben Maimon in 1135, served as physician and astronomer to Muslim royalty. He penned numerous medical tracts and a medical ethics oath still in use today in schools of medicine. He also wrote on astronomy, and it is this work, well documented with references to ancient and Arabic resources, to which Zacuto referred. Maimonides, then, was a twelfth century model of a Jew with worldly as well as spiritual eminence.[23] The model was demonstrated so well again three hundred years later by our Salamanca astronomer, as it was with Isaac Abravanel.

Although astrology and astronomy were treated as one in Zacuto's *Hajibbur*, he recognized differences in their applications. While medical care or planning for religious festivals were not his goals in preparing the almanac, Zacuto wrote that the data could be used for purposes beyond navigation, such as calculating the moment of conception and the first day of the new moon. "*Yo no ordene este libro sino por la sciencia y no por otro prouecho*," he affirmed, "I did not limit this book for use in science only and not for other uses."[24]

The death of Vivero in 1480 was a personal, as well as professional, loss

Opposite: Abraham Zacuto prepared *Hajibbur Hagadol*, The Great Essay, at the behest of his patron, Gonzalo de Vivero, the Bishop of Salamanca. An almanac charting the positions of sun and moon throughout the year, the tables would be used by Columbus, da Gama and other navigators. Originally prepared in 1478 in Hebrew, the work was later titled *Almanach Perpetuum*, translated into Latin by Joseph Vecinho and into Castillian by Juan Selayo. These pages are reproduced from a 1502 edition of the *Almanach*. (Abraham Zacuto. *Almanach Perpetuum* [1502], courtesy of Biblioteca General Histórica, Universidad de Salamanca, Spain.)

for Zacuto. He soon had a new patron, however, and took up residence in Gata in Extremadura to be near Don Juan de Zúñiga y Pimental, last Master of the Order of Alcántara, a descendant of the Dukes of Arévalo.

Don Juan's new protégé had this to say about him in the prologue to his next work, *Tratado de las Influencias del Cielo*:

> ... a great man from an illustrious lineage ... lover of the sciences and knowledgeable in all of them, it is noted, to his credit, that several wise and learned scholars have left their homelands to continue their work and fulfillment with his support and remuneration in true peace. He can be compared to King Solomon: "Your fame is attested to by all who hear your words."[25]

The interaction between mentor and protégé, as described in the Order's records, was amiable and fulfilling. Writing in *Crónica de la Orden de Alcántara*, his order's chronicle, Alonso de Torres y Tapia described how "el Judío astrólogo," the Jewish astrologer, read to Don Juan "about the earth's spheres and all that it was possible to know of his 'Art.'" The prelate was so enthralled with the subject that he had all the planets, constellations and signs of the zodiac painted on the high ceiling of one of his rooms.[26]

Zacuto's next project was *Tratado de las Influencias del Cielo*, Treatise on the Influences of Heaven, prepared at his patron's behest. This was more clearly a work of astrology than *Hajibbur Hagadol*. Like its predecessor, *Tratado* did not define astrology and astronomy and made no distinction between them. Although it seems the least scientific of Zacuto's works, again one must keep in mind the era in which it was written. In that context, it met the period's definition of scientific, citing significant resources, such as Hippocrates, Aristotle, Menaleus, Abenazar, Abumasar, Indian and Italian scholars and the Bible to support its contents.

Tratado made a case for the importance of astrology and astronomy in the practice of medicine and provided a manual of sorts for physicians of the day. As in *Hajibbur*, it described how planetary phases could be used to calculate the day of human conception. The work promised to provide "all that doctors need to know to use this science to manage treatments, even if they do not have special knowledge of astrology."[27] One can imagine physicians of the period poring over sections on birth phenomena and reviewing how astrological signs are manifest in the four elements and in human organs and limbs.

The original *Tratado* manuscript, found today in Sevilla's Columbina archives, has appended to it *Juicio de los Eclipses*, Opinion on Eclipses. In this work, Zacuto credits Ptolemy as his source, presents his views on how solar and lunar eclipses relate to specific planetary conjunctions and how eclipses relate to "good or bad planets," describing their specific effects on Earth, such as epidemics, war and death.

It is not known how long Zacuto remained in Gata under Don Juan's patronage after his completion of *Tratado* and *Juicio*. It is known that he was back in Salamanca at the end of 1486 and at the beginning of 1487, when Christopher Columbus came to the city to press his petition for a fleet of ships. As seen earlier, Fernando and Isabel were holding court there, and the rulers summoned scientists and cosmographers at the university for their opinions on the voyage. Zacuto was chief among these. *Hajibbur Hagadol* had made him an academic and navigational celebrity, with his views on related issues much sought after.

The astronomer gave a favorable prognosis to Columbus' proposal. They met during the navigator's visit to Salamanca and Zacuto opened his personal library to him. They discussed applications of the tables, which as described previously, would be very much in use during the voyage five years later. Columbus was said to have received a copy of Vicinho's Latin translation earlier, during his time in Lisbon looking for support.[28]

Five years later, on March 31, 1492, the same Catholic Majesties who had reconquered all of Spain utilizing the counsel, skills and resources of Sephardim such as Abraham Zacuto, Luís de Santángel, Abraham and Jehuda Cresques, Isaac Abravanel and Abraham Seneor, issued the Alhambra Decree, the edict of expulsion. It required all practicing Jews to choose between conversion to Christianity and permanent exile from Spain.

There was no choice for Zacuto. Conversion was not an option for one whose faith was the fiber of his life, and whose ancestors had consistently refused to convert, risking life rather than surrender their beliefs.

The difficulties facing the emigrés were great, however noble or courageous their motivations for leaving. The expulsion terms allowed very little to be taken along. In Zacuto's case, he had to sunder his connection with the most significant institution in the sciences, give up his magnificent library and separate from his professional and scholarly colleagues. Unlike the converts to Christianity, for whom the Inquisition and local church institutions kept records of baptisms, confirmations, marriages and deaths, there are few records of Zacuto's family and his wife's name and genealogy, although it is known that he had at least three sons, Jacob, Abraham and Benjamin. His family, about to be torn from two centuries-old roots, wrenched from relatives and friends, divested of possessions and keepsakes, faced the same obstacles as other exiles. However, the Zacuto family's situation was less unstable than most coreligionists planning to cross over into Portugal. They were one of thirty families invited, because of talent or wealth, to settle in that country after payment of a fee of one hundred cruzados. Other immigrants were to be temporary residents.

It does not seem likely that Zacuto and his family were in Zaragoza, as some historians claim, at the time of the expulsion, for they did not cross the nearest frontier into Navarra, as did Jews from northern Spain. It is more logical that he was in Salamanca, as Cantera Burgos averred. His status as the most prominent scientist in Sefarad could not protect him and his family, however, from the anguish, fear and terror around them. Cantera Burgos described the exodus:

> He must have been one of those 120,000 Israelites who ... sought refuge in the kingdom of João II, and probably could be found among the 35,000 who crossed the Portuguese frontier at Ciudad Rodrigo y Villar Formoso, meeting everywhere, as the exiled Isaac Abravanel wrote, sorrow, vast and gloomy darkness, severe distress, greed, loss and discouragement, weakness and poor health, hunger and pestilence.[29]

Some who could not pay the entry fee for the right to stay for eight months made their way furtively into Portugal by back roads and mountain crossings. Others took their chances and entered without the resources. All who could not pay would be declared slaves later by King João, then freed upon his death by his successor, Manoel.

While he was exposed to the terrors of the crossing, the celebrated astronomer did not have to experience the worst of it for long. As explained, his reputation in navigation had won a privileged position for him among the skilled or affluent Jews invited by João. Zacuto's rabbi and religious teacher, Isaac Aboab, had been one of those who negotiated with João for this dispensation. Also influential in smoothing the way for the Salamanca astronomer was former student Joseph Vecinho, who, as has been seen, was mathematician and scientific resource for João's court. Soon after his arrival, Zacuto was appointed Court Astronomer and was called upon to put his expertise at the services of Portuguese royalty and seamen. As mentioned earlier, Vecinho had translated *Hajibbur Hagadol* into Latin and Juan Selayo into Spanish, and it was already in use for navigation under the title *Almanach Perpetuum*.

João died the following year, in 1493. Manoel I succeeded to the throne after the suspicious drowning death of Crown Prince Affanso, who had been married to Isabel, daughter of Spain's Catholic Majesties. The new sovereign continued to encourage Zacuto's work and the use of *Almanach*'s navigational tables. Vecinho's Spanish translation, made in 1483, was finally published in 1496 in Leiria, a small Portuguese city, by *Magister* Samuel d'Ortas, a Jewish printer.[30]

We have seen earlier how Manoel had summoned Zacuto for his opinion of the proposed voyage to India, and that Zacuto had predicted success. The way was now clear for the journey of Vasco da Gama. As Court Astronomer, Zacuto was the acknowledged master adviser to Portuguese navigators. Much of his work was done at Sagres. As da Gama prepared his armada, he consulted frequently with the astronomer, who trained captain and crew in the use of the *Almanach* tables and the improved copper astrolabe, formerly made of wood. Predecessor of the sextant which is used by navigators today to measure the altitude of celestial bodies, the astrolabe had been pioneered by the Muslims. It was to contribute significantly to da Gama's success, earning a place of honor eighty-one years later in *Os Luciadas*, The Enlightened Ones, by Luís Vas de Camões, who highlighted it in his epic poem paying homage to Portugal's navigators.

Camões wrote in the first person, as if Vasco da Gama himself was describing his voyage. Here, the navigator describes the entrance of his ship into the Bay of Saint Helena, at the tip of South Africa:

> We began our discovery with
> the misty mountains we'd sighted,
> the heavy anchors light as ornaments,
> the sails had already been furled.

Next, he gives credit to the astrolabe and its inventor, describing how he went ashore to use Zacuto's new copper instrument to fix his location.

> And I, I hoped to learn more
> of the remote place we were,
> using the astrolabe, the new instrument
> created with fine skill and wisdom...

While the rest of the crew scatters to explore on land, da Gama stays

> beside the pilots on the sandy beach
> to compute the altitude of the sun
> to chart where we are,
> in the universal setting.

In the next stanza, da Gama says he's fixed their position as between the Tropic of Capricorn and the Antarctic, the part of the world he describes as least known to humans.[31]

In addition to the astrolabe and an updated *Almanach*, da Gama also carried Judah Cresques' maps and Vecinho's technique of measuring latitude, based on Zacuto's tables. Earlier navigational voyages had used a quadrant called *Cuadran Judaicus* after a Jewish inventor. It has been seen that Jews and New Christians contributed significantly to the journeys of Iberian navigators and would continue to do so into the future. Forty years after da Gama's voyage, in 1537, Portuguese mathematician Pedro Nunes, from the University of Coimbra, would lay the groundwork for a new approach to spherical cartography in his *Treatise on the Spheres*.

68   The Sephardic Jews of Spain and Portugal

The da Gama expedition was a great success, further elevating Zacuto's esteem with king, navigators and scientific colleagues. Alas, as in Spain only two years before, his services and achievements were not enough to keep the astronomer secure and settled in Portugal, as long as he chose to remain a practicing Jew. Again, the specter of conversion was raised. Knowing the deep

The astrolabe, in wood or metal, measured the altitude of the sun or heavenly bodies above the horizon and was used at sea to determine latitude. Abraham Zacuto designed an improved model in copper that was utilized by Vasco da Gama and honored by Luís de Camões for its value to the voyage in his epic sixteenth-century poem, *Os Lusíadas*. This mid-sixteenth century astrolabe bears a Hebrew inscription. (Courtesy of Adler Planetarium & Astronomy Museum, Chicago, Illinois. In Mann, Vivian B. *Convivencia* [New York: George Braziller, 1992], 82.)

commitment of Zacuto the Talmudist and Judaic scholar, the outcome regarding his future in Portugal could be predicted.

As explained earlier, most of the Jews admitted to Portugal at the time of the expulsion received residency for a short period, about eight months, with payment of an entrance fee. King João was said to have promised ships for their departure, but when the deadline came, there were few vessels provided. Most Jews, almost 100,000 souls, unable to pay for passage on their own, were declared slaves of the court.

Further, João had ordered all young men and women and the children of those unable to pay the tax to be seized from their parents and settled on Portugal's newly acquired island of São Tomé, to be raised as Christians. There, many died of starvation and exposure. Upon succession to the throne following João's death, Manoel I appeared at first to herald a reign of mercy. He released the enslaved Jews from bondage. Zacuto's influence at court was said to have played a role in this action. Shortly thereafter, however, the king began his own form of pressure on Jews to convert. He wanted to please his brother's widow, Isabel, now his intended bride, daughter of Spain's rulers, who had declared she would not marry him if Jews remained in the country. Manoel viewed the marriage as vital to his hopes for an eventual union with Spain, with him as ruler. To win this prize, he had to rid Portugal of Jews. He tried the expulsion approach first. On December 5, 1496, he signed a decree ordering Jews to convert or leave his country by the following October.

Soon he realized the considerable loss this would bring in financial resources and talent, and decided instead to tighten the pressure to convert. In March, he ordered all children between four and fourteen years taken from their parents, to be raised by Catholic families. The king expected parents to join their children at the baptismal fount, rather than have them taken away, but this followed only rarely. Jerónimo Osório, Portuguese bishop and professor, believed this to be "born out of laudable purposes" to save the souls of the children, yet he called it "unjust" and "unfair." He described the scene as all non-converting families lost their children, many torn away by force, some smothered by their own parents:

> ... the king did not accomplish this without great spiritual affliction. It was such a piteous thing to see the children being wrested from the breasts of their mothers, and the parents being dragged, struck, and whipped as they clutched their little children in their arms.... There were some among them who ... drowned their children in the wells; some of them fell into such madness that they killed themselves.[32]

In October, 20,000 Jews gathered in Lisbon as ordered, where they were herded together, and harangued by priests and converted Jews. Those who did not succumb were detained until past the deadline to depart, and told they were the king's slaves for failure to leave. More surrendered and were baptized, some dragged to the fount by force. The rest were sprinkled with holy water and declared Christians. It could be said there were no more Jews practicing in the open in Portugal.[33]

The king appeared to have removed the obstacles to his marriage, but not without losing Abraham Zacuto, his eminent navigational adviser and astronomer. Joseph Vecinho succumbed to the pressure to convert, taking the name Diogo Mendes Vecinho, but Zacuto stayed firm. Alas, even the high esteem in which the king held him could not keep the astronomer in Portugal at the price of his ancestral beliefs. The devoted Talmudist, descendant of a family that had kept their Jewish allegiance through massacre and persecution in Sefarad, had no recourse. To remain a Jew, he had to leave the country. Once again, he was giving up his exalted position and professional fulfillment, facing separation from most of his family and having to find a way to escape. One of his stature could not leave openly. He had long since said goodbye to his teacher—Isaac Aboab had died only seven months after negotiating the dispensation that brought Zacuto and his family to Portugal in 1492. Zacuto had recited the eulogy for the last *gaon* of Castilla.

Bound for Tunis in North Africa, a Muslim state friendly to Jews, he took with him his son Samuel, still a boy. What other family he had remained behind.[34] Son Jacob was later to find his way to Constantinople, where he published Zacuto's *Nehar Pishon* in 1538. Son Abraham took the name Duarte Diaz as a *Cristão Nuovo*.[35]

A century later, King Manoel II wrote this about Zacuto in his chronicles:

> Truly, the grand astrologer, certainly with the help of his disciple Vicinho, gave grand, enormous service to Portugal, his knowledge. Zacuto's science served not only the Portuguese, but also Spain, beginning with Columbus, who possessed a copy of *Almanach Perpetuum*....[36]

Indeed, Manoel I, later called The Fortunate, had much to thank Zacuto for. The increased trade and conquest that followed Da Gama's successful voyage made him the richest sovereign in Europe, and his country the ruler of many distant peoples, lands and seas until then largely unknown.

Ironically, in spite of expulsion from Spain and forced conversion in Portugal, enterprising Sephardic Jews, whether observers of Judaism or *conversos,* were to be involved in the lucrative spice trade that flourished with the sub–African routes in the next century. Chapter Two described Isaac Abravanel and his son representing Venice in negotiations with Portugal over trading rights, while Chapter Five will show the same trade adding to the wealth of the Nasi/Mendes family.

In 1497, however, the picture was not rosy for the astronomer from Salamanca. Zacuto's flight from Portugal was hazardous and prolonged. Ships carrying father and son were captured twice by pirates, the passengers imprisoned each time, and held for a total of two years. It is not certain how they were freed, but it is known that well-to-do Jews ransomed captured coreligionists whenever they could. We will learn more about this type of intercession in Chapter Five. Zacuto and Samuel finally reached Tunis, seven years later, in 1504, where a prosperous and learned Jewish community welcomed the fleeing emigrants.

It was to be the great astronomer's dark night of the soul. In the introduction to his *Crónica* he writes despairingly of his grim experiences.

> Because of my sins and the seriousness of persecutions, captivity and hunger, I have neither strength nor clarity of mind; my understanding has disappeared, I have lost my judgment.[37]

Eventually Zacuto recovered, spending his years in Tunis in relative tranquility. Although without books and other resources, he supported himself tutoring in astronomy and mathematics. It was clear, however, where his heart was. The eminent scientist gave way to the man of Judaic law and lore. Establishing himself as the Talmudist Moises Alaxcar, he dedicated his time to historical and spiritual work, particularly *Sefer Yohassin, Libro de las Genealogías* in Spanish, The Book of Lineage. It is believed that he began writing it before leaving Portugal in 1497. He may even have begun as early as 1480, while still at the university in Spain. He completed it in Tunis in 1510.[38]

This work has been credited with launching historiography as a genre for Jewish writers. It organizes and records the Judaic oral law in chronological order. Zacuto compiled the teachings of rabbis and sages, passed along through the ages, which he had studied from boyhood on, beginning with Moses, the prophets and the major authorities of the Mishnah and Talmud, from earliest times to his era. He included accounts of Israel's kings, the Babylonian captivity, the Second Temple and the ancient learning academies of Sura and Pumbedita.

Sefer Yohassin thus followed in the tradition of writers on the Torah, such as Maimonides, Sherira b. Hanina Gaon and Rabbi Abraham ibn David, the latter the author of *Sefer ha–Kabballah*, writing of Jewish mystical teachings. Zacuto was said to have been influenced also by Jewish medieval works such as *El Libro de la Cábala*, Book of the Kaballah, by Abraham de Torrutiel; *La Vara de Judá*, The Rod of Judah, by Ben Verga; and a work by Zaadic de Arévalo. He went further than these authors in attempting to organize, chronologically, an entire body of knowledge about Jewish religious tradition. He intended it to stimulate scholarly study and discussion, and to help Jews living among Christians be more knowledgeable when representing the history, traditions and beliefs of their faith.

Indeed, *Sefer Yohassin* was to be used by succeeding generations of Jewish scholars to stimulate debate and discourse among each other rather than with non–Jews. Historiography had come of age for Jewish authors. Cantera Burgos claims, however, that the work exhibits "a certain racial and religious intolerance," disparaging non–Jewish beliefs. Burgos compares this to *Hajibbur Hagadol* and *Tratado de las Influencias del Cielo*, written among and largely for Christians, from which these negative views about Gentile lore are absent. He suggests that the subsequent expulsions from Spain, then Portugal, and Zacuto's experiences thereafter, may explain the difference.[39]

In another work, *Hjosafot Lesefer ha–'Aruk*, Zacuto adds to and amends the Talmudic dictionary, *Ha-'Aruk*, by Natan ben Yehiel, which he completed after the year 1506. Here, he takes advantage of the commentary of Rabbi Semaj Gaon on ben Yehiel's work, enhances the latter's words and phrases in three hundred sixty cases, and adds sixty articles to the original.[40]

In 1513, Zacuto journeyed to Jerusalem, where he studied at the *yeshiva* of Rabbi Isaac Sholal, and wrote an almanac on biblical meteorology. In *Sefer Yohassin*, he described his desire to see the burial sites of holy men. He was able to indulge his wish in the Holy Land.

Two years later, Spanish conquest threatened the African coast, and a cautious Zacuto, who had returned to Tunis, left — this time for Damascus, which was under Turkish rule in the Ottoman Empire: another departure, another exile.

Historians disagree on the place of his death. Some say he died in Damascus, while others place him in Jerusalem. There is disagreement also on the year of his passing, which fell between 1510 and 1522. In the latter year, he would have been seventy years of age.[41]

In the following century, his great grandson, the honored Portuguese physician Manuel Alvares de Tavara, took his ancestor's name in Amsterdam upon conversion there to Judaism in 1625. History knows him as Zacutus Lusitanus, praised by poets and princes for his epic writings in medicine.[42]

How does one begin to assess the significance of a person's life and life work? With Abraham Zacuto, we have to answer two questions, each stemming from his twin connections with astronomy and Judaic studies. What was the impact of the astronomer from Salamanca on the history of science, navigation and exploration? What was the influence of the Talmudic disciple of the last *gaon* of Castilla on Judaic thinking and scholarship?

With regard to the first question, Cantera Burgos and Arías Barbosa call Zacuto and the Sephardic cartographer Yehuda Cresques the two loftiest figures in the history of fifteenth and sixteenth century navigational science.

Certainly, Zacuto himself was proud of his achievements, writing in *Yohassin* that

> I, Abraham Zacuto, the author, have corrected all the books [containing the earlier astronomical tables prepared by Alphonso X] in accordance with the tables that I have prepared, and my tables circulate throughout all Christian and even Muslim lands.[43]

We have shown earlier how the two celebrity explorers of the time appreciated his contributions to navigation. Columbus' diary recounts the value of Zacuto's tables to his voyage, and da Gama's voyage succeeded, thanks to the improved copper astrolabe and the *Almanach* tables, as feted later by poet and ship crewman Luís Vas de Camões.

The descendant of Manoel I, whose pressures to convert caused Zacuto to flee Portugal, is not hesitant in giving him great praise a century later. As seen previously, Manoel II calls Zacuto "the great astrologer" in his diary, who "gave great, enormous service to Portugal," as well as to Spain.[44]

He is recognized by today's scientists, who have named a large crater in the moon, discovered in the space explorations of the twentieth century, after him. He joins other greats so memorialized on lunar geography, such as Albert Einstein.

In the area of Judaic scholarship, *Sefer Yohassin* gave rise to Jewish historiography, and provided stimulus to generations of students in their debates and discussions on the impact of the sages' teachings. An evaluation of his writings indicates how Zacuto likely would have wanted to have his life seen as a testimonial for his spiritual commitment to his people's covenant with God. In the opening paragraphs for the *Almanach* he takes great pains to justify his involvement in the celestial tables as harmonious with *halacha*, Jewish law, and the teaching of Maimonides. Twice, in Spain and Portugal, he surrendered prestige, professional fulfillment and a comfortable lifestyle to remain a practicing Jew, and he also fled a third time, from more modest circumstances in North Africa, to do so. He endured piracy and prison, as well as hunger, poverty, and homelessness, as a price of his beliefs. He also lost the circle of his family, two of his sons remaining behind in Portugal as New Christians when Zacuto fled. The permanent separation from most of his family must have caused grief and loneliness. His story is another tale of one who risked everything to stand by his spiritual covenants. He was another who epitomized the mix of worldly skills and spiritual commitment that categorized so many notables of the Sephardic Golden Age.

Without his *Almanach* and astrolabe, Spain's empire in the New World and Portugal's primacy in trade with the orient might not be facts for students to learn about today. The Columbus and da Gama voyages might have produced different results from the ones recorded in history.

FOUR

Luís de Santángel: Spain's Disraeli and *Converso* Bridge to the New World

> *All who'd live by*
> *risk and resistance*
> *manage three things:*
> *high-sea commerce,*
> *excellent enemies*
> *and the company of kings.*

Schmu'el Hanagid, who penned in verse this portrait of the quintessential courtier or influential figure of his time and place, knew whereof he wrote. The Sephardic poet, whose life bridged the tenth and eleventh centuries, rose to be chief vizier of the Muslim kingdom of Granada and military commander of its armies, in addition to giving leadership to Jewish and Muslim literature and scholarship.[1] Project his words three hundred years into the future, and they describe the life of Luís de Santángel.

The grandson of Noah Chinillo of Daroca, who converted to Catholicism under pressure in the early part of the fifteenth century, Don Luís inherited a successful mercantile enterprise and became a favorite courtier of Fernando II, while living most of his life in the shadow of the Holy Office of the Inquisition. Despite his loyalty and much appreciated services for *Los Reyes Católicos*, he and family had no more immunity from arrest and interrogation than other prominent Sephardic *conversos* and their kin.

The story of Luís de Santángel has its beginnings in the violence of 1391 and the increasing persecution and proselytizing thereafter, which resulted in a wave of Jewish conversions to Catholicism in the early part of the fifteenth century. At first, many of these New Christians continued observing elements of Judaism forbidden to them. What rituals or customs were maintained were

Four. Luís de Santángel

His followers behind him, Dominican monk Vicente Ferrer bursts into Toledo's Ibn Shoshan Synagogue to force preaching of conversion to the congregation. In the early fifteenth century, church officials forced entry to Jewish gathering places, often accompanied by mobs threatening death to those who didn't convert. The building, renamed Santa María la Blanca, became church property after the massacre of 1391, and can be visited today. A contemporary view is seen on the cover. Painting on glass. (©Beth Hatefutsoth, Permanent Exhibition, Tel Aviv. Visual Documentation Center, Beth Hatefutsoth, Tel Aviv.)

those that could be hidden from prying eyes and practiced secretly. They were now required to attend mass and take part in other requirements of Catholic observance, but were able to abstain from pork, for example, in situations where it would not be noticed, or to fast to observe a holiday that could not be celebrated in the open. With care, they could even bathe and change linens on occasional Fridays. This was most difficult, however, to conceal in homes with Old Christian servants. Then in 1480, pressures on New Christian families intensified as the Holy Office of the Inquisition began its work, watching for those still practicing "the dead law of Moses," as they called the forbidden religion. Those suspected were called *judaizante*. Lists were posted specifying acts that might indicate backsliding from Catholic practice, and the seriousness of the inquisitors, as they made arrests and filled the prisons with suspects, dampened the desire of many a family or individual to continue risky observances from the past.

Upon conversion, New Christians gained the possibility of entry to professions, status and lifestyles previously prohibited to them as Jews. In those early days, some may have come to appreciate the adoption of the officially-sanctioned state religion as a doorway through which they and their descendants could elevate class and economic stature. If so, it was a Faustian bargain, for whatever new opportunity or status a New Christian earned could all be destroyed simply on the testimony of anyone coming forward to testify that the *converso* or someone in his family was seen observing ceremonies or customs of their former faith.

When Pedro Arbués, Chief Inquisitor of Zaragoza, was murdered in 1485 as he knelt in prayer, the names of those investigated for complicity in the deed read like a roll call of the most prominent and wealthy *conversos* of the kingdom. Many were courtiers of the king and officials in high positions of the Aragonese government: Gabriel Sánchez, Royal Treasurer of the Kingdom; Alfonso de la Caballería, Vice Chancellor; Sancho de Paternoy, Comptroller of the Royal Household; Jaime de Montesa, Deputy of the Zaragoza judiciary; Francisco de Santa Fé, Assessor to the Governor of Aragón. The latter was brother to Gerónimo de Santa Fé, *converso* churchman known for his zeal in attempting to convert Jews to Catholicism. Another on the list was Luís de Santángel, *escribano de ración* or Chancellor of the Royal Household of Aragón and Chief Accountant of Aragón.

Of these, Jaime de Montesa was to be convicted and die at an *auto de fé*, or act of faith, execution by fire, while Francisco de Santa Fé was arrested and committed suicide afterwards. The subsequent trial of Alfonso de la Caballería went on for two years. Roth writes of the Inquisition that "The names of the great families of Santángel and Sánchez appear with monotonous regularity in its records ... in the following years."[2] While Sánchez, de la Caballería and Santángel escaped conviction, there were kinsmen of each who did not fare so well, having to escape or be arrested and face death.

A judicial official with the same name as the king's *escribano de ración*, Luís de Santángel, was arrested and condemned to death. It is worth noting that he had been knighted for his military services and loyalty to John II in the Rebellion of 1462. That was insufficient to override the charge that he had hidden a Torah at home and was heard to say Hebrew prayers. When his brother, a high-ranking official of a monastery in nearby Daroca, tried to secure witnesses on behalf of the accused, he was sentenced to do penance.[3] Although their grandfathers had the same Sephardic surname, Chinillo, the condemned Santángel was not closely related to the Luís de Santángel of King Fernando's court, and perhaps was not even in the same bloodline. Their ancestors were probably converted by a churchman named Santángel two generations back, taking his name in the customary way *conversos* did when required to give up their Jewish surnames.[4]

The courtier Luís de Santángel, on whom this chapter will focus, was a favorite of the king. Fernando had expressed fondness and appreciation for his services, yet this did not bring him, or other Sephardic *converso* notables, immunity from the ubiquitous shadow of the Inquisition. Certainly the scope of arrests and the involvement of important families were portents of an investigation beyond regional boundaries. The tentacles of the Holy Office apparently had greater prey in mind. One would think that influence and loyal service to the crown would shield eminences, such as de la Caballería, Sánchez, de Paternoy, de Montesa and the jurist de Santángel, from suspicion, investigation and arrest. Of those in question, five held the highest positions in Aragón and the court. Surely Fernando valued their services, but the monarch had to play the power game with the Inquisition, whose work he encouraged, and it was not yet clear early on whether it would be big or little fish, or the whole species, that would be eliminated. It must have been pondered whether Arbués' murder would give the church and its allies an excuse to diminish the influence Jewish eminences had with the Catholic Majesties and have access to their wealth as well.

It will be seen that the king's own *escribano de ración* could not protect his own mother from arrest and interrogation later on. Don Luís de Santángel was typical of New Christians in high places: beloved of king or noble, yet still not safe from the Inquisition.

As was seen in Chapter One, the Santángels of Valencia were New Christians, whose conversion had come about two generations earlier in 1414, at the close of the Disputation of Tortosa.[5] The disputation was one of a series of so-called debates which Jews of the late Middle Ages were required to attend to hear churchmen and rabbis argue the superiority of their respective religions. These were not true debates, but rather staged events designed to favor the Christian position, to convince the audience of Christianity's superiority, and to request, threaten, or demand conversion of the captive audience. At Tortosa, Jewish spokesmen included the learned Vidal Benveniste, presenting his case in Latin, and Astruc ha–Levi, eloquent in rebutting attacks on the Talmud. The anti–pope himself, Benedict XII, presided, assisted by archbishops, bishops, abbots and knights.[6]

The disputation lasted a year and nine months, during which the influential Jews required to attend were prevented from returning home. A few years earlier, in 1411, Dominican Friar Vicente Ferrer had moved through Castilla in a major effort to convert Sephardim. He would appear in synagogues, a fiery figure, holding a Torah and a cross, and preach to the audience of Jews, with a mob usually present to support him, howling for conversion or death.

In Toledo alone, he stayed one month. There, in 1414, it was claimed that he converted 4,000 Jews in one day. In a few years, the efforts of Ferrer and the *converso* Gerónimo de Santa Fé are said to have resulted in 35,000 additional converts.[7]

In addition to the pressure of the disputations and Ferrer's efforts, Jews faced an abundance of new laws and regulations which radically restricted and made demands on their economic and social lives. Thus, extraordinary constraints and persecution, which were, at the least, harassment, and at the worst, life-threatening, were being applied to make Jews abandon their faith. In addition, vivid memories remained of the 1391 massacres, when major Jewish communities, such as those of Sevilla, Barcelona and Toledo, were wiped out by mobs, fired up by followers of the churchman Ferrán Martínez. All this undoubtedly made fertile soil for conversion.

Don Luís' grandfather, Noah Chinillo, was one of thousands to convert at the time of the Disputation at Tortosa. The first to be called Luís de Santángel, he was a successful clothing merchant from Daroca. In the years following the disputation, his work took him everywhere in Aragón and abroad to Naples, purchasing textiles and serving clients, many of them entitled nobility. In 1436, he moved his family and his now prosperous, decades-old business to Valencia, to take advantage of the greater opportunities and markets of the thriving Aragonese port city. He soon became a jurist, an appointed position given to men thought well of by royalty, serving the court of Alfonso V of Aragón.

The family of this first Don Luís was two generations removed from the personage of this chapter. His family consisted of wife Constanza and children Luís, Berenguer and Pedro Martín. To allay suspicion of *judaizante*, or the secret practice of Judaism, New Christian, or *converso*, families often prepared one son, usually the youngest, for the priesthood. Pedro Martín was Patriarch Don Luís' selection for this role. He eventually rose to the position of Bishop of Majorca and adviser to Juan II.

Much of the elder Santángel's wealth came from two enterprises. He was farmer of the de la Mata salt works, which he arranged by contract in 1472 for an annual rent, payable to one Juan de Ribasaltas. He was also farmer of customs and royal domains. This allowed him to amass a considerable fortune.

He died in 1444, eight years after settling in Valencia, having established family members as wealthy and influential entrepreneurs, and was looked on favorably by royalty and nobility. His will named his son Luís universal heir. In addition to legacies for wife and son Berenguer, he also provided a generous gift for Antonio de Santa Cruz, canon of the Cathedral Santa María de los Corporales in Daroca. This testified either to the sincere nature of the patriarch's conversion or his effort to make it appear so. It is one of many special

Four. Luís de Santángel   79

Representatives of the Santángel family mercantile enterprise most likely traded with those of other fifteenth century firms at Valencia's *La Lonja,* the commodity exchange, also called *Casa de Contratación,* House of Contracts. (Generalitat Valenciana, ed. *Lluís de Santàngel y su época: un nuevo hombre, un mundo nuevo* [Valencia: 1992], 229.)

favors to influentials that he had used so successfully through the years to establish good will for family and business.

His son Luís began his career first as partner with his father, then as heir and head of the family empire. On the elder's death, he secured the contract to farm the royal domains and customs, elevating him even more in status and wealth. He was subsequently appointed an attorney in the royal court. A trusted courtier, his influence and economic benefits increased even more. King Alfonso V of Aragón had recognized his father in 1450 for his services, particularly his loans to the monarchy. Later, the younger Luís served Juan II, and was honored with the title of *caballero* for gallantry at the Battle of Rubinat in 1462, in the War with Catalunya. He also made several large loans to the crown to help pay for the war.

The second Luís was married to Brianda Bessant, from a Darocan New Christian family. Their first son, born in 1439, was third in the line to be named Luís. Two more children followed, Jaime and Galcerán. This child Luís was his father's choice to follow in his footsteps, and when the elder Santángel received the lease on royal tolls and taxes in Valencia following the patriarch's death, his namesake was recorded as co-lessee.

This, then, is the lineage of the third Luís de Santángel, whom we met earlier as *escribano de ración* to Fernando. He was also appointed *contador mayor*, Chief Accountant, to the king, and was an influential figure in court and national affairs. He was among the most prosperous men in the Christian kingdoms as well. In three generations, the family had risen to great wealth and status, from Jewish clothing merchants of Daroca to New Christian favorites of royalty. Making this possible was the economic and political environment of Valencia in the first half of the fifteenth century. The port city was a thriving financial and commercial center of Aragón, due to the War with Catalunya and the economic needs of its rulers. This environment presented opportunities for social ascension for those with something to offer the monarchy. The family of the patriarch, Luís de Santángel from Daroca, was in the right place at the right time. Resourceful and adaptable, they were always ready to put themselves and their wealth at the service of rulers and highly placed people. Their success was based primarily on access to large amounts of capital and the willingness to finance royal projects. There was no mercantile arena of the day with which the Santángels were not involved, and their wealth and position as elites catapulted them onto the larger stage of political and social leadership.

On this proscenium, in the middle of the fifteenth century, the third Luís de Santángel, was co-lessee with his father of royal roads and taxes in his native Valencia, embarking on a career of commerce and statesmanship. The earliest record has him in Daroca in 1443, five years of age, with his

Four. Luís de Santángel

mother, Brianda, and maternal grandmother, Gracia. The source, for this, however, is Inquisition testimony, and the family had been well established already in Valencia by that date, seven years after moving from Daroca. One cannot be sure, therefore, that the child Luís had lived at all in Daroca. We do know that he was groomed early as family protégé and heir, and that he spent much time with father and grandfather in the thriving port city. After the patriarch's death in 1444, the youngest Luís was exposed increasingly to the activities of the family firm. He was honing the business and political skills that were to manifest themselves later as wealth, power and influence.[8]

Juana, daughter of Barcelona jurist Diego de Tarabau, was the young man's choice as wife. She was also related to the powerful de la Caballería *converso* family. The mid–1470's found the couple living in Barcelona with their four children: Luisa, Hernando, Jerónimo and Alfonso. The Santángels

An angel holds a flaming torch over a gold background in the *escudo*, or coat of arms, of the Santángel family. The image appears on *un azulejo de Manises*, a glazed colored tile, from the last third of the fifteenth century, when the house of Luís de Santángel was recorded to be located on *dels Castellví*, a street named after his prominent neighbors in Valencia's Santo Tomás parish. (Museo Nacional de Cerámica y Artes Suntuarias González Martí, Valencia, Spain. In Generalitat Valenciana, ed. *Lluís de Santàngel y su época: un nuevo hombre, un mundo nuevo* [Valencia: 1992], 259.)

returned to the family base in Valencia by the end of the decade, taking up residence near the Plaza de Villarrasa in the parish of Santo Tomás. Their house bordered the home of the Old Christian family of Mosén Castellví, on the street bearing his name. The neighborhood was near the *judería* and dominated by offices of government departments and the liberal professions.

Inquisition testimony made against Brianda and son later in the decade would describe the Santángel lifestyle vividly, including the numbers of servants and the average length of tenure. Maids for the neighboring Castellví family would tell of arguments between Luís' parents, overheard through open windows, even one between the *escribano de ración* and his mother. The Castellví house was obviously a good eagle's nest from which to spy on one's *vecinos*, or neighbors. Although the validity of the reports is unsure, coming as they did from Inquisition records, there were specifics about house layout and living patterns, observable from nearby windows, which seem factual enough. They described the bedrooms, a chapel for mass, even the laundry area. The kitchen was in a separate wing, with the dining room below. Of special interest, however, was the study, where the business of the powerful Santángels was conducted. Situated on a mezzanine-like area called the *entresuelo*, it was a hub of activity throughout the day, and often, the night.

The families of Luís and his brothers were close. When her husband died, Brianda assumed his role in the family business. The houses of the two generations, including Luís and siblings, were in close proximity. The family was described as chatting frequently from building to building through open windows. This afforded generous opportunities for unrelated neighbors to overhear conversations and observe comings and goings, dutifully reported or embellished years later before Inquisition proceedings.[9]

In the late 1470's, the youngest Santángel stepped out on his own onto the stage as royal courtier. His father and grandfather had served Juan II well, and the monarch's son, Fernando, saw to it that their heir received the same opportunities. Among Don Luís' first assignments was the settlement of an issue regarding customs duties and Genoese mariners in 1479. As head of the family firm, he had done business before with Genoese merchants. Court records show him also on a royal mission to pay for textiles from Lombardy. These interactions with seamen and merchants from Italian ports kept him informed on developments and explorations in navigation, which were invaluable when Christopher Columbus would enter the scene in the next decade.[10]

Don Luís continued to serve in various financial and state projects through the 1480's. By then, he had been conferred the titles and responsibilities of *escribano de ración* and *contador mayor*, and an effusive Fernando was heard referring to him in laudatory terms, such as "the good Aragonese, excellent, well-beloved councillor."[11] In 1487, he was sent to negotiate the ransom for several thousand Christians captured by the Muslims in Málaga and the sale, in turn, of Muslim captives to their rulers. Aragón's Royal Treasurer Gabriel Sánchez worked with him on this assignment. As has been seen, Sánchez was one of several important New Christian courtiers close to the king. His name appeared frequently as a creditor of the crown and receiver, in turn, of royal beneficence. Soon he, Don Luís and other *converso* and Jewish courtiers would again provide financial rescue for *Los Reyes Católicos*.

In 1489, only Granada remained as a stronghold of Iberian Muslim power, and the final campaigns of the *Reconquista* had placed the Crown in need of funds. Santángel negotiated several very important loans to support the war effort, totaling almost 50 million maravedis. His loan was the largest — just over 10 million maravedis. Other lenders included Isaac Abravanel, the Jewish financial adviser, as described earlier in Chapter Two, and New Christian and Jewish notables Gabriel Sánchez, Francisco Pinelo, Juan de Coloma, Rodrigo de Ulloa, and Sancho de Toledo.

To help repay the war debts, the Crown had levied several financial measures over the ten-year period ending in 1493. *Contador Mayor* Santángel directed measures to collect these assessments, called the Bull of the Crusade and the Ecclesiastical Tithe. In Chapter One, we visited the home of Isaac Abravanel in 1492, as Don Luís, sent by the king, repaid Don Isaac's Granada war loan of 1.5 million maravedis, as the latter prepared for exile. Abravenel's debt repayment came from the bull and tithe money.

Another assignment for Santángel was to serve as treasurer of the *Santa Hermandad,* a knight-like brotherhood order, a role which he exercised from 1490 to 1493. Together with Francisco Pinelo, he was responsible for administration and taxation for the Crown of Castilla. This gave Don Luís a kingdom-wide political and administrative presence, enhancing his experience and influence.

Much of Santángel's success came from his ability to marshal large sums of money from a variety of sources and to distribute them sagaciously to gatekeepers, who then made even more affluent sources available. Among them were especially good contacts in Sevilla and Valencia, particularly among merchants of Genoese origin.

Another skill was Santángel's sagacity in accomplishing such tasks effectively and in a politically astute manner. This required a delicate balancing act. It was important to restrain demonstration of his power so as not to threaten the important personages he dealt with, as this could lead to his downfall. At the same time, he took care to be noticed and remembered as a valuable and significant player. In such dealings, he knew that one had to be affable while tenacious, but not pushy. Aware of these requirements, Don Luís carried them out with élan.

In his assignment with the *Hermandad*, for example, he was to administer the order's treasury extending throughout Castilla. He developed good working relations with the *Hermandad* Council by nurturing cordial contacts early on with its gatekeeper, Accountant Alfonso de Quintanilla. This, in turn, opened the doors to *Hermandad* paymasters and captains, with each of whom he became on friendly terms. In another assignment carried out for the Catholic Majesties, as Collector of the Bull of the Crusade, he eventually developed a congenial working relationship with one of the era's principal church and political figures, the queen's confessor, Hernando de Talavera, bishop of Avila, later Archbishop of Granada. As with the *Hermandad*, this proved invaluable, the bishop facilitating his contacts with important regional clergy and laypeople, so necessary for the assignment's effective implementation.[12]

All these services, well performed, won fame for the Santángel scion and the appreciation of his rulers. However, his greatest gift to the Catholic Majesties, to Spain, and eventually to millions of beneficiaries from other lands, lay ahead. This was the vision propelling him to advocate support for Christopher Columbus' first voyage. It was possible that Santángel had met Columbus early on in numerous interchanges with Genoese mariners and merchants for king and for his family's firm. Among the most knowledgeable officials of the Court, Don Luís had been aware of the mariner's unsuccessful appeals for financial and official support over several decades.

Columbus' earlier efforts to secure funding were made in Portugal, where it was believed that he first thought about sailing west to reach China and India for reputed bounties of spices and gold. He may have been inspired also by 500-year-old tales of exploration that he heard about while on the Faeroe Islands, when crewing for a Portuguese vessel. The Faeroes, located between Britain and Iceland in the North Sea, were the perfect location from which to learn about Leif Ericson's westward voyage in the year 1,000, reaching a "new" land called Vineland. Knowledge of this discovery, which resulted in a brief settlement, had been disseminated abroad and reported to the pope by the Christian Norsemen. It was familiar knowledge to scientists, cartographers and navigators in Columbus' day, as well as to merchants and those plying the seas. None of these learned individuals, by the way, continued to believe that the world was flat.

It was likely that this contributed to Columbus' realization that more awaited discovery to the west than the spices of the Indies. However, the 1480's found Portuguese navigators and scientists focusing instead on sailing south and then east, around the tip of Africa. In 1484, Columbus petitioned Portugal's João II for ships and funding to reach the same rich lands by heading west. The king appointed a commission to study the proposal and report back. Joseph Vecinho, Jewish court mathematician and scientific adviser, whom we met in Chapter Two, was a member of the commission, which also included Court physician Rodrigo, Jewish mathematician Moses and the Bishop of Cueta. Reporting to the Council of State, the commission recommended against Columbus' proposal, presenting Vecinho's reasoning on it as the group's opinion. The navigator later blamed "the Jew Joseph" for the king's eventual refusal to support his voyage.

Vecinho and others preferred to continue the voyages throughout the decade to further explore and document the sub–African route. Chapter Three looked more closely at some of these, which eventually culminated in Vasco da Gama's successful journey later in the century around the Cape of Good Hope to the Indian subcontinent. Certainly, having invested time and identity with the African route over a significant period, one could not expect the members of King João's commission to surrender potential fame and fortune to a Neapolitan outsider.

With this rejection, Columbus then turned his attention to Spain, to Salamanca in 1486–87, where the Catholic Majesties were holding court.

Artist Zarza y Manchón portrays Christopher Columbus reviewing plans during his stay in the convent of La Rábida. Grateful for the efforts of Luís de Santángel in winning the queen's support, Columbus sent the first report of the voyage to the *converso* financier, as the flagship neared the end of the journey. (E. Cano. *Colón en el convento de la Rábida.* Zamora y Caballero. *La Historia General de España y sus posesiones en ultramar* [Valencia: 1874]. In Generalitat Valenciana, ed. *Lluís de Santàngel y su época: un nuevo hombre, un mundo nuevo* [Valencia: 1992], 255.)

There, he made his appeal. The royal couple consulted with eminent scientists, cartographers and navigation specialists. One of these, the Jewish astronomer Abraham Zacuto, who had developed the almanac and improved the astrolabe that was to be used later by Columbus and Portuguese navigators, gave a positive prognosis for the voyage, although he stressed its difficulties. The monarchs offered a warm reception, but did not accept the navigator's proposal at that time because of heavy costs in waging the Granada campaign.

Columbus bode his time for five years until 1492 and the fall of the last Muslim stronghold. He then appeared at court, which was now at the Alhambra. This time, the rulers negotiated seriously with him, and the mariner seemed almost in reach of his dream. He was reported, however, to have presented requests which Fernando deemed excessive, such as being appointed admiral and named viceroy and governor for life over lands of discovery. Columbus refused to compromise and the king suspended negotiations. Considering this the final rejection, the mariner left for France to try for support there.

An alarmed Santángel learned of his departure. Convinced of the viability of the voyage and the many benefits that would accrue to Spain, he became the prime force behind efforts to win Columbus support. Joining him were influential Aragonese, among them Royal Chamberlain Juan Cabrero, of Jewish lineage. Cabrero was a close friend and confidant of Fernando. The king thought so highly of this man, who had fought by his side in war, that he had made him executor of his will. Another important ally was Royal Treasurer Gábriel Sanchez.

It was Santángel's intervention at the last moment that turned the tide and won backing for Columbus. Don Luís had supported the idea since its 1487 hearing in Salamanca, and was willing to put his influence behind it. In the serious bargaining stages at Granada, perhaps even earlier at Salamanca, he spoke as an astute political and economic adviser and entrepreneur, and had convinced Fernando of the economic benefits to be gained.

In a dramatic meeting with the queen following Columbus' departure for France, Santángel emphasized the value of the voyage even if the navigator didn't reach the Indies: that there was much out there to discover and that Spain would be the richer for it. He described Columbus as an experienced sailor of good judgment, willing to risk his life to prove his theory. He cited the testimony of scientists, navigators and other counselors backing the venture, the eminent astronomer Zacuto among them, and claimed that the opposition had not been able to present convincing arguments to the contrary.

In making his case, Don Luís underscored that if the voyage were to be supported by another country, Spain would lose respect and suffer shame among nations. He stressed this point effectively. Kayserling summarizes the arguments he made:

> If the queen did not seize this opportunity, she would reproach herself all her life; her enemies would deride her, and her descendants would blame her; she would impair her honor and the renown of her royal name; she would injure her states and the welfare of her subjects.[13]

The queen was finally convinced, and declared her desire to support the project, but bemoaned the difficult financial condition, post–Granada, of the kingdom. Any remaining restraints dissolved, however, when Don Luís advanced a loan of almost five million maravedis for the voyage. This showed Isabel that the man she admired for his wise financial advice was willing to risk a fortune to back what he called a venture for Spain's greatness.

There is a legend that a convinced Isabel offered to pawn her jewels to pay for the voyage. This story is not true. In fact, her crown had already been encumbered by an unpaid loan from the City of Valencia for the battle of Granada.[14]

Columbus knew full well that he owed his good fortune to the royal *escribano de ración,* his persistent intervention on his behalf and his willingness to put his credibility and a vast sum of money on the line. Luís de Santángel was the first to receive a letter from the admiral as the journey neared its end on the return trip, "knowing the pleasure you will receive in hearing of the great victory which Our Lord has granted me in my voyages." The letter was addressed to "Comptroller of the King and Queen, giving a summary of the voyage," and explained that he was writing from Lisbon, where the ships had to take shelter after a fierce storm.

He described having "arrived at the Indies," after a voyage of seventy-one days. Then he wrote about the generosity of the people he found living there and their spiritual and material values.

> After they have shaken off their fear of us, they display a frankness and liberality in their behaviour which no one would believe without witnessing it. No request of anything from them is ever refused, but they rather invite acceptance of what they possess, and manifest such a generosity that they would give away their own hearts.

He claimed he had protected these innocent people who were trading much of their property to the sailors for worthless pieces of broken glass or broken hoops from casks. "I thought such traffic unjust, and therefore I forbade it," he wrote Santángel. Columbus added that his kindness was designed "to secure their affection ... that they may become Christians, and enter into the service of their Highnesses and the Castillian nation." What of the material wealth to be gained? He described finding "spices, cotton and rhubarb, cinnamon, aloe in as great abundance, and equal store of mastick, a production nowhere else found except in Greece and the island of Scio.... To these may be added slaves, as numerous as may be wished for."[15]

The next letter from the Admiral was to Gabriel Sánchez. The third, to the Catholic Majesties, bore similar descriptions of a successful voyage with prosperous portents. Needless to say, the monarchs were pleased. Fernando, in particular, referred gratefully to "his beloved councillor and *escribano de ración* Luís de Santángel," and asked Treasurer-General Sánchez to pay Don Luís 30,000 gold florins, of which 17,000 repaid the loan for the voyage and

13,000 was a gift. He also rewarded him with the right to import horses and wheat into the new lands. The king further showed his regard for Santángel by establishing equal rights in the New World for Aragonese as well as for Castillians, Don Luís having the identity of the former in a recently unified kingdom where the queen's kingdom still held slightly higher status.[16]

There were other tangible signs of Fernando's affection for his *escribano de ración*. In 1493, the king presented Santángel's daughter, Luisa, with a present of 30,000 sueldos upon her marriage to Angel de Villanueva, later named Governor of Sicily. The gift was made "in recognition of the many services which her father, the well-beloved councillor and *escribano de ración* of his household, had rendered and was still rendering him," recorded the royal archivist on May 10, 1494.

When a jealous Gabriel Sánchez reminded the monarch of his equally great services, Fernando presented a similar amount to the treasurer's son, Pedro, as a wedding gift.[17]

Early in this chapter it was seen how the Santángels had much to fear from the Holy Office and how the family name appeared with great frequency in Zaragoza's Inquisition records, along with references to four other prominent Aragonese *converso* families. Research showed that the Valencia Santángels may not have been kinsmen to those from Zaragoza; the name was taken at the time of conversion, probably after the church official who performed the ritual. As explained, while both families had ancestors several generations back surnamed Chinillo, they were not necessarily from the same line. The Zaragoza Santángels' ancestor was Azarias Chinillo of Catalayud; the Valencians were descended from Noah Chinillo of Daroca. Yet the Inquisition ignored the differences between families, ready to focus on anyone with the surname.[18]

Over the past five hundred years, scholars have presented differing genealogical pictures of the *escribano de ración*'s ancestors. Those who have described Luís as a relative of the namesake prosecuted in Zaragoza have been mistaken, according to more recent studies by Kerem, Bauza, Serrano, and Sánchez-Blanco, who claim that their predecessors relied too heavily on flawed Inquisition testimony as primary sources.[19]

Netanyahu, in particular, denounces colleagues' dependence on these records, and presents the case that courtiers such as Sánchez, de Paternoy, de la Caballería and the Zaragoza Santángels were too savvy politically to believe that the assassination of an Inquisitor could change Fernando's use of the Holy Office. In fact, Netanyahu proposes that the Holy Office itself might have been behind the assassination, acting with the foreknowledge of Fernando, using the murder to eliminate "the strong resistance he encountered to the Inquisition in Aragón, ... the *converso* leadership in that kingdom, as well as ... some of the *converso*s in his court."[20]

The Holy Office appeared to have used this as an opportunity to look into the family of the king's *escribano de ración*, particularly his mother, Brianda, for whom there was a reported *judaizante* trail. The closeness of the dates of the inquisitor's death, September 15, 1485, and the very beginning of the investigation of Brianda, January 2, 1486, seems to indicate a relationship between the two, although the matriarch was not implicated in the murder. On the latter date, the Holy Office was first recorded asking witnesses if they knew of her observing any of the Jewish practices so carefully outlined and posted for public awareness.

At her trial in 1487, two women told the Inquisition that they saw Luís, then five years old, accompany his mother and grandmother several times in 1443 and 1444 to visit a woman called Dueña La Morena in the *judería* of Daroca. These visits, said to have taken place over forty years previous on the "Sabbath and the Jewish Easter," were presented as testimony of *judaizante* against mother and grandmother.

Inquisition testimony made against Brianda vividly described the Santángel lifestyle, including numbers of servants and average length of service. Witnesses testified that Brianda's sons were displeased with their mother's alleged observance of Judaism. As described previously, there were reports of arguments between Luís' parents, allegedly witnessed by servants and members of the neighboring Castellví family.

One witness told of an argument overheard through an open window thirty years before, between Brianda and her husband. The latter was reported excoriating his wife for keeping the Sabbath. Further evidence, presented by the Collector for the Parish of San Nicolás, described a quarrel he claimed to have witnessed when visiting the family as part of his work. Brianda and her husband were described arguing over where she had put the tithe money he claimed to have given her. When she denied possession, the Collector reported that Don Luís had called his wife "*¡marrana judía!*" a term of derision referring to her as a converted Jew not to be trusted. She is alleged to have replied, "Yes, I'm holding on to this [the money] for the honor of my family." The inquisitors inferred that the reference to "honor" underscored her belief that she would betray her Jewish faith by paying a Christian tithe.[21]

As described earlier, Brianda made her home with Luís, her oldest son, after her husband's death. Inquisition testimony recorded that she took her meals upstairs by herself, in the *entresuelo*, instead of below in the dining room. The inference was that Brianda had taken pains to conceal her eating practices, which, presumably, followed Jewish dietary laws.

Brianda was arrested and placed in the prison of the royal palace on January 4, 1487, a year and four months after the assassination of the inquisitor in Zaragoza. The inquisitorial tribunal heard testimony in the case for five

months until May 8, when formal accusation was made that she had observed the Sabbath and followed Jewish dietary laws.

The mother of the *escribano de ración* strongly denied the charges and affirmed her loyalty to Christianity. The Holy Office then formally opened the trial. Meanwhile, her sons had prepared her defense with the services of an attorney and a solicitor. The inquisitors then submitted the proceedings to a church panel to weigh and rule on the case.

This was an unusual step for an inquisitional process. The king's influence was probably at work in this instance. Traditionally, torture would have been used at this point in a trial, in the belief that it extracted the truth from the accused, but it was probably abjured for Brianda because of Fernando's behind-the-scenes intervention. Some researchers connect the decision against torture to the high status of her family and her age.[22] Yet, the Holy Office did not take status and age into consideration with Jaime de Montessa, the aged and respected jurist, or Sancho de Paternoy, the Chief Treasurer of Aragón, both of whom were tortured and burned at the stake following the assassination of Arbués.

Since the inquisitor's murder and the subsequent escalation in accusations against prominent *conversos*, Fernando had to choose which of his accused courtiers to protect so they could continue their valued services to the crown. It is worth noting that neither Gabriel Sánchez nor Alfonso de la Caballería were ever formally accused although cases were begun for both, while considerable family members of each were exiled or tortured, jailed and executed. Obviously someone, probably the king, was protecting the king's most valued courtiers. The relative care shown in Brianda's case seems to reflect Fernando's plan to keep her son by his side. After all, Don Luís was a most useful courtier for whom he had special fondness.

Yes, the proceedings against Brianda had given the king much to consider. One can speculate how Fernando, who was in full support of pursuing accused *conversos* for the murder, protected his three most useful courtiers, Sánchez, de la Caballería and Santángel. The monarch, said to be Machiavelli's model for *The Prince,* stepped in eventually, to keep their much appreciated and dependable services. It would not have been expedient, either, to move firmly against Don Luís' mother.

The eleven persons on the judicial panel weighed the evidence presented against Brianda, and declared her innocent. This gave the inquisitors no

Opposite: The long arm of the Inquisition reached into the house of the king's own Chancellor of the Royal Household, with processes against Luís de Santángel's mother, Brianda, and grandmother, Gracia. This Holy Office document reports on Brianda's trial. (Generalitat Valenciana, ed. *Lluís de Santàngel y su època: un nuevo hombre, un mundo nuevo* [Valencia: 1992], 135.)

choice, and on May 1, 1488, after almost one year and five months in prison, she was freed and absolved of accusations. She was made, however, to swear publicly that she would not engage ever in the "errors" of which she had been accused but not convicted — Jewish dietary practices and observance of the Sabbath — and to swear once again her faith in the Holy Roman Church.

Still, stories about the family continued to abound, the way gossip accompanies celebrities of all eras. In 1491, the Holy Office turned its attention to Don Luís. Although he was not convicted of "error," he was made to appear on July 17, 1491 in the sanbenito, the hooded yellow robe of penitents.[23] We don't know what he must have thought of this turn of events, but it can be surmised that the pragmatist saw this temporary, one-day humiliation as a small price to pay for the life of his mother and the safety of his nuclear family. He was, after all, one whose success, like his father's and grandfather's before him, owed much to skillfulness in negotiation and resilience in adjusting to undesirable situations.

Surely, the great gift of Inquisition immunity, received a few years later in 1493, brought tremendous relief. The question still persists in reviewing the case, however: was Brianda *judaizante*? Was her son?

Although from a New Christian family, Brianda was only one generation removed from the original conversion. Those who changed their religious affiliation in fear or danger rarely did so from a true turning of heart and soul toward the new faith. From a secular perspective, however, there were substantial social and economic benefits accruing to Christians and denied to Jews of the fifteenth century. Most Jewish men experienced this daily, their livelihoods taking them out into the larger community, where they felt the sting of these inequities. While men of observant religious bent found it difficult, if not impossible, to give up the daily prayers and rituals that had set the clocks of their lives, those to whom Judaism was more simply a traditional, ethnic connection made an easier adjustment to the new reality. Of course, there was always the need to show one's family's devotion to the church ostentatiously by attending mass, confession and other rituals of Christianity. What a small price, however, to be no longer subject to the taxes and restrictions experienced as Jews. At last, families such as these could see themselves rising economically, able to move about freely, own land and work in formerly prohibited occupations.

This line of reasoning, however, was not the same for most women, for whom it was hard to let go of the significant roles they held in Jewish day-to-day life. Their year-round calendar was set by the preparation of meals for *Shabbat* and holidays and the carrying out of related familial and Jewish household rituals connected with food preparation and cleaning. In a patriarchal age, mothers treasured the Sephardic family role of the first educator for the children, responsible for teaching the basic observance of Judaism. This began in early childhood for youth of both sexes and continued for the boys until they began attending the *Talmud Torah* or Hebrew school around five or six and accompanying their fathers to the synagogue. Girls, however, remained at home to learn and repeat the female role cycle. Mothers continued being responsible for maintaining the family conformance to ritual and observance and to conserve Jewish values.

Whether changing faith willingly or by force, female converts were expected to give up that respected and valued charge, observing Christian ritual instead, at home and in public. It is easy to see, then, why *judaizante* practices persisted among women of even the most important *converso* families in Aragón and Castilla and continued in the centuries to come. Brianda and her mother may have followed this pattern. It is possible that they took five-year-old Luís along on their visits to the Daroca *judería* to expose him to *Shabbat* and Passover. As Brianda's first born, he would be the child considered most vital in preserving some knowledge of Judaism in the next generation. He fell under the more secular guidance of father and grandfather, however, when old enough to accompany them on their business in Valencia. Practical men who saw their fortune dependent on the good will of Christian royalty and influentials, it can be assumed that they took great care to show their Christianity openly and abjure any practice that would end the boundless opportunities.

It is probable, therefore, that Brianda was *judaizante*, most likely in the dietary and Sabbath rituals that could be more easily hidden than other observances, and that her son, Luís, *escribano de ración* and *contador mayor*, a favorite of the king and trusted financial adviser to both rulers, was not.[24]

It is recognized, however, that while the celebrity Santángel could adjust outwardly to the realities of the era, the inner man still had to confront the conflicts raised. What price did Luís de Santángel and other New Christian notables pay to conform in behavior to the requirements of public life and continue the appearance of loyalty, while witnessing those with the same surname be accused, tortured, even executed — while witnessing one's own mother in danger of same? To keep his lofty position and family status, he, and other public figures such as Sánchez and de la Caballería, had to appear unruffled; they most certainly could not protest. Santángel was serving a king and queen who had shown by the expulsion and the establishment of the Inquisition their lack of gratitude for the crucial support received from Jews and *conversos* in the *Reconquista* and the daily needs of royalty. At least fifteen individuals with the name Santángel would be punished by the Inquisition by the year 1499. By 1503, fourteen Sánchez family members would meet the same fate, although the royal treasurer remained free.[25]

Answers to these questions are merely conjectures, based on the personalities, histories and situations of the *dramatis personae*. Here is the probable Machiavellian model for the quintessential absolute monarch. While there are no records on whether Fernando communicated in any way with his *escribano de ración* on the issues, we do know the king's guiding principle was expediency. What politically-safe message could Fernando have communicated to calm "his much loved councillor," a loyal New Christian, while his mother remained in prison?

Netanyahu portrays the monarchy in power struggles with three groups; the nobility of Castilla and Aragón, the prelates of the Holy Roman Church and the growing Old Christian middle and merchant classes. All of these stood to profit by the stricture, even the elimination, of Jews. Add to these a fourth element: the general populace supplying the mobs for the conversionary efforts of Ferrán Martínez and Vincente Ferrer, argues Netanyahu, and you had a monarchy that had to please these groups to keep control. This explains, sometimes in greater, sometimes lesser, degrees, the seesawing policies of rulers towards Jews from the late fourteenth through the end of the fifteenth centuries — sometimes protectors, sometimes persecutors or the allies of persecutors, but always ready to accept Jewish services and resources when useful.[26]

With this perspective and his known affection for Santángel, one can visualize Fernando in thought over how to protect him and Brianda when the time was right. After all, how could Don Luís continue effective performance of his services with his mother in prison and his family endangered? Santángel endured the seventeen-month incarceration of Brianda, the fear about potential torture, which fortunately did not materialize, and the anxiety awaiting the appointed council's decision. Presumably, the hand of the king could be seen in her release. Surely, eventually freeing the Santángels from inquisitorial concerns for thirty years was the greatest reward Fernando could bestow, a significant "thank you" for service through harrowing times.

This leads us to consider if there was more to Santángel's support of the Columbus voyage than the glory of Spain and his own enrichment. There has been much supposition about the backing the seaman received from Jews and *conversos*, who included, as has been pointed out, Sánchez, de la Caballería, Cabrero and Abravanel. Did they support an opportunity to settle new lands, with relative freedom far from Spanish shores? We have acknowledged that few men of learning still believed that the earth was flat, and that they would probably be familiar with the Norse settlement one-half millennium earlier. Did the courtiers view the voyage's success as initiating a possible route to safety and opportunity? As yet, researchers have found nothing definitive on whether Columbus was, indeed, of Jewish background, nor whether there was more than economic opportunity and pro–Spanish patriotism behind the support of his voyage by Jews and *conversos*. Everything else is hypothesis or speculation.[27]

In 1496, Santángel received the assignment to represent *Los Reyes Católicos* in purchasing the dowry of their daughter, *La Infanta* Doña Juana, for her marriage to Archduke Philip of Habsburg, the future Philip I of Spain. This was a lucrative appointment, a further token of appreciation for his well-executed services.[28]

Luís de Santángel lived five more years after Columbus' return from his first voyage. He lived those years in relative peace, knowing that he and his family were safe from inquisitorial harassment. He died in 1498 at age fifty-seven. Wife Juana was blessed with long life, surviving Luís by one-quarter of a century, and living to see her sons and daughters marry nobility, prosper and continue to serve the crown. She died in 1523.

After Don Luís' death, his brother Jaime was named *escribano de ración*. Luís' son Hernando, also called Fernando, was appointed to the position upon his uncle's death in 1512. Each received the annual salary of 8,000 sueldos and accompanying perquisites.[29]

Successive monarchs continued to call on Don Luís' descendants after Fernando's death, who, like the "much loved councillor," had been groomed for royal service. Noah Chinillo's heirs had gone from merchant status to nobility in three generations. Public opinion varied, however, on their value to Spain and the use of their services, depending on the economic, political and social circumstances of the beholder. Some Old Christian aristocracy, as well as members of the burgeoning middle class, resented the substantial wealth and influence achieved by the increasingly ennobled Santángel family, and considered them and other prominent *conversos* to be "polluting" the *limpieza de sangre*, or purity of blood, of the titled families into which they married. The same resentment was directed against any talented *converso* with political savvy and financial resources, who, no longer technically Jewish, could rise to the level of his potential without legal restrictions.

In the middle of the fifteenth century, the City of Toledo enacted ordinances differentiating between Old and New Christians, and prohibiting the latter from access to positions in church and government. Although Pope Nicholas V overruled these, holding that "all Catholics are one in body according to the teachings of our faith," the king, nevertheless, approved them. Soon, there were purity of blood laws everywhere. By the middle of the next century, no one with Jewish ancestry was able to enter public employment in Spain and Portugal.[30]

To enhance their positions in the face of *limpieza de sangre*, prosperous and influential *conversos* strengthened Christian identity by arranging marriages for their children into entitled Old Christian families. This appeared to be a beneficial exchange for all. New Christians improved their status, building a multi-generational case for *limpieza de sangre*, and gaining influential Old Christian relatives. In turn, titled families gained access to much needed wealth to help them better cope with the changing economic realities of the early modern period and the growing concentration of capital and political power in the hands of the new burghers.

This was the case with the Santángels. Jaime, brother of *the escribano de ración*, was the first descendent of the Jewish clothing merchant from Daroca to take the high road to nobility. Jaime's father, Luis II, arranged his marriage to Francina de Centelles, from the family of the Counts of Oliva.[31] Through this liaison, he became landed gentry, called Lord Redován of Orihuela, and bearer of the additional title of *baile general* of the region. Holders of this title represented the crown in their local communities. Jaime's heir, son Miguel Jerónimo, inherited his father's titles and married Doña Esperanza Despés of a noble family. Continuing through the generations, Diego, Miguel Jerónimo's son, who further inherited the lordship and *baile* titles, linked the family once again with the Centelles when he married Doña Juana, daughter of the Count of Gallano.

The *escribano de ración* himself began the ennoblement process for his nuclear family with daughter Luisa's marriage in 1494 to Don Angel de Villanueva, who became Viceroy of Sicily in 1515. Son Alfonso married a daughter of the Lord of Carlet, Doña Jerónima del Castellví. Their son, Francisco, would serve later in the court of Phillip II. It is ironic that Alfonso's in-laws, the Castellví, were the same neighboring family whose servants gave testimony in 1486 against his great-grandmother Brianda. Alfonso's other son, Jerónimo, was probably the *caballero* of the same name who married Isabel, daughter of Don Tomás de Próxita.

Hernando, Luís de Santángel's heir, continued the ennoblement effort, wedding Beatriz de Fenollet, daughter of Don Luis de Fenollet, high official in the court of John II. Their daughter Isabel married Don Hernando de Ayala of Toledo. One of the descendents of this marriage, Don Diego López de Ayala, was to be a candidate for Canon of the Cathedral of Toledo, and join the Cabildo, or Chapter of the Cathedral. The Cabildo was known for its adherence to *limpieza de sangre*, so the descendent of Noah Chinillo had done very well indeed.[32]

Why should we remember Luís de Santángel? What were the achievements of this most powerful New Christian merchant and courtier? Coming first to mind is his success in making the voyage of Columbus possible through his strong advocacy, while risking fortune and reputation. Columbus had left the Alhambra, convinced that Spanish support was out of the question, and was headed for the French court to open his case anew, when Santángel presented his loan to Isabel and won over the monarchs. He brought the mariner back to Granada to receive his sought-after commission. Perhaps France, looking for colonial riches, would have had the wisdom to see the potential of this expedition. Or in default, England, whose navy was quietly developing into a major force, might have acted to support the voyage. In either case, the success of the expedition for England or France would have diminished Spain's colonial potential. And, therefore, the migratory pattern of settlement in the New World would undoubtedly have been very different. The ancestors of many of today's Americans might not have crossed the seas, had the national scenario played out differently.

There is debate about the glory of the voyage, given the decimation of indigenous peoples and the despoiling of natural lands and life. Yet, we defer to the lessons of hindsight, when we can see the horrors of the past from the perspective of a more judicious present. We defer to Octavio Paz, who reminds us that human greatness, *la grandeza humana*, lies in turning nightmare into vision.[33] We are always awed, for example, by the concern for human values demonstrated today by the descendants of the very Vikings who once marauded, conquered, raped, murdered and pillaged their way through Europe and Asia, reaching even North America. Surely the unfolding vision of democracy and freedom that epitomizes much of the Americas is the present transformation of the nightmare.

We know little about the values and ethics of Luís de Santángel. Most probably, as a prosperous merchant and important courtier, he epitomized the behaviors, attitudes and values of a man of his class, status and era. We know he was practical, resourceful and flexible, and more inclined toward action to improve one's family wealth and status than toward reasoning based on the highest good for all concerned. As a merchant, he was competitive in nature, trying to outdistance rival mercantile houses, while being wary and cognizant of royal and aristocratic politics and its dangers. He was capable of negotiation, of the give and take required for a New Christian, thriving in both business and court.

There are some clues as to his family values. At one time, there were three young people living in the household of the *escribano de ración*, two of whom were said to be his illegitimate offspring. Sánchez-Blanco identifies them as Brianda and Tecla, with a third, Angela, who was either Luís' or brother Galcerán's child. This was typical of the marital behavior of prominent Jews and *conversos* of the period, but it was unusual, however, to see a progenitor and his family providing direct support for his out-of-wedlock offspring in their own home.[34]

Some historians report him intervening occasionally on behalf of some

New Christians endangered by the Inquisition. In 1482, Santángel urged Fernando to intercede in the case of a *converso* who had confessed his sins when the Holy Office in Valencia had urged individuals to come forth during a period of grace. The king subsequently wrote the inquisitor to be compassionate and "to be lenient in his penalties" on behalf of the individual.[35]

It has been seen that much of Santángel's success in royal service came from his skills in procuring funds for the needs of rulers and influentials. He was a talented facilitator and networker. He was pleasant and agreeable, while tenacious in pursuing his goals. He knew how to make friends and avoid making enemies, no small task for a New Christian in an era of inquisitorial activity and emerging burgher classes. It is probable that, like other wealthy persons of his time and place, he made payments to important people when it would help his family's business, its welfare and perhaps the welfare of *converso* friends and kinsmen.

Kayserling eloquently assesses our subject's contributions, comparing him to Benjamin Disraeli, Prime Minister of England of *converso* Sephardic background, and calling him "the Beaconsfield of Spain," adapting Disraeli's title.

> Like that English statesman — who was of Jewish stock and whose ancestors were also persecuted by the Inquisition and driven from Spain — Luís was characterized at once by particularism and universalism, enthusiasm and sagacity, subjective patriotism and objective devotion to other nationalities. He was a good Aragonese, and yet he worked for the unity of Spain; he was ardently devoted to his country and he carefully considered the advantages which it would derive from maritime discoveries.[36]

His image appears on monuments and statues in Valencia, Granada and Barcelona, in tribute to his contributions to the Columbus voyage. However, there were those such as Isaac Abravanel, who were critical of successful converts, believing them to be traitors to their faith and opportunists reaping economic and social gain. Yet, Judaism teaches forgiveness for the *anusim*, the forced ones. The text of *Kol Nidre*, the solemn service the night before *Yom Kippur*, the Jewish Day of Atonement, wipes the slate clean for *conversos*, as it does for all men and women, releasing them from the vows sworn under force:

> Concerning all vows, oaths, covenants, promises and all manner of bindings of soul with which I will bind and limit myself, constrain and confine myself from this Yom Kippur until the next Yom Kippur, I proclaim: I hereby recant, release, disavow, and declare null and void from this time forward.
>
> The bindings shall not bind me, the roles I take on shall not constrain me, and the limitations shall not in any way limit my power.

The congregants then ask forgiveness of God.

Four. Luís de Santángel 99

This sculpture, on the monument to Columbus in Barcelona, portrays a beneficent Luís de Santángel placing a box in the hands of a page, containing funds loaned to the Catholic Majesties to finance the navigator's first voyage. (Generalitat Valenciana, ed., *Lluís de Santàngel y su época: un nuevo hombre, un mundo nuevo* [Valencia: 1992], 272.)

May all be forgiven of the entire people of Israel, and of all the gentiles who dwell among them, for we assume that all have sinned by error and not by malice. Pardon the errors of this people, according to your abundant loving-kindness, just as you have forgiven this people since they left the confinements of Egypt and until now. In the Bible, it is written: "And God said, 'I have pardoned, as you have asked.'"[37]

Many a descendant of *conversos*, returning to Judaism, awaits these words yearly with gratitude and relief, to help relieve the five-centuries-old burden of guilt and a sense of not truly belonging anywhere. "The gentiles who dwell among" us are included in the amnesty, on an equal par for forgiveness with professing Jews.

Luís de Santángel showed resiliency in the human dilemma facing Sephardic Jews in the middle ages and early modern period, and was able to demonstrate loyalty and a high level of performance in serving family, king and country. We suggest he be seen as an embodiment of the plight of Jews who converted to Christianity under pressure and fear. That he and his antecedents were able to turn this around to their benefit aroused both admiration and censure in their day from former coreligionists. Increasingly, one learns today — in popular media, at academic conferences, through word-of mouth — about numerous individuals with Spanish and Portuguese ancestry coming forth to explore genealogy and DNA results in search of possible or probable Jewish ancestry. Luís de Santángel and his progeny seem less and less a tale from the past and more and more at home on the contemporary American continents, in the mountains and cities of Portugal and Spain and in the places of Sephardic diaspora in Europe and Asia.

✥ FIVE ✥

Doña Gracia Nasi: "Piety of Miriam, strength of Judith"

It is easy to come under the spell of Gracia Nasi. Inspirational, and revered in her day by Jews and *conversos* alike, this figure from post-expulsion, sixteenth-century Sephardic history appeals to the twenty-first century enchantment with women who have expanded the gender boundaries of their eras.

Even today, it is not regarded as typical for a woman not yet thirty to assume leadership of one of the largest banking and trading enterprises of the day, with little preparation for the task, and manage it well for the rest of her life. Gracia Nasi not only accomplished this while the tenacious middle ages still influenced the dominant thinking and behavior in many parts of Europe and the Ottoman Empire, but she also applied her power to protect her people and initiate reprisal against their enemies. Widowed, she continued to use her great fortune and company's ships to support a rescue operation initiated by her late husband and brother-in-law, to help Portuguese New Christians in danger of persecution flee for safer lands. She funded the building of synagogues, schools, hospitals. She served as patron to worthy literary efforts, some of which are still regarded as classics. She was the driving force behind an economic boycott of the Italian port of Ancona to avenge the burning at the stake of twenty-four *conversos*. And she initiated a resettlement effort, designed to bring Jews from throughout the diaspora to Tiberius in the Holy Land.

For all her achievements, Gracia Nasi was no saint. Convinced of the validity of the causes she espoused, she could be imperious, impatient and threatening with those who advocated paths differing from hers. Nevertheless, she won respect from many an opponent. When she died, Joshua Soncino, distinguished rabbi with whom she had clashed over the Ancona boycott, added his voice to the eulogies, declaring "her righteousness will stand forever."[1]

In his definitive biography of Doña Gracia, Historian Cecil Roth reminds us that

> The sixteenth century was in fact, the age of famous women — Elizabeth, Mary, and Mary Queen of Scots in Great Britain, Lucrezia Borgia, Isabel d'Este, Caterina Sforza, Vittoria Colonna and a score of others in Italy, Catherine de' Medicis in France, and many more. It is noteworthy that Gracia Nasi belonged to the same age.[2]

He calls her "one of the outstanding figures of Jewish history, not of her own day alone, but of all time."[3] This is all the more remarkable given the challenge of having to hide her beliefs and intentions while very much in the public eye as a celebrity. Still, this judaizing New Christian was able to cheat the Inquisition of more victims and shepherd the House of Mendes successfully while in flight, literally and rhetorically, for seventeen years.

It is useful to examine this life so well lived for her family and her people. Was there any indication that the baby girl, Beatriz de Luna, born into a prosperous New Christian family in the Lisbon of 1510, would someday become known as the legendary Gracia Nasi, humanist, philanthropist and political and economic strategist?

Her birth came almost two decades after the expulsion from Spain. In an ideal time or place, she would have been known as Jana or Hannah, meaning grace in Hebrew — Gracia in the family's native Spanish tongue. But the second decade of the sixteenth century was not the ideal time and place. This was Portugal, thirteen years after her parents, like all Jews, were forcibly converted to Christianity in 1497, five years after the expulsion from Spain. And it was four years after the Riots of 1506, when thousands of Jews in Lisbon were slaughtered by rampaging mobs. The girl child entered a New Christian setting in Lisbon, and was baptized Beatriz. Her surname, de Luna, could have been selected to honor her parents' baptizing churchman or Old Christian godfather, or it could have been chosen in honor of Alvaro de Luna, a benefactor of Jews a century before. Brooks tells us that it is possible that Luna was "the family's village of origin. Her mother used the surname de Luna while historians are divided over her father's between de Luna and Miguez."[4]

Born into wealth and a distinguished family, Beatriz received the typical education of a woman of her class and economic position, preparing her with the cultural background she would draw from someday as wife of a prominent and successful man and *dama de casa* of his residence and household staff. The typical curriculum of the day included studies of music and a musical instrument, the favored arts of the era and the necessary math, language and management skills to host eminences and run a large household, with servants, retainers and providers in the hundreds.

To the outside world, the family was Catholic, attending mass and being shriven, observing holy days of obligation and all Christian rites. Their home bore the icons of Christianity: sculpture and portraits of the Holy Family and saints. There may even have been a statue of the Virgin at the entry door in the typical manner, so all who passed in and out could pay her homage. Beatriz's brother, Aghostino, was physician in the royal court, so it can be assured that the family was visibly Catholic.[5]

However, Beatriz de Luna's family was *judaizante*, observing in secret what Judaic ritual they could, with great care to avoid detection. Before coming to Portugal, her father was called *el nací*, or *nasi*, a tax farmer from Briviesca, near Burgos. *Nasi* in Hebrew means prince, a term of respect. He and others like him were so called because they represented their Jewish communities before rulers and administrators.

The young Beatriz grew up with a strong sense of Jewish identity, which had been carefully cultivated in secret by her parents. Jewish women had carried the traditional role of responsibility for the Judaic and secular education of their children, and her parents assured that their outwardly Catholic daughter knew the basics of Judaic life and practice. Again, any practice of ritual and customs had to be observed in secret. For although the Portuguese Inquisition would not be established until 1536, the practice of Judaism had been illegal since the forced conversion in 1497.

As we have seen earlier, New Christian families were also called *marranos*, meaning swine; *conversos*, converts; or *Nuovos Cristianos*, New Christians. Many of them, like Beatriz's, retained a secret identity with their Jewish roots. During this era, *judaizante conversos* yearned for the coming of the messiah to rescue them from fear, danger and homelessness. It was the general belief that the trials of persecution and expulsion were God's way to purify his people and ready them for messianic delivery. They hoped and prayed to be able to observe Judaism openly someday. In the meantime, they observed those rituals whose practices they took care to hide. These included fasting at the seasons of traditional Jewish holidays such as *Yom Kippur* and *Purim* and not eating pork when possible. Unfortunately, even these were often almost all too visible to servants and visitors, as Inquisition records in Spain and Portugal would attest.[6]

At the time of Beatriz's birth, more than a decade had passed since synagogues and rabbis had been extant. The rites and rituals that *judaizante* New Christians observed, therefore, took on individual and family peculiarities, based on oral history from elders. Historian David Gitlitz quotes a woman in Toledo who was interrogated by the Spanish Inquisition in 1527, illustrating the doubts of practitioners about the accuracy of their observance:

The things I did not do was because I did not know when the festivals were, or what things I was supposed to do. Sometimes I omitted doing them because I was afraid. But I did them in my heart and I would have done more, because I know that my salvation depends on it.[7]

Judaizante New Christians shared three beliefs: that the messiah would come to deliver them; that God is One, not tripartite; and that loyalty to the Law of Moses is required for salvation. As observed in the chapter on Don Isaac Abravanel, unhappy circumstances made many vulnerable to the claims of individuals fraudulently declaring themselves to be the messiah or his emissary. A young Beatriz must have heard of David Reubeni, the imposter who presented himself as representative of a king of Israel from the Levant and was received at the Portuguese royal court where her brother was royal physician. He was much talked about by New Christians like her family, who hoped that the coming of the messiah was close at hand. Brooks writes that "Such hoopla and its glorious potential could not have failed to impress the teenage Doña Gracia who lived in daily fear of her neighbors." Whether they actually met face to face is not known, but it is highly possible; Reubeni was known to have visited the homes of the leading *converso* families of the day.[8] Afterward, when Reubeni was unmasked, Beatriz surely would have witnessed, even experienced herself, the subsequent discouragement of fellow Jews. One wonders if this could have influenced her proclivity, later in life, toward direct action rather than prayer and ransom, in dealing with the enemies of Jews.

At the age of fifteen, Beatriz took charge of the education of her nephews, João and Agostinho, upon the sudden death of their father. The young aunt assumed the traditional female responsibility to pass on the fundamentals of Jewish practice — in secret of course. Thus began a close relationship between Beatriz and the young João, whose path would later come to parallel hers. Their future teamwork on an international scale would become legendary, as they safeguarded familial interests and protected Jews and *conversos*.

In 1528, Beatriz became the wife of Francisco Mendes. We met Francisco in Chapter One. Originally named Semah, he and his brother, Meir, came to Portugal at the time of the expulsion with their family, the Benvenistes, becoming Francisco and Diogo Mendes during the Christian conversion of 1497.

Partner with Diogo of the powerful House of Mendes, Francisco was a good bit older than his wife. It was probable that he and Beatriz were related. Roth conjectures that Beatriz's family was "perhaps allied long before to that of Beneveniste,"[9] while Brooks cites documents describing Francisco as brother to Beatriz's mother, hence the young woman's uncle.[10] It was customary among wealthy and prominent *conversos* for immediate family members to marry as this not only safeguarded family fortunes, but assured more protection in keeping Jewish practices secret. In Chapter Two, we saw Isaac Abravanel's son, Samuel, wed his first cousin, Benvenida. Aside from this, there is little documentation describing Francisco. Roth quotes a contemporary source referring to him as "a Rabbi Anuss," from the Hebrew word for forced, considering him a scholar, respected by his peers, who hid his Jewish identity behind a Christian veneer.[11] If so, Francisco must have attained sufficient Judaic scholarship and respect to earn the title. As we witnessed in earlier chapters about Isaac Abravanel and Abraham Zacuto, Francisco also personified that quality of leadership Roth calls "the traditional Jewish fashion," which "combines worldly and intellectual eminence."[12]

On coming of age, Francisco and Diogo inherited a considerable fortune and a respected position in the *converso* community. They shepherded this well. Their House of Mendes had become a successful banking and mercantile enterprise, with a fleet of ships in international trade. The firm eventually cornered the spice trade for Portugal, and also held dominance in gems and textiles, which would make them fabulously rich. In Chapter Four, we saw that the Portuguese lead in this trade was what Venetian leaders hoped to reduce when they retained Isaac and Joseph Abravanel to negotiate more favorable terms.

As bankers, the Mendes firm used its ships to carry letters of credit for their clients, facilitating the exchange of assets and cargoes and the transfer of funds. They were also generous and much sought-after lenders, with clients among European royalty. Diogo Mendes had been based in Antwerp in the Low Countries, a vital trade crossroads, since 1512. From there, he stewarded his part of the firm's affairs.

There was still another facet of the House of Mendes, kept hidden for very good reasons. Although the Inquisition had not yet been established in Portugal, Francisco in Lisbon and Diogo in Antwerp were secretly utilizing their ships and assets to help *conversos* flee the increasingly severe oppression and threats, while transferring the fugitives' funds to safety. In every port with Mendes agents, there were resources and contacts to help the travelers find their way to relatively safe destinations. When a fugitive had no funds, the firm covered the cost of the journey, usually made in one of its ships which plied the Atlantic and the Mediterranean regularly. The agents met arriving ships at each port, and supervised disposition of the commercial, as well as human, cargoes. They even boarded the incoming Portuguese spice ships of other firms when *conversos* were aboard, to advise them about relative safety on shore. In England, for example, Mendes factor Christopher Fernandes was dispatched frequently to Southampton or Plymouth to meet the ships. Antonio de la Ronha, another Mendes agent, helped fugitives transform property into funds, and then into Antwerp bills of exchange. A network of agents arranged safe housing for the fugitives, as they made their way to desired destinations in the Lowlands, Italy or the Ottoman Empire. Even an occasional Old Christian, such as burgher Daniel Bomberg, aided in the venture. Bomberg managed the escape project in Venice, assuring that assets transported by Mendes ships eventually reached their owners. Behind it all were Francisco in Lisbon and Diogo in Antwerp.[13]

The Mendes lifestyle in both cities was one of splendor, elegantly furnished mansions, with retainers and suppliers of food, tradesmen and artisans passing in and out. In Lisbon, visitors in the arts, philosophy, science and commerce, came to share their ideas with the learned and influential couple.

Soon a daughter was born. Researchers differ on the baptismal name of Beatriz's daughter — Ana or Brianda.[14] We do know that she was secretly called Reyna, a popular name for Jewish girls.

We don't know how much Beatriz had learned of the different aspects of family empire, the trade in spices, gems and textiles, and the commercial mechanisms moving the fleet and operating the offices from India and the Far East to Iberia and Western Europe. Nevertheless, Francisco had specified in his will that she share with Diogo leadership of the firm should he pass away. This came to pass all too soon, as Francisco fell ill and died in 1536, leaving behind his twenty-six-year-old widow and their six-year-old daughter. As he lay dying, Beatriz promised to honor his request for his remains to rest in the Holy Land some day. For the present, however, she was compelled to bury him with Christian rites.

It was, at the very least, a challenging time for Beatriz. It was certainly transformational, signaling her emergence as a celebrity of the century. Now co-owner and partner with her brother-in-law of one of the richest and most powerful trading and financial organizations in Europe, she had to make decisions on her own as a significant public personality. It will be seen later how the strong ties and loyalties within the Nasi and Mendes clans supported her in this role, and where they fell short.

In addition to her maternal responsibilities, Beatriz continued to serve as guardian of nephews João and Agostinho, who had come of age but deferred to their aunt as adviser and family matriarch. She played a protective role as well with her younger sister, who, like her daughter, also carried the names Brianda publicly and Reyna in secret.

Despite increasing danger in Lisbon, Francisco had probably chosen to remain there to safeguard his empire and continue his clandestine beneficent activities. Upon his death, his widow made plans to join Diogo in Antwerp via England. With the Holy Inquisition about to be established in Portugal, it was likely that the Lisbon part of the secret escape network would be exposed and no longer protected by those eager to please the generous creditor that the House of Mendes had become. With daughter Brianda, sister Brianda and nephews João and Agostinho, Beatriz set sail on a Mendes ship, the cargo hiding most of their fortune. The considerable wealth and inventory of the family's commercial empire made such an escape possible. And yet, great pains had to be taken to make it appear not a flight, but merely a business journey to take care of family matters.

Thus began a legendary journey over land and sea for Beatriz and her loved ones. Before reaching their planned final destination of Constantinople, seventeen years later, they would have traveled perhaps 3,000 miles, crossing through at least eight countries, including England, Belgium, the Netherlands, France, Venice, Ferrara, Ragusa (now Dubrovnik) and Greece, before settling at last in the Ottoman Empire, a land of relative freedom and safety for Jews. Most of the journey would be perilous; traveling outwardly as observant Catholics, but secret Jews, they would live in constant fear of detection or betrayal. Also, Portuguese New Christians were prohibited from interchange with Muslim countries and from fleeing to another state. The risk of discovery was that much greater for Beatriz and nephew João, the latter having become an international celebrity like his aunt. They were always in the spotlight, in frequent social contact with royalty and nobility. While their great wealth gave them the wherewithal to travel by land and sea, it was also cause for jealousy and resentment, and, as will be seen, for betrayal and imprisonment. At the same time, it could, and did, buy escape from peril and provided safe conduct passes along the way.

In the long odyssey toward the Ottoman Empire, England was the first step for the young widow, her family and entourage. In Constantinople, Sultan Suleiman the Magnificent had extended the welcome to fleeing Jews and *conversos*, aware, like his predecessor, Bayazid II, of how beneficial their skills, experience and resources would be to his empire. The Mendes family, however, had to move cautiously and gradually so as not to endanger life and fortune, always maintaining a Catholic presence. Choosing the longer, but safer, sea route from Portugal, rather than a shorter overland journey, it was necessary to have a viable excuse for stopping in England before moving on. Through contacts between Diogo and Thomas Cromwell, chancellor and chief financial adviser to Henry VIII, the firm's agent in London secured an English safe conduct for Beatriz and her family to stop there on the way to Antwerp for business with her brother-in-law. France and the Holy Roman Empire were at war, and it was deemed too risky to go overland. The business referred to was the rumored wedding of Diogo to Beatriz's sister, Brianda. Surely, they hoped, this family matter would serve as a good pretext, and raise no suspicion by Portugal's King Manoel about the sudden departure. The king, it will be remembered, enabled the dominant position of the House of Mendes in the lucrative spice trade and would certainly not have wanted the widow and her fortune, often available to him in much-needed loans, out of his control.

England's Henry VIII had taken his island kingdom out of the Catholic Church over his divorce from Catherine of Aragón. He had no reason to help a Catholic ruler regain his subjects, especially since the latter were agreeable creditors. England had become a temporary safe haven for the *converso* refugee community, even though practicing Jews had been legally banned for centuries. Henry, then, welcomed the head of the great enterprise which had become his generous creditor.

So, Beatriz de Luna arrived in London with family and entourage. Roth quotes a contemporary source as referring to their stay there as "of some duration."[15] It had to be long enough so as not to arouse suspicion. A wealthy and successful commercial leader and a baptized Christian, she was welcomed in the English capital by *converso* and Christian alike.

When the time was deemed right, the family and its retainers moved on to Antwerp, where Diogo directed the House of Mendes as the dominant commercial force in the trade in spices, textiles and precious stones. He was also a major creditor to royalty of several nations. The House would buy the spices in bulk, for cash, from Portugal's king and sell them to European merchants. Thus, a considerable amount of money had been pouring into Portuguese coffers. The Crown relied on this trade as a source of revenue, making it financially dependent on the House of Mendes.

Even in the relatively tolerant atmosphere of Antwerp, however, Diogo had been imprisoned twice for *judaizante* and smuggling of *conversos*, but released both times, thanks to intervention by Portugal's Manoel and England's Henry, showing appreciation for their New Christian creditor. There were also protests by likewise dependent nobles and burghers. The Portuguese *converso* community benefited from the commercial success it had brought everyone from royalty and nobility to burghers and ordinary people. The arts and sciences flourished as well. For the *converso*, Antwerp was a tolerant and prosperous environment. Cecil Roth paints a colorful picture of the vitality of life in New Christian circles. Even prominent non–Jews, such as Albrecht Dürer, the great painter from Nuremberg, sought out the community and enjoyed its social and artistic offerings. Roth pictures Dürer as perhaps hoping for a commission from the prosperous *converso*, Diogo Mendes, as he visited frequently in the great mansion.[16] And Diogo, indeed, flourished at the heart of this intellectual, scientific and commercial community.

Into this environment came Doña Beatriz and entourage. Eighteen months after their arrival, sister Brianda and brother-in-law Diogo became man and wife. As pointed out earlier, *judaizers* took great pains to marry only other *judaizante* New Christians. This often resulted in endogamy, marrying within families for security, while still being sure to attend mass and confession regularly, and keeping up other appearances of Catholic observance. This pattern would be repeated later within the family.

The business and family relationship between Beatriz and Diogo was harmonious. True partners, they maintained the day-to-day operations of the empire, including coordination of the *converso* escape routes, with which Francisco had played such a vital part in Lisbon. The importance placed on serving in this clandestine role was probably the main reason why the Mendes family did not leave Antwerp sooner in the direction of their planned-for resettlement in the Ottoman Empire.

Charles V, Holy Roman Emperor, ruled over Flanders and the Low Countries, the Hapsburg lands and Italian cities in the south. He was also Charles II, king of Spain. Growing repression from church and monarchy, and the possibility of another arrest for Diogo, made it clear to Beatriz and her brother-in-law that it was time to move on. All was in jeopardy in Antwerp, and they shared the desire to practice Judaism openly.

However, Diogo died suddenly in 1542 or 1543, before this could be effectuated. His will affirmed Beatriz's half of the firm's assets, as provided by his brother and appointed her administrator of his half, to be passed on to his young daughter, named Beatriz after her aunt, upon marriage or coming of age. Now sole head of the fabled Mendes Empire, Beatriz used some of the funds for payments to Emperor Charles V so he, in turn, would withdraw all charges of heresy against Diogo.

As before, the death of a near and dear one had elevated the relatively young matriarch into a more visible place on the stage of European power, as undisputed head of one of the richest, most powerful commercial empires of the early Renaissance. In their day, the House of Mendes was, indeed, comparable to the Rothschilds of two centuries later.

Keeping up Catholic and social appearances made the widow de Luna a desired presence in the court of Marie, regent of the Lowlands, sister of Charles V. Nephew João, now a charming and socially attractive young man, had become jousting partner and favorite of Prince Maximilian. Aunt and nephew had begun a life-long relationship, working together toward family and commercial goals. João would soon be called upon to effectuate the withdrawal of the family and its assets from Antwerp.

Meanwhile, Beatriz's daughter, Brianda, had come to the attention of Don Francisco of Aragón, an illegitimate but titled descendant of the Spanish royal family. He promised Marie and Charles financial payments to enlist support for his courtship of the young woman. Doña Beatriz resisted the Regent's importuning as long as possible, and when the marriage was finally formally proposed, she was reported to have said that she would rather see her daughter dead.

Marie and Don Francisco continued their efforts, nevertheless. Beatriz gave the suitor's advanced age and questionable reputation as reasons for her refusal. Realistically, she could not hold them off much longer and feared such a marriage would unmask her Jewish identity, endanger their lives and decimate the family fortune. Soon, it was discovered that Doña Beatriz, her sister and their daughters were no longer at home in the great house in Antwerp. They had left, presumably to take the waters at Aix-la-Chapelle, in France. By the time of the discovery, however, they were well past the fabled health resort and on their way to Venice, via Lyon, for resettlement, carrying with them as many valuables as possible.

It fell to nephew João to press for release of the considerable, remaining Mendes assets, which had been placed in embargo by regent and emperor. After protracted negotiations over two years, a settlement was reached, confiscating much of the fortune, but canceling criminal and heresy charges against Diogo and Beatriz. In addition, the monarchs received a large, interest-free loan. Even with the considerable financial loss, however, the Mendes firm and its owners were still wealthy beyond the day's standard.

And so, Phase Three was underway of the legendary passage of the de Luna-Mendes clan. Venetian safe conduct in hand, the sisters made their way, first, to Lyon. After a stay of unknown length, they moved on to Venice, Queen of the Sea, taking up residency in a great house in the center of the city. Still presenting themselves as Christians, they did not have to live in the ghetto with professing Jews. Established in 1516, the ghetto was the first of its kind, restricting Jewish residency in Renaissance cities to a limited area. It was named after the foundry that once operated in the district.

Long the prosperous hub of Mediterranean trade from Muslim countries, the Far East and countries and cities to the north, Venice had benefited for centuries from the resulting diverse cultural influences. But as the sixteenth century moved toward its midpoint, Venetian hegemony was threatened by the loss of commerce to Atlantic ports, growing prosperous from new trade

Opposite: Doña Gracia Nasi and nephew Joseph Nasi look out from the pages of Ludwig Lewisohn's 1931 novel, *The Last Days of Shylock*, in which they were portrayed as defenders of Jews endangered by persecution. Arthur Szyk illustrated the book with drawings centered on personages and events in sixteenth-century Europe and the Ottoman Empire. (*The Last Days of Shylock* [New York: Harper & Brothers, 1931], facing 56. Reproduced with the cooperation of Alexandra Szyk Bracie and Historicana, Burlingame, California, www.historicana.com.)

routes to west and east, following the discovery of the New World and the sub-African passage. At the same time, Mediterranean trade was increasingly threatened by Turkish armed power. Further, the Protestant Reformation was making headway, with increasing conversions in Northern Europe.

Thus, the de Luna-Mendes clan had come to an edgy Venice, its economic, political and spiritual crisis masked by its glittering veneer. Despite the slow decline, the city was in the midst of its golden cultural century, characterized by artistic giants such as Titian and Tintoretto. It was also a garden of sensory delights, and the setting for contemporary European high style. In this environment, impending family conflict between Beatriz and Sister Brianda would put the family in jeopardy.

Diego's will had designated Beatriz as administrator of his half of the Mendes wealth and firm until his young daughter would marry or come of age. His widow, Brianda, continued to express her dissatisfaction with the arrangement, demanding control of the portion, perhaps, surmises Cecil Roth, so she could better enjoy Venice. Beatriz turned down this request, believing her sister would not be a responsible custodian of the large sum. The angry Brianda then denounced her sister to the authorities as *judaizante*, planning to take her fortune from Venice to the Ottoman Empire and practice Judaism.

With doubt cast on Beatriz, Brianda hoped she could win her legal case for custody over the funds. It did not turn out that way. Again historians and researchers differ. Roth and Birnbaum have Beatriz imprisoned and the two young daughters placed in a nunnery, with an embargo on all Mendes assets, in Venice as well as in France. Brianda herself was denounced as *judaizante* by a disgruntled agent she had retained to help her.[17] Brooks has Beatriz fleeing to Ferrara temporarily with much of her treasure to protect it from Brianda, as the latter asked a Venetian court for a judgment to put her in charge of her daughter's inheritance.[18]

Once more, the partnership of aunt and nephew saved the day. João had won the support of Moses Hamon, Sephardic physician to the sultan of the Ottoman Empire. It was rumored that Hamon hoped that the young Brianda would wed his son Joseph, as part of the arrangement for his help. He presented the petition for intervention to Suleiman the Magnificent, who notified Venetian authorities that members of Beatriz de Luna's family were his intended subjects, demanding her release and the freeing of her property. A messenger was dispatched to Venice on her behalf. Shortly after, Beatriz was released and reunited with her daughter. Still, she had been endangered for almost two years, and no longer feeling safe, Beatriz and daughter left for Ferrara in 1549, with a safe conduct from its duke, Ercole II. It is worth noting that after her departure, Venetian authorities considered expelling all *conversos* to avoid further conflicts with the Ottoman Empire.

Soon after Beatriz's arrival in Ferrara, Brianda left Venice to follow, and the two sisters were reconciled. It is interesting to read Roth's explanations for Brianda's return to the family. He reviews the obvious ones — disenchantment with Christian deed and greed and realization that Turkey offered the only viable future refuge, with real freedom. Then he postulates that it may have been a plan by the women themselves "to secure the family property to one of the two sisters by vindicating her unquestioned orthodoxy, with results that had gone further than what was originally anticipated."[19] This seems unlikely, too risky an undertaking for someone as politically wise as Beatriz. Besides, João would have most probably vetoed such an idea, for the same reasons.

Beatriz's willingness to forgive and embrace Brianda upon the latter's appearance in Ferrara demonstrated her nobility and ability to see beyond personal and familial injuries. After all, the betrayal had endangered lives and fortune, caused two years of life-threatening conditions and separation of the daughters from their mothers. For the Mendes/de Luna matriarch, however, the larger picture was family and spiritual preservation. This capacity for moral greatness would be manifested again as we follow her path.

Under letters-patent issued by Duke Ercole of the House of Este, Beatriz and daughter were welcomed in Ferrara and permitted to practice Judaism without reprisal. Henceforth, they would be known as Nasi, the honorary surname from Spain, passed down in her father's line. Daughter Brianda became Reyna. And with true grace, Beatriz de Luna, whose Hebrew name Hanna translated as Gracia, began her new life as Doña Gracia Nasi, practicing the rites of her ancestors in the open.

Renaissance Ferrara was a glorious respite for a family that had lived in dread for a lifetime. They entered a world where art, music and literature flourished with commerce and trade, in the fertile soil of tolerance and relative freedom. It was also home to *conversos* and Jews who had flocked there to live in peace.

Ercole's letters-patent granted considerable protection to the Nasi family, stating that if a future duke were to cancel the letters, they would have eighteen months to leave with their possessions and without an exit tax.[20] In this setting, Doña Gracia emerged as philanthropist and patron of Jewish learning, art and culture, finally able to direct her gifts openly to strengthen her people's practice of their religion. For over forty years, Portuguese *conversos* had been prohibited from the public observation of Judaism. Without rabbis or congregations, the recent residents of Ferrara and other places of shelter had little or no knowledge of authentic Jewish ritual and practice. There were no bibles or prayer books. To fill this gap, Doña Gracia promoted the publication of the Hebrew Bible in the Spanish vernacular by printers

As it was the fashionable thing to do in 1558, Doña Gracia's niece, known as Gracia *La Chica*, the Younger, had this medal struck during her stay in Ferrara. Pastorino di Giovan Mechele de' Pastorini. Medal of Gracia Nasi the Younger, Ferrara: 1558 (New York: ©The Jewish Museum) FB77. (Jewish Museum, New York /Art Resource, New York.)

Yomtob Athias and Abraham Usque, known previously by their *converso* names, Jerónimo de Vargas and Duarte Pinel, respectively. Published in 1553, the bible had two editions. The one for Christians and the general public was dedicated to Duke Ercole, and bore the *converso* names of the publishers. The other, for Jews, listed the two publishers by their Hebrew names, and was dedicated to Doña Gracia, "the noble-hearted Jewess ... so noble and magnanimous, that it would adorn her nobility."

It further described her "as being a person whose merits have always earned the most sublime place among all of our people — both because your greatness deserves it, and because your own birth and love of your land imposes this well-deserved obligation upon us." It is curious to note in both editions an imprimatur, stating that they have been "seen and examined by the Office of the Inquisition."[21]

Doña Gracia was praised in print again that year when Samuel Usque's epic prose poem, written in Portuguese, was published under her patronage by Abraham Usque, who may have been a relation of the author. Called *Consolaçam as tribulaçoens de Israel*, Consolation for the Tribulations of Israel, its purpose was to lift the spirits of Jews and *conversos*, presenting hope for deliverance as comfort for centuries of suffering and martyrdom. It was to become a classic, read by Portuguese schoolchildren well into the twentieth century. Probably drawing upon his own experiences in the flight from Portugal, Usque's dedication to Doña Gracia described her activities in providing for the escape and care of "your necessitous sons." He declared that "the wide pinions and outspread wings of this eagle have saved a great part of your sons in their flight from the cruelty of the Portuguese, so that she thus imitated the Lord at the time of the Exodus from Egypt."[22]

During her stay in Ferrara, Doña Gracia came into contact with other notable Jewish women living there, among them, Benvenida Abravanel. Wife of Don Isaac's son Samuel, Benvenida was already well known by the time of Gracia's arrival, and highly regarded for her charitable acts — ransoming Jewish prisoners, supporting arts and letters and generosity with paupers. She is said to have welcomed the newcomer upon her return to Judaism.

Once again, as in Lisbon, London and Antwerp, the great house of Doña Gracia was frequented by distinguished men and women of all talents, Jews as well as Christians. It was in fashion to have one's portrait struck in metal, and following along was Gracia *la Chica*, young Gracia, the niece. The famous medal by Pastorino di Giovan Michele de' Pastorini, shows an attractive young lady about eighteen years old, dressed in the high style of the age. It is particularly interesting that the letters surrounding the image on the medal are in Hebrew.[23]

Despite the relative safety and freedom of Ferrara, there were experiences and ill omens which turned the Nasi/Mendes clan to look once again toward Turkey. When popular belief blamed Jews for an outbreak of the plague, Doña Gracia had to seek temporary shelter in Venice, where she was placed under house arrest. As before, the sultan came to the rescue, requesting her release. She was freed and returned to Ferrara, where there were indications, however, that even the city that had sheltered the exiles would eventually fall prey to changes in popes and policy, bringing repression. It was finally time to complete the journey. With the path well laid ahead, and safe conduct to the Ottoman Empire in hand, she left Ferrara in August, 1552 for Constantinople.

Doña Gracia was forty-three years old at the time of her entry the following year into the city on the Bosporus. Here she would live out her remaining years. As befitted their wealth, the party traveled like nobility, with family and servants in four large coaches, surrounded by forty mounted and armed men. The journey took them through the Balkans and Ragusa, which would be called Dubrovnik in later years. The last major city before Constantinople was prosperous Salonika in Greece, where Jews made up a significant portion of the population. There were synagogues representing every cultural group and city of origin. It was a center of rabbinic learning, of literature, medicine, philosophy and commerce, very Jewish and very cosmopolitan, and it was to remain so until the Nazi exterminations of World War II.

We can imagine the excitement of Doña Gracia and her party, seeing Jews not only practice their religion openly, but flourish in their diversity. Salonika had become a haven for refugees from all over Europe, as word spread of the freedom and opportunity offered.[24] It truly evidenced the wisdom of the royal policy of welcoming and appreciating Jews, so well-reflected in former Sultan Bayazid's oft-quoted remark that Spain's King Fernando "has impoverished his dominions in order to enrich mine."[25]

After Salonika, the road took them to Constantinople, where people lined the streets to see the impressive party of four coaches and forty horsemen. Long awaited at the Royal Porte, Doña Gracia was welcomed at court receptions. Henceforth, the great wealth and resources of the House of Mendes would enrich the economic and political position of the Empire, at the expense of former oppressors. Many came to pay respects at her splendid home, Belvedere, which was more like a palace. They included rabbis and representatives of prominent Jewish families, as well as artists, physicians, philosophers and businessmen. It was like Lisbon, London, Antwerp and Ferrara, with one great exception. This was more than a temporary resting place. Although Doña Gracia had nurtured thought to ending her days in the Holy Land, Constantinople was a major goal achieved, following seventeen years of exile. The family was no longer itinerant, moving from place to place, having to act out on the public stage the drama of belonging, while not belonging at all. They were home.

They received authority to live in the wealthy European suburb, Galata, also called Pera, rather than in Constantinople, where most of the Jewish population were housed. Family and household, including retainers and servants, were permitted to dress in Venetian style, rather than the garments and headdresses of Jewish men and women of the day. The atmosphere was the European-style mansion of a powerful personage. Portuguese and Spanish were spoken within its walls, and the cuisine of their countries prepared in its kitchens.

Safe and secure at last, Doña Gracia did not forget the less fortunate. She became known for her charity throughout the Ottoman Empire and Western Europe. Every day, she provided meals for eighty poor people at her own table. Paupers, as well as princely and powerful persons passed through the palatial doors and were treated with equal dignity.

She also continued the rescue work with *conversos* needing to flee Spain and Portugal, and was known for joining other wealthy Jews from Salonika and Constantinople in ransoming coreligionists captured at sea by the Knights of Malta and other marauders. Her support extended to hospitals and to Jews of slender means. She was a willing and generous patron of synagogues, *yeshivas* and scholars. One such beneficiary was an academy that brought ordinary people, as well as scholars, together to study. They came to learn and to worship, eventually forming a house of prayer and attracting many who had frequented other synagogues. It became known as *La Sinagoga de La Señora*, after Doña Gracia, who was becoming recognized for her deeds throughout the diaspora as "The Lady," or in Hebrew, *ha–Gaveret*.

One house of worship, called Synagogue of the Spanish Exiles, feared loss of congregants to *La Sinagoga de la Señora*, and asked a rabbinic court, or *beit din*, to forbid people from worshipping in centers other than their synagogue of origin. The rabbis ruled against this as a practice without precedent, and, moreover, impractical, given the diversity of the Jewish religious community. *La Sinagoga de La Señora* continued to flourish, as did its *yeshiva*. Prominent scholars and philosophers would become its principals through the years. The building still stands in twenty-first century Izmir, near Constantinople, or present day Istanbul.

La Señora founded other synagogues and institutions of learning throughout the Empire. In Salonika, *Livyat Hen*, the Chaplet of Grace, was known more familiarly as The Wayfarers' Synagogue after the well-to-do *conversos* from Lisbon who had become its congregants. Also, a unique *midrash* was founded in Salonika, where the city's rabbis studied Hebraic literature, while continuing their congregational duties, a rarity for a day when Judaic scholars were not expected to work.

A house of study was founded in Tiberius in the Holy Land, with the intention of energizing a Jewish settlement, preparatory to Doña Gracia's hoped for resettlement there. It will be recalled that the dying Francisco Mendes had asked his wife to bury him someday in the Jewish ancestral homeland. While in Venice, she received permission from the pope to have his remains disinterred from the grave in Lisbon, ostensibly so they could be placed in a private chapel she claimed to be preparing. She planned secretly to eventually rebury him in the Valley of Jehoshaphat, near Tiberius. One can imagine the activities that made this undertaking possible, the intrigue and payments required to move the remains of a prominent, baptized Catholic by his wife, a suspected judaizer. Safe conducts and other necessary documents were needed for the land and sea voyage to the distant burial site. All this, so the widow could fulfill her promise to her beloved.

Her intention was to follow Francisco to their ancestral land, but there was much to delay her in business, family and charitable callings. João finally arrived in Constantinople in 1554, in a magnificent entry that became legendary, matching his aunt's the year before. On close social and diplomatic terms with royalty and nobility throughout Europe, the lifestyle of *La Señora*'s nephew showed his great wealth and influence. He was accompanied by twenty servants on horseback, preceded by two Turkish janissaries, "with staves, as mounted lackeys, as is the Turkish custom, in order that nothing should happen to him," reported contemporary German observer Hans Dernschwam, describing the young man in "silk clothes lined with sable."[26]

João had served the House of Mendes well in a variety of circumstances, including negotiating the return of family possessions from embargo in Antwerp and France and winning the sultan's intervention in Doña Gracia's two Venetian crises. He had also played a significant role in the underground rescue operation. Soon after his arrival, he arranged circumcision for himself and his male retinue, taking the name Joseph Nasi, and becoming a practitioner of the Judaism so long denied him.

He soon wed his cousin Reyna, no longer called Brianda, long rumored to be the intended of court physician Moses Hamon's son. Thus, *La Señora* had settled her most important obligation after the Jewish burial of her husband: the marriage of her daughter to her nephew. It followed the endogamy practice of prosperous *conversos*, indeed, of the bride's own parents. Grim past experience had conditioned them to regard all feelings of security as temporary. Joseph's brother, Samuel, had wed his cousin, Gracia *la Chica*, the daughter of Doña Gracia's sister, formerly called Beatriz. It was rumored that the two had long been in love. They had stayed behind in Ferrara to take care of business and now awaited exit permits.

The family had been in Turkey only two years, when the repressive situation in the Italian port of Ancona brought Doña Gracia once again to international attention. Paul IV had become pope in 1555, determined to rid his Papal States of New Christians openly observing Judaism. The entire Ancona community of Portuguese *conversos*— about one hundred individuals — had been arrested and tortured, preparatory to execution by fire. Among them was the local representative of the House of Mendes. Upon learning of the arrests, Doña Gracia won Sultan Selim's support. He interceded to ask for the release of the prisoners and all seized goods. The pope rejected the effort, and twenty-eight individuals, including an old woman and a boy, were burned at the stake.

With others, Doña Gracia desired revenge against the papal city, a prosperous seaport, and used her considerable influence at The Grande Porte and throughout the Ottoman Empire to secure support for an economic boycott, diverting goods instead to nearby Pesaro, in the duchy of Urbino. There, the duke had sheltered those *conversos* who had managed to escape from Ancona. The original proposal was for an eight-month boycott, after which the principals would decide whether to continue.

The boycott was opposed, however, by the prominent rabbi of Salonika, Joshua Soncino, who feared reprisals against the older, non-*converso* Jewish community that had not been harmed thus far because of its non–Christian background. He interpreted Talmud to call the boycott illegal. Doña Gracia and her followers, on the other hand, pointed out the danger that failure of the boycott would bring to those who had fled to Pesaro. There, she feared, the duke, disappointed at the undelivered promise of increased trade after making expensive harbor preparations, would no longer refuse to hand the Ancona exiles over to the pope.

Soncino won the support of enough merchants and rabbis, many of whom had previously backed the effort, to destroy the unity required for the boycott's success. Subsequently, more and more trade began to return to Ancona.

Doña Gracia had predicted correctly. The enraged Duke of Urbino soon banished all *conversos* from Pesaro, even those who had been long settled there. The refugees were preyed upon by ships from Ancona, one group captured and sold into slavery. The pope was able to prevail upon even the relatively liberal Duke Ercole of Ferrara to destroy copies of the elegy on the Ancona executions, written by poet Jacob da Fano, and close the press of its publisher, Abraham Usque. It was Usque who had printed the Spanish bible dedicated to his patron, Doña Gracia.

Roth singles out the boycott as perhaps the first time Jews had applied pro-active, unified political and economic action to defend Jewish interests, rather than take the more traditional route of financial payments and prayer. He holds the boycott's failure responsible for the belief that was to persist in the centuries to follow: that Jews would never unite to fight their oppressors. The generations to come were to witness unending persecution and agony for Jews in the Papal States and in Christian Europe.[27]

Study of these events illuminates the character and methods of *La Señora*, who used power to get cooperating rabbis to excommunicate merchants breaking the boycott, and who summoned influentials before her in the manner of royalty, demanding and cajoling them for their support. Synagogues not yet committed were warned of losing the Nasi stipends they had been receiving. Even the redoubtable Rabbi Soncino was called to her palace in the same manner as lesser religious and commercial leaders, but to no avail. "It was amazing that it was a woman who had taken the lead in this gallant demonstration that it was not always necessary for Jews to suffer passively," Roth asserts.[28]

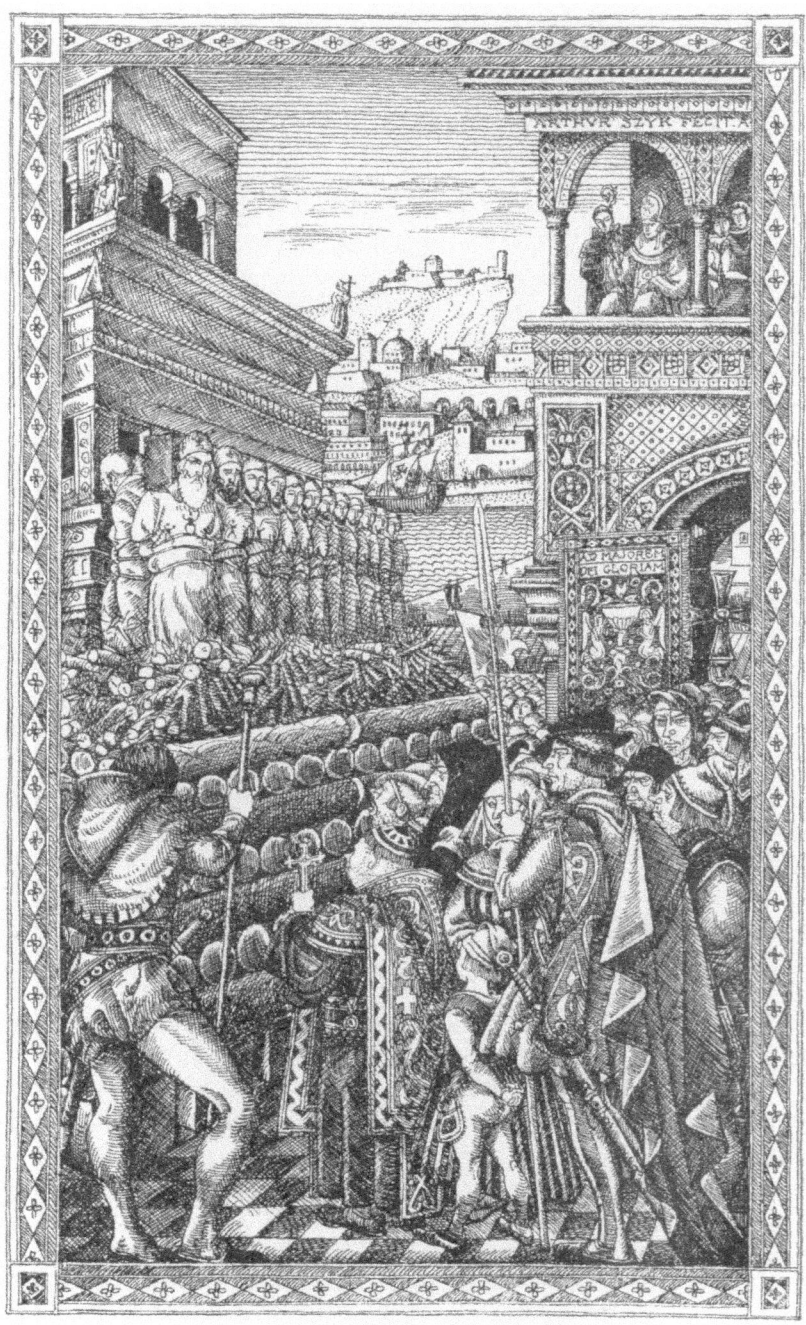

Five. Doña Gracia Nasi 121

Opposite and above: When the demands of Pope Paul IV resulted in the public burning of twenty-four Portuguese *marranos* in Ancona in 1555 (left), representatives of the city's exile community met in Constantinople with Doña Gracia (above), who spearheaded a trading and shipping boycott of the Italian seaport. (Left [drawing of Ancona auto da fé]: Ludwig Lewisohn. *The Last Days of Shylock* [New York: Harper & Brothers, 1931], facing 88. Reproduced with the cooperation of Alexandra Szyk Bracie and Historicana, Burlingame, California, www.historicana.com. Above [Jewish leaders meeting with Doña Gracia]: Glass painting by Simon Dray, London [1977]. ©Beth Hatefutsoth, Permanent Exhibition, Tel Aviv. Visual Documentation Center, Beth Hatefutsoth, Tel Aviv.)

In a rabbinic court case held later to settle the issue of niece Gracia's inheritance, the very same Rabbi Soncino who had so opposed the boycott, headed the *beit din* that ruled in favor of *La Señora*'s position. It is remarkable to see two such prominent figures, at loggerheads over one issue, able to separate principles from personalities in another.

La Señora continued to manage the affairs of her far flung merchant empire in the years following. All family members outside Portugal were safe at last on Turkish soil, with Gracia *la Chica* and husband Samuel finally permitted to leave Ferrara in 1556. Doña Gracia remained without a mate. Throughout the unfolding of her story, one wonders if romantic love had ever been present in Gracia's life since her widowhood at twenty-six, a young age even for the era. Given the widow's great wealth and rumored beauty, one would imagine suitors galore. Brooks hypothesizes a possible attraction for brother-in-law Diogo before his marriage to her sister. No romantic interests appear in other source literature, although, as we will see, two television writers in the twentieth century will weave love and lust into their dramatic portrayals of *La Señora*.

As explained earlier, it was the custom in Sephardic *converso* families for a brother-in-law to marry his deceased sibling's wife. Following this, one wonders why Gracia did not wed Diogo after leaving Lisbon. His marriage with younger sister Brianda may have been long planned, while Francisco's death was not expected. In looking back over events in her life, it is easy to see how a formal marriage with anyone else would have been unwise during the family's seventeen-year-long flight from Lisbon to Constantinople. Unless they were sure that the groom-to-be could pass several requirements, wisdom would mitigate against it. He would have to be *judaizante*, and a person with whom the family's secret Judaism could be entrusted while they appeared in public frequently as wealthy, New Christian supporters and trading partners of royalty, nobility and clergy. A review of both Mendes and de Luna families reveals no relative who could have been a potential match. In addition, there was the responsibility Doña Gracia carried as chief executive officer of a vast international commercial and banking empire, and her need, as matriarch, to protect and provide for the well-being of family wealth. All these weighed against a marriage for *La Señora*.

What about a lover or romantic relationship? Again, there is no record of anything of this nature, or a shred of gossip. It would have been near impossible for such a thing to have been kept from prying eyes, given the celebrity nature of Doña Gracia. Such an alliance would have been most risky before reaching the relative safety of Ferrara, and would have endangered the family's secret religious practices and the goal of settlement in the Ottoman Empire.

As the decade of the 1560s progressed, *La Señora* appeared less and less in public, and it was thought that ill health was bringing about this withdrawal. Nephew and son-in-law Joseph, who had been named Duke of Naxos by Sultan Selim as a reward for his loyalty and services, was in the spotlight alone, more and more. One wonders if the endogamous marriages of cousins and close relatives, practiced over several generations, had reinforced genetic traits, mirrored in poor health and few, if any, children for *La Señora* and her family. A life peppered with danger, stress and flight must surely have taken its toll on health and strength.

As observed earlier, Doña Gracia long hoped to end her days in the Holy Land, buried next to her beloved Francisco. In her early days in Constantinople, she had paid the sultan for the right to establish a settlement in Tiberius, and had arranged for a grand house to be built there. Nephew Joseph was appointed Governor of Tiberius. He organized a project to rebuild the city walls, which was completed in 1564. The way was prepared for the thousands of expected Jewish settlers, with construction of residences, synagogues and bath houses. A planned economy got a good start with the planting of mulberry trees for silk production and the importing of sheep. The arrival of *ha–Gaveret* was greatly anticipated.

Although there is no documentation regarding her death, one can assume from the dates of eulogies in her honor that it came sometime in 1569. She was fifty-nine, an advanced age for the period. Her death caused a remarkable outpouring of grief throughout the Ottoman Empire and Europe, where her works had become legendary. Alas, the *conversos* of Portugal and Jews everywhere had lost a great benefactor.

Many were the eulogies for *La Señora*. In his tribute, delivered at the synagogue *Livyat Hen* that she had founded in Salonika, Rabbi Moses Almosnino compared her to the great women of the Bible; Miriam, Deborah and Esther. A poet of Salonika's Hebrew-Hispanic school, probably Saadiah Longo, laments that "She is no longer, the noble princess, Israel's glory, the splendid flower of exile who built her house with purity and holiness. She protected the poor and saved the afflicted, bringing happiness to this world and rejoicing for posterity."[29]

We do not know where she lies buried. There is a street in Tiberius that bears her name to this day, as well as ruins of a water reservoir supposed to have been built under Doña Gracia's aegis, but there is no evidence of a final resting place for her in that city. It is possible that Joseph Nasi had her interred in the Holy Land, next to Francisco. Knowing his hegemony in Tiberius and his devotion to his aunt, it is logical to suppose that this was the case. It is also possible that she succeeded in spending her final days in Tiberius, as little was heard of her in Constantinople after the beginning of the 1560s, and nothing in the years just before her death.

She is still remembered and honored in Tiberius to this day. In December of 1990, the city and the Women's International Zionist Organization (WIZO) commemorated *ha–Gaveret* with a special event attended by 1,000 members and guests from the Turkish Jewish community. In a booklet dedicated to her, Dahlia Gottan of World WIZO writes that "for the first time in over 400 years, the city of Tiberius paid homage to its one-time patron and saluted its beloved *Señora*," and adds her praise to the eulogies for this remarkable woman.

"Her untiring devotion, the heroic efforts made on behalf of her compatriots and her munificent contributions to the many institutions of Jewish culture and learning she had established, earned her the designation of 'Heart of her People.'"[30] This was first bestowed on Doña Gracia by Samuel Usque, whose epic poem was published in Ferrara thanks to her patronage.[31]

As indicated earlier, Joseph Nasi was well versed in the affairs of the economic and political rivals of the Ottoman Empire through his activities with the House of Mendes and his earlier closeness with European royalty. On his arrival in the Sublime Porte, he put this experience at the disposal of the sultan and became a favorite at court. As described earlier, he was granted the title of Duke of Naxos as reward for his generosity and usefulness to the empire and his amiability and friendship with the sultan's son Selim. He became a most influential and powerful member of the court, holding this position for two decades.

We have seen that his authority extended to Tiberius. Although he supported his aunt's plan to develop that area into a region for Jews returning to the Holy Land, various historical events and circumstances limited the project's success, leading to its fading away after the matriarch's death.

Joseph was much affected by the loss of his aunt, his mentor since early childhood, who had provided love, knowledgeable support and a focus to his direction. This was compounded by the death soon after of his brother Samuel, who had been by the duke's side since his arrival from Ferrara. These mammoth personal losses within one year were especially painful, coming at a time when powerful enemies were working for his downfall, which would come in only five years' time.

In 1574, Murad III ascended the throne. He departed from previous sultans in their relations with Jews, putting restrictions on Jewish life. He showed contempt for Nasi, and ended his influence in the Empire. The duke, however, was allowed to keep his titles and means of securing revenues.

Joseph retired to his palace, Belvedere, where he and Reyna shared a princely lifestyle. It must have been most difficult for the leader of Turkish Jewry, the man who had wielded so much influence in the courts of Europe and the Ottoman Empire, to adjust to the quieter, intellectual life. He died soon after, on August 2, 1579, eighty-seven years to the day after the expulsion of the Jews from Spain.

His widow continued the family tradition of benevolence. Truly Doña Gracia's daughter, Reyna carried on the legacy of charitable acts until the end of her long and fruitful life. Her major interests were intellectual. She opened her husband's great library to scholars and researchers, and generously supported Hebrew printing, founding a printing press at Belvedere and one outside the city. It is worth noting the vision of the Nasis and the printers with whom they had worked in the Grand Porte and, previously, in Ferrara. Barely one century since the invention of movable type, they were in the forefront of those using books and literature to help rebuild Jewish religious and community life.

There is no record of Reyna's activities after 1599, and it is assumed that she died in that year. It was thirty years since her mother's death, twenty since her husband's. And as the sixteenth century drew to a close, it appeared that the Nasi/Mendes dynasty had ended with Reyna.

Belvedere still stands, probably rebuilt several times, its grandeur on the Bosporus preserved as a popular tourist site. Visitors report no mention of the Duke of Naxos or his once very prominent and revered aunt during palace tours. One can still attend services at *Sinyora Geveret Synagogue*, originally established by Doña Gracia, and referred to earlier as *La Sinagoga de La Señora*. The wooden structure has been rebuilt several times during its 450-year life and still houses an active congregation.

It is possible that there are direct descendants living today, although we have no evidence of their existence. We know that neither Reyna and Joseph Nasi nor Gracia la Chica and Samuel Nasi bore children who lived beyond their youth. There is no record of Doña Gracia's sister Reyna after her arrival in Ferrara. Roth assumes she followed to Turkey, but we know nothing more. Brooks' genealogical studies show Doña Gracia having another sister, Giomar, whose marriage with Francisco Vas Beirão created a daughter, Lisabona, who herself had a daughter, Alumbra. Family tree charts show no children or grandchildren continuing Giomar's line further.[32]

The adventure and emotion in the life of Joseph Nasi have inspired fictional works, some as early as the sixteenth century. The authors either eulogize or demonize their subjects. It is thought that the character of the Jew Barabas in Christopher Marlowe's *The Jew of Malta*, first produced in 1592, was modeled after the unflattering Christian view of the Duke of Naxos:

> I am not of the tribe of Levi, I,
> That can so soon forget an injury,
> We Jews can fawn like spaniels when we please:
> And when we grin we bite; yet are our looks
> As innocent and harmless as a lamb's.[33]

In contrast, a favorable portrayal of the Jewish character appears in Ludwig Lewisohn's 1931 historical novel, *The Last Days of Shylock*, which picks up where *The Merchant of Venice* ends. The money lender is portrayed as a sympathetic and devout member of the Jewish community, escaping Venice on a Mendes ship to avoid the demands of forced conversion. His life, in contrast to Shakespeare's vindictive version, becomes one of service to Doña Gracia and the Duke of Naxos.[34]

Doña Gracia of the House of Nasi, the script for a yet-to-be produced television drama by Emilie Roi and Rochelle Furstenberg, took first prize in Israeli Television's 1992 national TV contest. While the story closely follows history, the play fictionalizes possible areas of attraction and conflict between *La Señora* and Joseph. It portrays her bitter disappointment at the end of her life at her nephew's failure to support her vision of the Tiberius project, and her grief at the death of her lone grandchild, born to Reyna and Joseph. The authors then have her setting out alone for Tiberius and the Holy Land.[35]

Naomi Ragen's 1998 novel, *The Ghost of Hannah Mendes*, focuses on the effect of a discovered diary, supposedly kept by Doña Gracia, on a contemporary New York family of Sephardic background.[36] The revelations of *La Señora*'s love and dedication have a transformational effect on the sophisticated modern characters of Ragen's work.

Undoubtedly, we will hear more of this remarkable woman in today's media, with increasing research into her life and actions. Searches may reveal more remaining sites attributed to her presence or influence: in Turkey, Greece and Tiberius; in Ferrara, Venice, Antwerp and London; yes, in Lisbon also. If one closes one's eyes momentarily during a stroll through the Rossio, the Portuguese capital's main square near the waterfront, one can almost hear the clatter of carriages, carrying wealthy *converso* merchants of the 1530s from their elegant mansions nearby to dock-side warehouses and offices to take care of business.

Regardless of what may be learned eventually about bloodline descendants, perhaps the greater truth is that all those whose lives manifest courage, love, generosity and loyalty can claim kinship with her, whose life epitomized those qualities: *La Señora, ha–Gaveret*, Doña Gracia Nasi.

❧ SIX ❧

"Thou preparest a table before me": Jewish Life in Cities, Towns, Countryside

This chapter begins our focus on the day-to-day affairs and life patterns of ordinary Jewish men, women and children at the time of the expulsion. Unlike the subjects of the earlier chapters, they were not known for kingdom-wide or large-scale celebrity. While many were familiar names in their *juderías* or *calls*, the areas where the Jews lived, they would not have been recognized outside their local regions.

Most of the exiles-to-be left behind little, if any, literature or tangible materials for future generations to access — only limited records of commercial and property matters and legal proceedings. Some documents are also available that illuminate the interactions of Jewish communities or individuals with the Crown and local government. These have helped scholars reconstruct portraits of Sephardic Jewish life in the family, school and community. The documents give some picture of how tens of thousand of families practiced the Jewish faith, what role the synagogue played in their daily lives, how people were educated and earned their living and how they supported the poor, the stranger and the traveler. They also contain information on what people did for fun, describing games and entertainment activities like festivals and special events of the period. We draw upon the documentation unearthed by historians, anthropologists and folklorists to enhance understanding of their lives and times.[1]

What was life like for the less prominent Sephardim as the fifteenth century entered its final decade? What social positions did they occupy in the divisions of class and status in Jewish and Spanish life? What were their rights and privileges, restrictions and limitations? Could they move about freely, engage in work of their choice, and reside wherever desire and economic capacity suited them? What were their relations like with Christian and Muslim neighbors and local government?

To answer these questions, we'll look at records of life in *juderías* and *calls* from representative Spanish communities. They include Trujillo, a textile center in Extremadura, to the west near Portugal; Tortosa, a northeastern Aragonese port city in Catalunya, then considered the commercial rival of Barcelona; and Valencia, important commercial, southeastern coastal center, and its many surrounding communities. Descriptions of life at home, in school, in synagogue and in community will put human faces on facts, with a portrait of everyday life for Sephardim before the expulsion. This portrait, then, gives witness to their everyday lives, describing familial, educational, religious, occupational, social and political realities for them in the last days of Jewish Sefarad.

We'll begin with Trujillo, now a city of just under 10,000 in west central Castilla. Chances are that today's travelers, motoring on the modern four-lane highway passing through the city, are on their way to Portugal or Sevilla and beyond. They might be put off from more than a cursory food stop by the modern guidebooks that tend to paint its region of Extremadura as bare of vegetation and very hot in summer.[2] Some perhaps may stop long enough for a one- or two-hour walkabout after reading that the city in west central Castilla was birthplace to two prominent conquistadores, who earned their fame in the New World of Spain's sixteenth-century empire.[3] Few travel guides, however, will tell them that an active Jewish community thrived here in the Middle Ages, before the year of the expulsion. This omission is being remedied more recently as Spanish tourism officials discover the economic benefits of attracting increasing numbers of visitors interested in these sites.[4]

The first record of Jewish settlement in Trujillo was in 1290, when the Jewish community was included in an archival tax list. The historian Beinart reasons that if the assessment for the community was 3,769 maravedis, a considerable amount at that time, and was "based on the real means of each community," then it "must have already been in existence for some years."[5] So we see that Jews were firmly established in the area at the close of the thirteenth century.

Trujillo had been in Christian hands since 1231, when Fernando III of Castilla captured it from the Muslims. We don't know its Jewish population before that, when it was part of Muslim Spain. In November of 1491, it was home to about 50 Jewish families, similar to Segovia and other medium population cities.[6] Many of the residents earned their living in the thriving commerce in textiles. Located near Caceres, a busy commercial hub for the region, Trujillo merchants frequented weekly markets in both towns, offering cloth woven in their shops or homes for purchase by town folk and nobility alike.

Six. *"Thou preparest a table before me"* 129

Some, like the Cohen family, had large scale operations by the day's standards, employing apprentices and salesmen, and contracting with local families for weaving to be done in their homes. The Cohens were a prominent clan in Trujillo, and their name appeared often in the legal documents and records of the community. Before long, the success of such merchants enabled them to build large houses, some near Trujillo's plaza, symbolizing Jewish prosperity. It was the pattern for many young men to apprentice in the textile enterprise of a relative, then advance into sales or the tasks to be carried out in running businesses. Others were occupied in additional forms of commerce and in agriculture and crafts. Jews also owned and traded in land, both urban and pastoral.[7]

Each community throughout Spain had its particular demographics, depending on its history in the panorama of Christian and Muslim conquests and civilizations and on the local climate and resources that determined how people lived and worked. In November of 1491, however, Trujillo's Jews were probably no different from other coreligionists in Sefarad, even those in high places, who appeared to have had little, if any, suspicion that in a few short

The niche at the entry to a home in the Portuguese village of Monsaraz is presumed to have held a *mezuzah* before the forced conversion of 1497. Containing the *Shemah*, the statement of belief in one god, it was placed near the door, as it is today among observant Jews. The source is Deuteronomy 4-9: "...and these words which I command you this day ... you shall write them upon the doorposts of your house and on your gates." One can find remains of these recesses 500 years after the practice of Judaism had been forbidden in Spain and Portugal. (©2000 Cary Herz.)

months, their present way of life, their surroundings, everything, would be transformed irrevocably, their ancestral roots in Sefarad torn out forever. As we saw in Chapter Two, even the most informed, well-placed courtiers did not seem to expect such an extreme course of action as expulsion by monarchs they had so recently supported with their loans and services.[8]

It was life as usual throughout Sefarad. Boys were studying on long wooden tables in the *Talmud Torah* of each *aljama*, or Jewish community, while girls were learning about responsibility for home and family under the tutelage of their mothers. Children were playing and doing the usual things that young ones did during the few hours when not in school or with family. Adults were going about the business of home and livelihood; local councils and rabbinical courts, *beit din*, were taking care of matters between Jew and Jew. Rabbis and scholars were reading and discoursing on the fine points of Talmud and Mishnah. It was business as usual for the powerful Jewish courtiers who served king and queen, benefiting the Crown and further enhancing their own financial and political empires. Certainly, they were sounding no alarms. As the Catholic Majesties prepared to take possession of Granada, the last piece of land to be wrested from Muslim control, did anyone foresee that, in less than nine months from this November day, practicing Jews in Sefarad would be gone from the land forever?

Jews at this time were living at the end of a hundred year period, soon to be enclosed chronologically between the two great bookends of Sephardic tragedy: the massacres of 1391 and the expulsion of 1492. Both were large scale attacks intended to reduce the perceived influence of the Jews on both rulers and ruled and to convert them to Christianity. The latter of these disasters awaited them barely seven months ahead. Few communities or their Jewish residents had escaped the ravages of 1391, and none would evade the expulsion. Those whose great-grandparents had survived 1391 were trying to normalize life in 1491, even given the severe limitations on their freedom. Thousands had converted when threatened. More than 1,500 years in the Iberian diaspora had certainly taught approximately 60 generations of Jews how to accommodate themselves to the needs and whims of whichever ruler was occupying the throne.

It is important to realize that Sephardic culture at the time of the expulsion had been in decline from what is referred to as its golden age, beginning with the effects of the 1391 massacres, which destroyed whole viable and culturally rich Jewish communities, such as Sevilla, Toledo and Barcelona.[9] The massacres were the culmination of over one hundred years of efforts by the Church to convert Jews to Christianity, and were contemporaneous with the *Reconquista*, the military conquest by Christian rulers that drove the Muslims out of Spain. Earlier in the century, the pope had established the religious

Six. "Thou preparest a table before me"

orders of Franciscan and Dominican priests, with the mission of preaching to and converting unbelievers. Valencia alone had five different schools of these orders, with Barcelona not far behind. Priests thus trained accompanied the mobs in the 1391 assaults on Jewish communities.[10]

The outbreaks began in the city of Sevilla, spearheaded by Ferrán Martínez, the local archdeacon. He had been preaching actively against the Jewish faith and its followers, with such actions as ordering the nearby communities of Ecija, Alcalá de Guadaira, Coría and Cantillana to destroy their local synagogues. Then he turned his attention to Sevilla, encouraging attacks by mobs in that city. Soon, the violence spread to Córdoba and throughout Andalucía. It was not long before Toledo, the Castillian center of learning esteemed throughout the Jewish diaspora, fell prey. The attacks then spread north to Madrid, to Segovia, and then through intervening communities to Burgos. To the east, riots took hold in the Aragonese port city of Valencia, and spread throughout the region. Only one nearby community, Morvedre, appeared to have missed the sacking and slaughter. Soon, there were outbreaks in Palma, Barcelona, Gerona, Lérida and Perpignan, and in the west as well. Beinart tells us that the riots "did not bypass Trujillo, but we lack information on their extent."[11]

It was a rare community that escaped the onslaught. Like Morvedre, Tortosa, an Aragonese trading center in Catalunya north and east of the Valencia region, was one of these. It escaped the onslaught thanks to a strong stand by local authorities, who first actively protected the *judería*, then moved its residents to a local fortress, and finally placed them in individual Christian homes. A massacre had been prevented, although there was a price to pay: Jews were then pressured to convert to Christianity.[12]

Whole Jewish communities, such as Sevilla, Toledo, Valencia, Burgos and Barcelona, were destroyed by the 1391 outbreaks. They never recovered. The massacres and accompanying forced mass conversions created a physical and psychological reality, which escalated the decline of Sephardic culture.

Well before 1391, Spanish kings and queens had found it in their best interests to protect Jewish communities threatened with attack and to quash inter-religious conflicts. The goal was to prevent local disagreements from spreading to the general population. The 1391 outbreaks showed what happened when these policies failed to work, or even to be applied. After that, royalty attempted to keep control over discontent from the Church, nobility and the growing middle class to prevent future violent conflicts.[13] Increasing political upheaval in the fifteenth century made this harder and harder. In attempts to calm opposition demands for Jewish suppression, rulers sometimes departed from their protective policies. As we saw in Chapter Two, Fernando himself had recently attempted to convince the Aragón *Cortés*, a parliamentary body made up of nobles, to expel Jews from the kingdom. Although this failed to win the support the king had expected, it was surely an omen of things to come.

In November of 1491, all Jews knew well of the growing activity of the Inquisition, established in 1480 to root out heresy, or beliefs other than those sanctioned by the Catholic Church. In its early days, many among practicing Jews erroneously believed that the Holy Office was a threat only to converts to Christianity, who might be discovered secretly observing Judaism. They failed to foresee that the spotlight of blame would be more and more focused on them. Observant Jews were being accused increasingly of aiding and abetting New Christian converts to maintain links with their ancestral religion. Indeed, the edict of expulsion, which would be issued in March of the coming spring, would name their alleged influence on the *conversos* as the reason for exiling them from Spain.

A review of the Jews' legal position in the Christian kingdom shows enshrinement of the long-established principle that they were the property of the Crown. Whenever a new monarch ascended the throne, each *aljama*, as the local Jewish, semiautonomous, governmental entity, had to renegotiate its charter, which set forth the relationship between the sovereign and the community. For example, in 1477, Solomon Romi, then *procurador* or attorney for the Trujillo *aljama*, petitioned Queen Isabel to renew support of its charter. Like other communities with charters from the rulers, the community had limited powers in governing Jewish residents. In the 1477 appeal, Romi had to be represented by a Christian, so Fernán Díaz de Toledo, a *converso*, was retained to bring it before the queen. Isabel renewed the privileges the community had received earlier in 1454 from her father, John II, and affirmed that since Jews were "her property and enjoy her protection, it is her duty to protect and maintain them." The *aljama* and the Jewish community, she continued, have the right to the same "privileges, charters, charters upon charters given and ordered by me to the Jewish communities of Kingdoms and seigniories, or their copies signed by public notaries which shall be shown to you by the Jewish community of that town."[14]

Although, like Trujillo, communities throughout Sefarad were relieved to have their charters renewed, they did not look so favorably at the additional taxes and assessments that the monarch's show of benevolence carried with it. Rulers used the reissuing process to charge substantial fees in return for the grants of limited self-rule. Moreover, they could order review of an *aljama*'s charter at any time, assuring themselves a fresh influx of funds.

Under Muslim rule, Jews and Christians had an established, legitimate place, and were recognized as children of the Book, believers in the same God as followers of Islam. They were also respected as descendants of Abraham,

Six. *"Thou preparest a table before me"*

an important figure in the origin of all three religions. Although *dhimmis*, unbelievers, were subject to additional taxes, Jews were largely unrestricted in residential and professional choices, and could move about with relative freedom, subject only to prescribed limitations on matters such as clothing and other minor items. Christian rule changed that, bringing with it the concept of Jews as property, and increasingly restricting where they could live, what occupations they could work at and under what conditions they could relate to Old and New Christians.

How well did the queen and rulers before her take care of their human property, each Jewish community, within their kingdoms? Sometimes with fairness and justice, other times with unequal restrictions and neglect. An example of the former took place the day after the queen had assured the Trujillo community of its renewed legitimacy, when Isabel responded to another *aljama* appeal. A new petition protested actions against Jews by civil and military forces of the Crown, then occupying the town after winning it back from a rebellious nobleman, the Marques of Villena, and his followers, who had had held it briefly during an insurgency in 1475. The *aljama*'s appeal accused local Crown officials of forcing Jews to provide lodging for new tax collectors and for the armed horsemen, called *caballeros*, brought into the area. They were also compelled to feed the military and their horses, to guard the town walls and to pay the salaries of judges and prosecutors sent to punish the rebels. The queen supported the *aljama*'s appeal, eliminating the monetary compensation forced on the community for the rebellion. She ruled that only those who had joined the rebellion should be punished and that those who had remained loyal to the Crown should no longer be compelled to provide the services enumerated. Supporters of the Marquis, however, who included members of the *aljama*'s influential Barchillon family, were to have their property confiscated.[15]

The queen appeared to have acted judiciously and fairly in this case. What about other situations? We spoke earlier about Crown policy to maintain law and order, used to keep control over those who hoped to turn religious and group conflict to their advantage. In an increasingly volatile time, the monarchs' success in managing power required vigilance against anti–Jewish outbreaks. Hoping to discourage civil disorder, then, the Crown usually responded favorably to Jewish petitions for protection. This had been widened to apply to other violations, such as bodily assault, kidnapping for ransom and cattle and property theft.[16] Rulers feared that local conflicts could spread and become general uprisings.

Having established that the rulers protected their human property for their own best interests, we look closer at the institution of the *aljama* and the limited self-rule that it provided in internal judicial, religious and social

Jews and Muslims engage in a game of dice in this thirteenth-century work commissioned by Alfonso X, called *El Sabio*, The Wise. Jews moved about with few restrictions on residency, livelihood and interaction with others during much of the period of Muslim hegemony. This continued to some degree during Alfonso's reign, which saw the conclusion of the *Reconquista* in Castilla. (Alfonso X El Sabio, *Libro de ajuedrez, dados, y tablas,* Book of Chess, Backgammon and Dice [Sevilla: 1283]. In Mann, Vivian B. *Convivencia* [New York: George Braziller, 1992], title page.)

matters. Derived from the Arabic term *al yamaa*, or assembly, the institution represented continuing Jewish civil self-governance under both Muslim and Christian rule.

Each *aljama* had a governing body, elected by members of the community. In Valencia and Trujillo, the head officer was called *adelantado*, or secretary. In Tortosa, the title, in Catalán, was *adelantats*. The chief financial officer was the *clavario* (Valencia and Trujillo) or *clavarius* (Tortosa), supervising tax collections and finances. The two positions wielded significant influence as the chief administrative officers designated to carry out policies set by the *councillors* or *counsellers*, an elected council of sorts intended to represent all elements of the population.[17]

Indeed, Crown regulations required that all *aljama* officers represent the three economic and social classes of the community. The majority, however, came from the wealthiest and most influential families, a hallmark of most Jewish communities in Spain. The undue influence of an economic minority and conflicts among its members often led to disputes concerning elections. For example, several conflicts over power issues can be found in Tortosa's archives from the fourteenth century on, where there are cases of Crown authorities intervening when an election was in question, as in 1436 and 1437. They were also known to step in when they disapproved of election results. Queen Maria objected, for example, to the election of En Salomon Nathan in 1437, resulting in the office going to the candidate preferred by the Crown.[18]

Valencia, as well, had seen its share of election discord. As in Tortosa, control stayed in the hands of a few powerful individuals. The historian Hinojosa Montalvo describes how this was achieved by those retiring from office appointing their own successors and selecting members of their families. Another way to keep control, in operation since 1297, was to require a special fee of anyone wanting to be *adelantado*, making this office affordable for wealthy individuals only.[19]

Hinojosa Montalvo points to Crown intervention in 1403 in the Valencian community of Morvedre, where the regional *baile general*, the Crown's legal representative, suspended results for the elections of *adelantado* and *clavario* when he thought they had not followed prescribed procedures. A half-century later, in 1456, and again in 1459, the *baile* intervened at the request of some *aljama* residents, who had complained that the outgoing *adelantado* had appointed his son to the position.[20]

The Morvedre position of *adelantado* carried with it the prerogative to expel anyone from the community that the office holder deemed a danger to it. This opened the door to abuse. In Burriana, near Valencia, the *adelantado* tried to expel a petitioner to prevent him from using royal law in a specific case, which the office holder believed would threaten his particular actions. The *baile* ruled for the petitioner on appeal.[21]

It can be seen, therefore, that all was not always harmonious between Jew and Jew, and not only in a few regions. During the two decades before 1491, the Trujillo *judería* had witnessed several explosive conflicts among its occupants, with swords drawn and fighting erupting in the synagogue. One such conflict took place in the presence of the town mayor and the *baile*. They were present, coincidentally, to investigate an earlier quarrel in the synagogue to which local Christian *caballeros* had been attracted, taking sides and joining in the fighting. The town officials intervened in both cases, penalizing the participants with loss of property and putting them under civil court supervision.

Some of the conflicts in Trujillo's *judería* involved members of the Barchillon family and their allies, who were often in opposition to the interests of members of the equally influential Cohen clan. One altercation reached into the very halls of the Catholic Majesties, resulting in the intervention of the powerful Jewish courtier Abraham Seneor, who, as Crown Rabbi appointed by the monarchs, was the court of final appeal in conflicts among Jews. The conflict began in 1485, when Schlomo Barchillon went directly to the town's chief magistrate, the *corregidor*, instead of to the *beit din*, the rabbinical court, accusing Rabbi Moshe Javali of witchcraft. In so doing, he was exercising his option to bypass the Jewish institutions legally responsible, but not exclusively, in cases of Jew versus Jew. The accused rabbi appealed subsequently to Seneor, described in earlier chapters in his other roles as chief tax farmer and royal adviser, who ruled in favor of Javali. Barchillon then appealed directly to the Crown, claiming that, since his case had originated with an officer of the king and queen, the *corregidor*, rather than with the *aljama*, the former, not the court rabbi, had jurisdiction. The Crown agreed, overruling Seneor, and directing the case back to the *corregidor*, even though the *aljama*'s charter gave it dominion in conflicts between Jews.

It is revealing to see various elements of the relationship between the powerful court rabbi, an influential courtier, and *aljama* officials of a small town, and how even the man considered the most powerful Jewish courtier could be overruled by the Crown when it felt the need to assert royal prerogatives. The rulers bypassed the *aljama*'s and even their own court rabbi's jurisdiction when the complaining party had dealt directly with the government and its administrators.

In the past, the Crown had supported and enforced Seneor's judgment when the conflict between Jews had initiated in the *aljama* court. In a contrasting case, the Court Rabbi was asked to rule on a disagreement between the Cohen and Barchillon factions on the legitimacy of adding a stairway to

Six. *"Thou preparest a table before me"* 137

the synagogue. Seneor's decision, which had favored those opposed to the steps, was subsequently ignored by those who wanted them, who added the steps anyway. The Crown then intervened to assess fines for those who had violated Seneor's ruling.[22] Similar cases occurred in other parts of the kingdom as well, showing government intervention in areas of *aljama* jurisdiction for a variety of reasons. These ranged from keeping the peace to flexing the monarchy's power as supreme authority.

Despite declared intentions to protect its Jewish "property," against threats to the peace, there are notable examples when the Crown's justice was either delayed or capricious. Rulers certainly failed to protect their Jewish property from mob action in the disasters of 1391. Almost a century later, they appeared to penalize the victim instead of the aggressor in the case of an attack on the Trujillo *judería* during Easter Week in 1486, by a stone-throwing mob. There was considerable property damage. Afterwards, the *aljama* petitioned the Crown, asking it to prevent reoccurrence. The monarchs took almost one year to respond, doing so shortly before the following Easter. In order to prevent opportunities for contact with Christians, which they thought would

The caricature of a circumcised rat, with beard and hat characteristic of those worn by Jews in the fourteenth century, was discovered sketched on the blank pages in the back of a fifteenth-century book from the Justicia Civil of Valencia. It is assumed that the unknown artist was a Christian visitor, portraying his perception of Jews as unclean animals, meriting scorn and ridicule. (Generalitat Valenciana, ed. *Lluís de Santàngel y su época: un nuevo hombre, un mundo nuevo* [Valencia: 1992], 189.)

avoid rioting, their decision restricted the Jews' freedom. They were required to stay indoors and were prohibited from work outside the home on specific days of the Holy Week. The monarchs' response to Christian acts of provocation, then, was to isolate the victims, rather than prosecute the offenders.[23]

Indeed, isolation and separation had been used more and more for civil control since the large-scale conversions following the 1391 massacres and the Disputation at Tortosa. Observant Jews were accused increasingly of tempting *conversos* to practice their former religion. The desire to keep the former coreligionists apart led to regulations requiring separate living quarters for Jews, as well as for Christians and Muslims. Those living outside the residential areas newly-designated for their group had to give up their homes, which, in many cases, had been family property for generations. Complaints of inequity led the *Cortés* of Toledo to pass additional regulations in an effort to make property exchange, purchase and sale more equitable.

After the new regulations for separate areas went into effect, Jewish residents in Trujillo appealed to the Crown, claiming they were being relocated by force. In response, the monarchs issued clarifications on the regulations to encourage peaceful exchange. These became the model for relocation procedures throughout the kingdom. One must note, however, that some affluent Jews utilized their influence and wealth to receive exemptions, which allowed them to live outside the appointed *juderías*.

Sometimes physical barriers were erected to reinforce the separation of residential areas, making it difficult for Jews to move freely through the city or town outside the *judería*. Trujillo's Jewish quarter, for example, had two gates. In the early days of separation, only one could be used, as the other was blocked by a house, which a co-owner refused to sell. An appeal to the Crown, while eventually providing a favorable outcome for the Jewish community, took four years to resolve. In another case, the monarchs ordered their representative, *Corregidor* Diego López de Ayala, to buy or confiscate a house that was preventing direct access to the town's plaza and business district.

The gates of the Trujillo *judería* were closed at nine every night. This, plus the ever-present danger of attack or kidnapping, severely limited Jewish freedom of movement. It can be seen how living in an ever-threatening environment, with isolation, restricted movement and limited economic opportunities, no doubt exacerbated already shortened tempers and edgy relations among Jews, examples of which we have seen earlier.[24]

Now we turn to the observation of Judaism and its institutions and the role they played in the religious and secular life of the Jews this last decade of the fifteenth century. Foremost, all communities had the right to observe the Jewish religion and to have jurisdiction over social and family matters, such as marriage and inheritance. This was assured in the charters of all Spanish *aljamas*, which also permitted observation of festivals and the Sabbath. In addition, the charters specified certain protections on those days, such as preventing imprisonment for nonpayment of taxes or depriving Jews of kosher food. The *aljamas* also had the right to produce or buy their own wine, and to have the wine vessels protected in the event of prosecution for nonpayment of taxes.[25]

The synagogue was the center of religious and secular life throughout Sefarad. In addition to prayer and study, it hosted meetings, council elections and other events. In Valencia, as in many communities, it also served as a hospice for travelers, a hospital for those needing special care and a center where public proclamations were announced. Synagogue seats were sold to members and could be resold or passed on by inheritance, a common practice throughout Spain.[26]

The consent of the Crown or its representative was required to establish, construct and operate a synagogue, whether a special building designated for that purpose or an installation in a private home. Historian Hinojosa Montalvo describes a petition for a synagogue and its results:

> We know that in 1378, the bishop of Valencia, Don Jaime de Aragón, granted a permit for the installing in the home of Aaron, bordering on the city wall, of a house of prayer, similar to the already existing one ... with the necessary sections, benches and rostrums. Another similar concession was made by Pedro IV in 1379 at the instance of Esdra, Jew of Valencia.[27]

Restrictions also governed the size and decoration of the building and specified rules covering its relationship to other structures. "The Jews may not enlarge, elevate or beautify their synagogues," read a 1261 decree by Alfonso X, still in force in 1492. Since prohibitions like these prevented synagogues from meeting the Talmudic injunction to be the tallest structure in the community, congregants often added small extensions to the roof as symbolic compliance.[28]

Royal or civil authorities sometimes went beyond prescribing size and architectural elements, and intervened directly in synagogue operation. An example was the queen's proposal in 1465 to give the Torah scrolls of the Valencia regional community of Burriana to neighboring Castellón, because the former's Jewish population had declined. Burriana's *baile* argued against this and prevailed. Twenty years later, as the Burriana *aljama* became even weaker, local judges tried to seize synagogue ornaments. This time, Crown and *baile* were on the same side in protecting the property, and the desired items were presented to the *adelantado* in the Morvedre *aljama* for safekeeping.[29]

Despite the weakening of Jewish communities after 1391, synagogues continued to be popular centers. They also attracted visitors from outside their congregations, such as traveling coreligionists from foreign places, visiting rabbinical students with news from Toledo or Córdoba, merchants and artisans peddling goods or looking for new places to settle and work, *chazzans* or singers of Jewish ritual music with new devotional songs and pilgrims on their way to the Holy Land. These visitors kept local residents aware of conditions affecting other communities and informed them about changing attitudes beyond town walls.[30]

The rabbi, preferably married, was an important leader in each community. In addition to religious and social tasks, such as officiating at marriages, circumcisions and birth registrations, he served the judicial function of validating dietary and other practices harmonious with Jewish law. In Morvedre, as in some other communities, he was also a notary. Fluent in Hebrew, the rabbi supervised Jewish education, and performed literary services. He prepared *ketubahs*, the marriage contracts, and other documents. He also authorized animal slaughter according to Jewish law, sometimes serving as *shohet*. Occasionally, a rabbi had more than one profession, such as medicine. Always, he was moral counselor to his people.[31]

Elections of rabbis sometimes resulted in factional squabbles within *aljamas*, and when Jewish leaders could not resolve them, royal representatives stepped into this non-secular arena. In 1459, for example, the queen took an active role in Morvedre by supporting the prevailing candidate for rabbi, which resulted in his election.[32]

It is important to observe the effect of religious teachings on social practices and behavior and the role the synagogue played in disseminating them. A good example is the Jewish emphasis on personal cleanliness. A typical *judería* street was narrow, congested and hard to keep clean, due to its location, usually in the oldest part of the city, and the inadequate space provided for its residents. Despite this, religious requirements for cleanliness, dignity, kindness and propriety in dress and manner were taken seriously and carried over into everyday behavior. Here is an excerpt from the will of a fourteenth century Jew, instructing his family on treatment of his remains after death and how he wished them to behave at his burial service.

> Be one of the first in the synagogue. Do not speak during prayers but repeat the responses, and after the service, do acts of kindness....Wash me clean, comb my hair as in my lifetime, in order that I may go clean to my eternal resting place, just as I used to go every Sabbath evening to the synagogue.[33]

The insistence on cleanliness in the teachings of the sages won this characteristic a place on the Inquisition's list of *judaizante* behaviors for non Jews to look for in identifying heretics. Washing oneself on Friday before sundown was suspect in Christian Spain, where infrequent bathing was the norm and

Six. *"Thou preparest a table before me"* 141

The retablo by San Estéban of the Los Serra painters portrays a Christian view of Jews as mysterious persons, with strange, even occult, customs. The passion of four Jewish scholars is displayed as they discuss the significance of Hebrew letters in a portion of scripture. (Generalitat Valenciana, ed. ***Lluís de Santàngel y su época: un nuevo hombre, un mundo nuevo*** [Valencia: 1992], 181.)

popular legend had the queen herself to have boasted at one time that she had taken only two baths thus far.

In the Sefarad of 1491, men and women were separated in the synagogue. Before the thirteenth century, however, they were not. Abrahams reports that women had their own court in the Jerusalem Temple of antiquity, and that "it is not impossible that they prayed together with the men in Talmudic times." In the fourteenth century, they were separated for social events, such as home celebrations and banquet, as well as for prayer.[34] In some communities, women had their own prayer meetings with female leaders, in separate areas apart from the main sanctuary. In others, they occupied a section adjacent to the men, separated by a curtain or structural device. A window or balcony was often used for communication between the two groups. Larger synagogues, as in Toledo, had a women's gallery above the main floor.

Most Jewish women did not know Hebrew, and therefore prayed in Spanish, and Passover rituals were often translated by the father for the rest of his family. Vernacular use first appeared in the synagogue as a result of women's needs and, occasionally, lessons from the prophets were translated into Spanish. A ninth century document, called a treatise *Soferim*, made it a responsibility to translate weekly readings from Torah and prophets before the end of the service. In the fourteenth century, however, this came into question in Zaragoza, when the newly appointed rabbi, Isaac ben Sheshet, discovered that the Book of Esther was being read in Spanish on Purim. He ended the custom, arguing that while it was within the law for women to hear holy prayers and readings in the vernacular, it was not so for men. The latter were presumed to have studied Hebrew, and were therefore restricted to that language in formal worship, the rabbi argued.[35]

In keeping with their traditional responsibility for the education of the young of both sexes, women continued to pass on Jewish rituals, customs and beliefs through the generations. Guided by their mothers, children joined in home observances, lighting *Shabbat* candles and performing *yahrzeit*, the honoring of the dead. They helped prepare for feast and fast days such as *Rosh Hashanah, Yom Kippur, Passover* and *Purim*. Both boys and girls received their earliest training in Judaica by their mothers' sides. This significant maternal teaching role was often maintained in secret in families who had converted to the Church. The practices were so embedded in the warp and woof of daily life, that women continued to observe them, tending to be the adults in *converso* families who passed on any hidden practices of Jewish ritual.[36] When the boys left around five years of age to attend *Talmud Torah*, the girls continued their tutelage in preparing food, keeping the home in order, and spinning the cloth for family clothing.

The riots of 1391 severely diminished cohesive Jewish life in many communities, ending the very presence of the religious institution of the synagogue. In Valencia, for example, the synagogue building became the Church of San Cristobal in order to serve the large numbers of New Christians who had been converted during the attacks. The Jewish quarter had lost its geographic integrity when authorities took down its gates, ostensibly to aid in financial assistance to victims of the violence.[37] In Toledo, two great synagogues standing today also became Church property and still go by their Catholic names, *Santa María la Blanca* and *el Tránsito*. Large-scale conversions from aggressive Christian preaching and disputations severely diminished synagogue population throughout Sefarad. The loss of the great centers of Jewish scholarship, such as Toledo, Córdoba and Gerona, undoubtedly contributed to the decline in learning, although there continued to be local scholarship centers. We have referred before to Isaac Aboab, the *gaon*, or great Hebrew scholar of Castilla, who continued to meet daily with students at his *yeshiva* in the city of Guadalajara, some of them as prominent as the astronomer Abraham Zacuto and the statesman Isaac Abravanel.[38]

Historian Abrahams describes the mournful poems and elegies that were frequently presented in synagogues, with subjects such as "persecution and cruelty, even unto death." These accompanied prayer and ritual, and had been long part of Jewish services. He cites these as examples of how Jews have chosen to emphasize endurance during harrowing times, leaving vengeance to God, and hails the liturgies as "a call to courage and devotion."

> They moved ordinary men and women to play the parts of heroes; they made devoted priests of them, ready to sacrifice their children to save them from apostasy; they inspired them with courage to endure all things for that which they held more precious than all things.[39]

The litanies in these hymns, both verbal and written, often presented persecution as punishment for wrongs that the Jewish people had committed, some of them since ancient times. Many looked to the coming of the messiah for salvation from continuing and intensified oppression, as we learned in Chapters Two and Five. Religious leaders advised them to pray for this, rather than to take action against their persecutors. In Chapter Five, focus on the messiah is cited as an important factor in the defeat of the 1547 Ancona trade boycott and the failure of a mid–sixteenth century Jewish settlement in Tiberius. This prayerful approach to persecution continued to predominate among Jews throughout Europe for many centuries, fed by the hopelessness and despair over ever worsening conditions.[40]

How did communities take care of Jewish travelers passing through? Each *aljama* provided shelter in privately owned facilities called hospices. Visitors to Trujillo, for example, often stayed in the hostel owned by Ysaque Romero and David Cohen. Some visitors chose to stay in the more prosperous homes when available.[41]

Some *aljamas* had their own slaughterhouses for the preparation of meat, while others shared theirs with Muslims. Some rented space in facilities also used by Christians. Local authorities occasionally got involved in deciding where and under what conditions Jews could establish or share them with Muslims or Christians. In 1322, Jews in Tortosa who had previously shared a slaughterhouse next to the Muslims,' were permitted to set up their own facility next door. The Christian lease-holder of the old building was named the same on the new one, and to prevent competition with the landlord, Jews were prohibited from setting up another in the *call*.[42]

Family practices were strongly influenced by Talmudic injunctions and *responsas*, or rabbinical opinions on moral and theological issues, setting standards for marriage and home life. Jewish courts, or *beit din*, used them as guides for judging cases which involved relations between men and women, such as marriage, divorce and parent-child issues. The *beit din* had the sole authority over divorce.

Despite the jurisdiction given to rabbinical courts in these matters, Jews often used the Crown's local civil courts or notaries instead of the *beit din* to resolve monetary questions, particularly in cases such as those involving dowries. Jewish law guaranteed the provisions for the bride's dowry and the gifts, set forth in the *ketubah*, or marriage contract. It gave the wife first claim on the husband's estate in the event of his death or their divorce. Still, couples often notarized their marriage contracts at the local civil court, as well as the *aljama* court, for extra security. The *beit din* enforced monogamy and fidelity, enjoining men to treat their wives with endearment and respect. Religious law was replete with the principle that "Jewish husbands must honor their wives more than themselves." There were even provisions to protect wives from desertion.[43]

The emphasis on chastity and its prevalence was due in large measure to the custom of arranging marriage at early ages. This widespread practice did not conform with the Talmudic teaching that "A man must not betrothe [sic] his daughter while she is a minor; he must wait until she attains her majority and says 'I love this man.'"[44] This was rarely observed at the end of the fifteenth century, and a Jewish girl was rarely, if ever, consulted on choice of husband. Female legal majority began the first day of the thirteenth year, yet many were betrothed while yet twelve. A provision was often inserted in the *ketubah*, specifying which adults were responsible to provide housing for the adolescent couple.[45]

Jews shared some superstitions of the period with their medieval neighbors. One of these advised that marriage take place when the moon is new. Because of the lunar calendar, this time of the month also took on importance in such matters as setting dates for holidays, feasts and fast days.[46]

Weddings often became community events with the procession to the synagogue for the ceremony. In earlier centuries, the custom was to transport the bride to her husband's home. At the end of the fifteenth century, the procession would often develop into a symbolic tourney, with jousting and lance-breaking mimicked on horseback.[47]

Nuptials combined joyous celebration with yearning for return to the holy land. The philosopher and poet Judah Halevi epitomized this in an ode:

> The day at last is here
> Filled full of love's sweet fire;
> The twain shall soon be one,
> Shall stay their fond desire.
> Ah! Would my tribe should chance
> On such deliverance![48]

As described earlier, women were their children's first educators and carried forth until male offspring reached the age of five. The Statutes of

Valladolid, drawn up in 1432 by an assembly of scholars and leaders of the Jewish communities in Castilla, required every town or village of fifteen families to maintain a teacher for the children, and in those villages with forty or more families, the teacher was "to impart instruction in 'Talmud, *halakhoth* and *haggadoth*.' All such scholars shall maintain 'permanent *yeshivot* where they could teach all who wished to learn *Halakhah* from them.'"[49] In most cases the rabbi served as appointed teacher for the *aljama*. The male child continued the next phase of his education when he moved his study base from home to the *yeshiva*. Long school hours began before dawn and ended after evening prayer in synagogue or school. This regimen continued until the boy's thirteenth or fifteenth year. At this point, those destined for non-professional vocations moved into the world of work or apprenticeship, while others went on to study and live in *yeshivot* near their instructor or principal, continuing professional and religious studies.

In addition to literacy and religious studies, schools emphasized poetry. Writing verses was deemed significant in developing spirituality.[50] Reading was also highly respected, indeed fundamental, in Jewish life due to the injunction to read Talmud and Torah. Male literacy was the norm from early childhood on, regardless of class or economic station. Perhaps this quotation from a thirteenth century father, Judah Ibn Tibbon, to his son said it all:

> Avoid bad society, but make your books your companions. Let your book-cases and shelves be your gardens and your pleasure-grounds. Pluck the fruit that grows therein, gather the roses, the spices, and the myrrh. If your soul be satiate and weary, change from garden to garden, from furrow to furrow, from sight to sight. Then will your desire renew itself, and your soul be satisfied with delight.[51]

Thus, although diminished from its former splendor, scholarship and vitality, a resilient Jewish life continued after the massacres of 1391, in spite of incessant attempts to convert practitioners through mob action or preaching. Learning had priority, with required education for all males, and communities enjoyed a limited form of autonomy in *aljamas* throughout Sefarad. The next chapter looks at relations with the greater community and with each other in the world of work and occupations, including money lending and customs affecting day-to-day life, such as clothing and the identifying badge. Attention will be given to how Jews took care of each other, providing dowries, supporting the sick and burying the dead, and what they did for recreation and social activities.

⚘ SEVEN ⚘

"In the presence of my enemies": Work, Usury, Clothing and Entertainment

The work or school day for the Jews of Sefarad began early, sometimes even before daylight could start to erase the early morning shadows. It could not have been different in the chilly late autumn of 1491. As the streets brightened, fathers and sons were leaving their homes or the synagogues where they had gone for morning prayer. Boys throughout Sefarad were setting off in the semi-light for another long day of school in the *Talmud Torah*, while girls and mothers centered on family needs, already involved with the daily tasks of household and community. Men were on their way to the shops, offices, factories, warehouses and marketplaces where they earned their living. Most were leaving small and crowded living quarters in the narrow, congested and often grimy streets of the *juderías* and *calls*. A few in each village prepared for the daily walk from comfortable homes near the town's plaza to their work sites, while a very few stepped into carriages to be taken to their places of business.

What were the occupations and professions of Spain's Sephardic Jews near the end of the fifteenth century? How important were they in the economic picture of the late middle ages: in the service of states and local government, such as administrators and customs officials; in the professions, such as medicine, astronomy and cartography; in the crafts, such as printing, carpentry, and metalworking; in the trades, such as textiles, spices and gemstones; and in agriculture and livestock, such as breeding, growing, harvesting and distributing products for food and clothing?

Records show a significant economic role for Jews in this period as businessmen. In Trujillo, for example, a textile merchant could be involved at many points in the movement of goods, from supplier of raw materials to manufacturer of finished products, and from factory or shop to consumer. In some cases, he was manufacturer as well. Sometimes he owned the sources of his products, such as the sheep from which he got the wool; sometimes he simply bought the raw materials and produced an intermediate product, such as cloth, which he marketed at fairs. Merchants from the town of Trujillo traveled frequently to fairs at nearby Caceres and to Badajoz, a day's journey away near the Portuguese border, attracting customers for the firm's yarn, thread and fabric. Others sold directly to small manufacturers and housewives, the latter using the cloth to make clothing for their families. The businessman could also be a distributor, getting his or others' products out to retailers who would sell them at the local level.[1]

Tailors occupied a related vocation, fashioning textiles into finished clothing. Like merchants, they often retained employees to serve as apprentices as they learned the trade. Assis describes an apprenticeship contract in 1383, between one Jafuda Abec of Tortosa and the parents of Jaffuda Condi, who was about to enter the tailor's service for a four-year apprenticeship.

> The apprentice undertook to obey the master and live with him. The master promised to provide him with food and footwear. While instructing him in tailoring, he would also pay him a salary of 70 sueldos for three years and in the last year 23s 8d.[2]

Jaffuda's service was his means of entry into the vocation of his master. He and others like him would fill the need by *comerciantes* and *artesanos* for assistants to help them in preparing their products, as well as warehousing and transporting the goods to buyers or serving as salesmen.

The process itself of weaving yarn or thread into the cloth, usually took place in home settings. This was considered preferable to using shops or factories, for the customs of the day discouraged having men and women in close proximity except for formal family settings. Therefore, Jewish women and children not at the *Talmud Torah* were often at home spinning cloth from wool or cotton.

Although the law forbade Jewish merchants from doing business with Christians and Muslims, this was rarely enforced. From records of period court cases, Hinojosa Montalvo is able to paint a picture of Jews from Morvedre traveling to Petres to trade with its Muslim inhabitants. One Salamo Zalmero is described selling a parcel of indigo to Valencia Muslim Abraham Zeyt in 1474, and subsequently going to court to get payment.[3] Christian authorities were often customers as well, as in Villareal, where local church officials were recorded purchasing materials such as plaster, fabrics and lead from Jewish merchants.[4]

Like their coreligionists in Italy, Spanish and Portuguese Jews took very

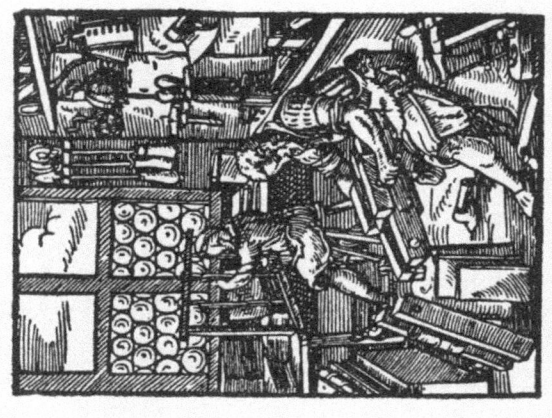

The invention of movable type in the fifteenth century revolutionized the production of books. Jews quickly recognized the educational, cultural and religious benefits from the ability to print numerous copies of a work and distribute it, at much lower cost, to more of an audience than had been previously possible. The vocation of printer was eagerly taken up, with philanthropists such as Doña Gracia Nasi, Benvenida Abravanel and Esther Kiera funding the publication of books to advance Judaic learning. These 1568 woodcuts by Jost Amman show stages in the production of a book. (Geoffrey Ashall Glaister. *Encyclopedia of the Book* [New Castle, Delaware: Oak Knoll Press and the British Library, 1996], 9, Z118.G55 1996. Courtesy of the Library of the Jewish Theological Seminary and Oak Knoll Press.)

quickly to printing, seeing it as a useful tool for religious learning, educational achievement and cultural preservation. The vocation was fairly new, having developed in 1452 when Johann Gutenberg used moveable type for the first time to publish a bible. His process cast letters in metal, then combined them into the desired words and sentences and imprinted them on paper. It became possible to replace the laborious task of hand lettering and illumination for multiple volumes, with the ability to reproduce many copies of the same work in a comparatively short time. Perhaps the relative youth of the occupation allowed some of its work aspects to differ from the local custom concerning separation of the sexes, for occasionally women were seen alongside men as compositors in print shops.[5]

Traditionally, Jews led in the manufacture of wine for use in Hebrew rituals and festivals. Often, they supplied the local churches as well. In fact, the role of wine in Jewish religious practice was recognized in *aljama* charters, where non–Jewish town officials were limited in their prosecution of Jews for alleged wrongdoing if the action endangered the ceremonial wine vessels and their contents.

Most Jews lived in towns and villages and were engaged in crafts, the trades and money lending. This pattern, repeated throughout the *aljamas* in Sefarad, appears "almost a constant throughout history," we learn from Sebastia and Nom de Dieu.[6] Under the Muslims, they became expert in the process of damascene, where gold is inlaid in decorative designs, mostly for jewelry and objects of art. They were also skilled in other handicrafts, and their work continued to be highly valued under Christian rule. Based mainly in Toledo and Andalucía, they were excluded from the Old Christian guilds, which played a significant role in governing production and sale. The Jews, therefore, often created their own associations, as in Tortosa, for example, where Assis reports that "As in some other communities, such as Perpignan where the Jewish tailors formed their own guild, there were several tailors working at the time."[7]

Jews were involved in a variety of other trades and crafts. For example, Astruch Saporta and Vidal Benvenist appeared in Tortosa notarial records as jerkin makers. There were also Jewish furriers in the city and in a neighboring village.[8] Most of the Jews in Sevilla applied their skills to crafts and hand fashioning products. In Toledo, as well, crafts were an important source of livelihood. This was common, in greater or lesser degree, throughout Sefarad. Hinojosa Montalvo describes "the transformation industries, such as the textile industry, and the small occupations of tailors or shoemakers, among others as the main support of the lower classes of the Jewish quarters."[9]

Jews were likewise involved in agriculture, owning vineyards supplying the grapes for wine, and livestock such as sheep and goats. Baer describes these enterprises as appearing in tax records of the Aragonese communities of Borja, Huesca, Barbastro, Fariza and Rueda. Like their Christian counterparts in other towns in Aragón and parts of Castilla, the Jewish communities continued to be semi-agrarian throughout the fifteenth century.[10]

Thus we see quite a diversity represented in the spread of occupations. Again, one wonders how significant the role of Jews was overall in Spanish commerce and trade. The overwhelming majority of historians believe it was notable, considerably influencing the manufacture and sale of goods and services. Certainly, this assumption was maintained by Christian critics in court, church, *cortés*, guild or street, where one heard frequent complaints of unfair competition from the Jews. Yet scholars disagree on the extent of the influence.

Assis points to Jews as significantly integrated into the local economy in Tortosa. Records throughout Spain show active Jewish involvement in pursuing vocations and paying their taxes and duties. And as showed previously, Christians and Jews had working agreements when it suited their interests, in spite of laws and efforts to restrict this. Jews were often the creditors of local Christian and Muslim merchants, which will be covered below in more detail.[11]

Beinart claims that Jewish merchants influenced the operation of business throughout the kingdom. He describes Jews in Trujillo as involved in a large number of different trades, despite the restrictions of the 1480's which limited work with jurisdiction over Christians. They were particularly active in the cloth-making industry, for which the town was known, as well as in other businesses. They were also the tax collectors and money lenders.

The pace of business life in Trujillo, as elsewhere in Castilla, was set to a large extent by the Jewish population's activities and its relations with the Christian community. Beinart quotes one inhabitant of Trujillo as observing that "all or most of the business of the town was in their hands." He was not alone in his opinion. Again, it appears that the numerous prohibitions did not prevent various commercial joint ventures between Jews and Christians. Trujillo's Jewish butchers and workers rented the local slaughterhouse, for example, and their meat was often sold to Christians. So varied were the vocations of Jews, and so frequent the working relationships between Jews and Christians, that Beinart declares "what havoc must have been wrought in Trujillo, as elsewhere in Spain, when the Jews were expelled in 1492."[12]

Hinojosa Montalvo, however, differs notably, and points to critics of this view of Jewish dominance, who consider it exaggerated. He claims there was no reason why Spanish Jewry should be more influential in the economy of the medieval world than Jews in other parts of Europe, with very similar activities found in all Jewish communities.[13]

Influential or not, Jewish merchants and owners of property and livestock had to be alert to the possibility of physical and other threats and abuses

Members of the different religious groups found ways to continue doing business together through the centuries, even when laws or decrees forbade it. In "A Christian and a Jew Transacting the Sale of a Golden Goblet," the thirteenth-century illuminator shows a vessel changing hands twice as the Christian buyer uses the overvalued item, bought from a Jewish merchant, to back up a loan from a Jewish money lender. (The J. Paul Getty Museum, Los Angeles, Ms. Ludwig XIV 6, fol. 180. Michael Lupi de Çandiu, Spain, "A Christian and a Jew Transacting the Sale of a Golden Goblet," ca. 1290–1310." Tempera, gold leaf and ink on parchment, bound between wood boards, covered with modern green morocco, 36.5 × 24 cm [14⅜ × 9⁷⁄₁₆ in].)

from Christians. Beinart describes the frequent occurrence of theft of single heads of livestock from Jewish herds in and around Trujillo. In other cases, whole or partial herds were affected. An example was the theft of 900 sheep around 1460 by Luís de Chávez and his band from a herd belonging to Alvaro de Escobar. It took twenty years for the Crown to respond to Escobar's plea for justice. In another case recorded in June, 1492, the Crown ordered a shepherd to return the herd stolen from Yaacov Abravanel.[14]

Kidnapping and holding Jews for ransom was not rare in Trujillo or throughout Sefarad. In one example, Yuce Arrobas of Trujillo was abducted on his way to the fair in Medina del Campo, and held for nine days by Nuno Yerro of Avila. He was freed after paying the ransom of 14,000 maravedis. Nevertheless, Jews continued to take the risks and do business away from their home bases, as commercial records and documented travel accounts evidence.[15]

In countries under Spanish hegemony, Jewish workers developed expertise in specific trades. They made up most of the skilled ironworkers in Sicily, for example, producing agricultural tools, horseshoes and ships. Christian leaders there were to plead for exemption from the expulsion edict when it came, fearing the effect the potential loss of skilled craftsmen would have on supply and prices.[16]

Assis calls attention to the "striking" number of Jewish physicians and surgeons in Tortosa, beyond the one doctor retained by the community to assure care for ordinary citizens, regardless of ability to pay. He names several who appear in the records over the years: Homar Tahuell, also an *aljama* leader, in 1383; Issach Salomo, in the mid 1400's; Salomon Tavys, medical student, in 1487; and Samuel Maneti, *aljama* treasurer, no date given. One physician, Magister Juceff Saltell Cabrit, performed the double professions of surgery and finance in the 1380s.

In 1437, Church leaders asked the sovereign to limit the activity of Jewish physicians, disturbed by their high status and the large number of Christians using their services. Queen María subsequently gave the vicar general the power to limit Jewish or Muslim doctors from treating Christians whenever he deemed it necessary.[17]

What about the occupation of money lending, in which Jews had become proficient over the centuries, thanks, or no thanks, to church condemnation of this work? Prohibition of this activity for Christians stemmed from the church dictum that charging interest for the loaning of money was immoral. Hinojosa Montalvo reminds us that "One of the deepest causes of anti–Semitism is to be found in usury, to the extent that the words usurer, Jew and enemy of Christ are used synonymously."[18] On the other hand, Spanish monarchs had always benefited from loans from Jews as sources of royal revenue,

Seven. "In the presence of my enemies" 153

AMATUS LUSITANUS

Ein Arzt von Castelblanco einer Stadt in Portugall gebürtig, hies eigentlich Johanne Rodriguez de Castelblanco, lebte in der Mitte des 16 Jahrhunderts, und bekante sich zu Thessalonich zur Jüdischen Religion.

(O original d'este retrato pertence ao Exmo Snr. Annibal Fernandes Thomaz)

The journeys of Amatus Lusitanus, prominent sixteenth-century physician and scientist, mirrored those of fellow *marranos* seeking safety from persecution. Born João Rodrigues de Castelo-Branco in Portugal in 1511 to forcibly converted parents, he found his way to several cities and principalities in the Lowlands and Italy throughout his life and was hailed for his achievements in each. His final haven was Salonika, in the Ottoman Empire. (Photograph copied from seventeenth-century engraving. ©Schwadron Portrait Collection, The National Library of Israel, Jerusalem. Photograph courtesy of Beth Hatefutsoth, Photo Archive, Tel Aviv. Visual Documentation Center, Beth Hatefutsoth, Tel Aviv.)

which is why they generally protected efforts to collect on debts, assuring the continuing prosperity of their ever-ready creditors. In most communities, the *baile general* of the Crown, not the *aljama's beit din*, was the final arbiter of cases regarding debt, financial claims or fraud.[19]

Lenders tended to operate as individual proprietors, loaning their own capital. While a few had ten or more clients, most were limited to less, with the preponderance serving one to four. Notarial resources in Valencia show that the main clients of Jewish moneylenders came from rural areas, where the largest number of loans was usually executed in autumn. This was the season when farmers had to arrange for seeds, when manor payments were due and when it was popular to schedule marriages. City dwellers from Valencia, working in textiles, fisheries and related crafts, made up the next largest money lending client group. It is important to note that *aljamas*, as well as individuals and firms, were often lenders to Christian merchants and that borrowers included Jews as well as Christians.[20]

Thus it can be seen that Jews in the last century before the expulsion supported themselves in a mostly urban setting, with concentration in services areas of business and commerce: in professions and vocations such as medicine and administration, finance and real estate, and the crafts and trades. Their involvement in agriculture largely serviced nearby in-town needs, such as production to support the making of wine for ceremonial use.

Turning now to customs affecting everyday life, those originating with the Jews or those forced on them, we look next at clothing and the garments worn outside the home. Significant restrictions and impositions on dress were standard throughout Europe at the end of the fifteenth century. How did Jews in Sefarad fare?

Under Muslim rule, Jews and Christians had to follow a prescribed style of dress so that their clothing did not resemble that of believers. Rabbis and scholars donned the cope, a long robe similar to the priest's ecclesiastical vestment, while women wore a head covering like a wimple. Under Christian hegemony, likewise, laws requiring that Jews wear different clothing from Christians had always existed, whether in threat or actuality.

In the early thirteenth century, the Lateran Council in Rome decreed that Jews and Muslims were to be distinguished from others by a badge attached to their clothing. Pope Innocent III, the power behind the edict, explained it as a way to prevent intermarriage or cohabitation. The badge took the form of a circle, and its color, location on the garment and fabric or material was left to the decision of each country.[21] Although the Jews of Aragón had been ordered previously to wear the badge and cover their clothing with a long robe called a *caps*, James I relieved them of the badge in 1268. He maintained the compulsory cape or robe for all Jewish males except those who were courtiers and officials.[22] In 1371, Castillian Jews were ordered by the *Cortés* at Toro to wear the badge, an order rescinded by the next monarch. Kingdoms and regions continued to require Jews to dress differently from Christians and Muslims, and legislation throughout Sefarad resulted in Jews being limited to the roughest fabrics.

In 1393, two years after the riots and mass conversions, such regulations were revived by John I, who initiated laws requiring Jews and *conversos* to eat and live apart. In later years, he mitigated these requirements for those traveling on the high road. In 1412, the Jews of León, France, were ordered, in laws aimed at separating them from Christians, to dress humbly and let their hair and beards grow. This action was paralleled in many parts of Spain, as part of a long period alternating between revocation of such laws by some rulers and their subsequent reinstatement by other rulers under political pressure.

Abrahams points to the wearing of the badge and restrictions on color and clothing expression as a "system of branding the Jews as a pariah class," marking the Jew for "the meanest of insults." He asserts, nevertheless, that Jews in Sefarad seemed spared centuries of the intense degradation suffered by coreligionists in other countries, lamenting that this was to end in 1492.[23]

Turning next to customs and practices within the *aljamas*, one notes that the Talmud places acts of charity and concern for the needs of others as second only to Torah study.[24] Sephardim were known for their communal systems of support for those without financial, health, educational, burial and other necessities. The following, from the *Mishnah*, rabbinical commentaries on observance, is chanted daily in morning prayers:

> These are the things, the fruits of which a man enjoys in this world, while the stock remains for him for the world to come: viz. honouring father and mother, the practice of charity, timely attendance at the house of study morning and evening, hospitality to wayfarers, visiting the sick, dowering the bride, attending the dead to the grave, devotion in prayer, and making peace between man and his fellow; but the study of the Law is equal to them all.[25]

The Bible is eloquent on providing for the poor. Jews are advised to leave the borders of fields and a remnant of grapes unharvested, with the gleanings lying in the fields. The Book of Leviticus tells them to "leave them for the poor and the sojourner."[26] Further, they are to honor the stranger among them, "and you shall love him as yourself; for you were strangers in the land of Egypt."[27] In addition, the Book of Proverbs urges them to speak out for the less fortunate: "Open your mouth for the voiceless ... judge righteously, and plead the cause of the poor and needy."[28] These teachings of charity, benevolence and service are embodied in Jewish practice. They are reflected in the simplest acts of kindness and care for the sick and needy, as well as in the grandest service of ransoming captives seized on the high roads or the high seas. One role model in this regard is an unnamed fifteenth century Jew, referred to by Abraham, who put aside a gold piece for charity whenever he had a pleasurable experience, such as an extra glass of wine, "the enjoyment of a tasteful dish, or a good bargain, or the birth of a child, or the marrying of a daughter." He also contributed to his kitty for the poor when he neglected a required religious injunction. During the high holidays each year, this individual calculated his annual profits and prepared a tithe for the poor.[29] Tithing has its roots in biblical text, and came, through the centuries, to mean one-tenth of one's income for the benefit of the less fortunate. Its applications are treated in the Talmud and in the teachings of the sages, among them Maimonides, who wrote that each Jew is expected to contribute a tithe of his income. The synagogue was the chief dispenser of this charity.[30]

In 1346, Rabbi Asher ben Yechiel left Germany to settle in Toledo. There, he and his sons agreed to the following pledge to continue the practice of tithing:

> ... to the poor one-tenth of our profits earned in business, derived from the loan of capital or from commercial undertakings. Three-fourths of this tithe we will hand over to a *kupah* [or general fund], which shall be administered by two treasurers.[31]

The belief that Jews are rich was contributed to, no doubt, by the absence of Jewish beggars in public places. There may have been some resident beggars within the *juderías* and *calls*, but generally the needy were taken care of through the benevolence programs of *aljamas* and synagogues. The sages have looked down upon giving alms to prevent shaming the beggar and avoid the ostentation of public giving. Consideration for the poor is also a reason for Talmudic restrictions on lavish clothing for the wealthy. Attention is given to what Maimonides calls the highest form of charity: "he who helps the poor to sustain himself by giving a loan or taking him into business with him." [32]

As a result of increased persecution and restrictions, traveling beggars became more common in the late fifteenth century in *juderías* and *calls*. They were offered shelter in the homes of the wealthy or in the Jewish communities' inns or hostels. Communal inns became common after the Crusades, when attacks on Jewish communities had resulted in an increase in homelessness. *Aljama* or community funds usually paid the innkeepers for these arrangements. Benevolent organizations also extended more and more help to homeless travelers. Many synagogue congregations, such as that of Rabbi ben Yehiel of Toledo, assured that travelers passing through their area, including those ill or poor, received succor. Travelers without resources were often housed by families, giving rise to the family table being called the altar of God. The tables of the rich often provided food for large numbers of hungry people.³³ Previous chapters recount the activities of Doña Gracia Nasi and Doña Benvenida Abravanel in this regard, the former feeding more than 80 persons daily in her palatial residences in Ferrara and Constantinople.

Matzo and wine for Passover and ceremonial use were always distributed to the poor. At the Feast of Esther, gifts of food for the poor were larger than those sent to the more fortunate friends and relatives. Collections were often made as well for orphaned girls needing dowries or for poor fathers for the weddings of their daughters.³⁴

The Talmud regards the gift of one's own services as a higher blessing than bestowing property or money. Care and concern for the ill and less fortunate came under this heading. Jewish physicians often took care of poor patients without charge.

Following Saturday prayers, synagogue members in some communities made a practice of visiting the homes of those unable to attend services, following a code of behavior when doing so. Guests were urged to make visits brief, to avoid going when the patient's pain was severe and to cheer the ill person by talking of pleasant subjects.

There existed also a general belief that one should also assure respect and proper attention to the deceased and their families. Charitable organizations called Holy Leagues took charge of the care of the sick and all attendant aspects of the burial of the dead. Funds for the relief of the poor often came from special taxes. In addition, every synagogue had a poor box or *kupah*, to which Jews contributed on joyful or sad occasions, such as weddings or funerals.

It is worth noting that not all obligations had to do with the solemn times in one's life. One happy dictum made it important to be present at weddings and to participate fully. The wedding was a true community event.³⁵

No description of concern for fellow Jews can omit the dedication by prosperous Jews, referred to earlier, to the ransoming and freeing of coreligionists kidnapped while traveling overland or by ship. This practice increased markedly after the expulsion, when large numbers of exiles on ships were held captive by pirates or sold as slaves. The Talmud and the writings of Maimonides refer several times to the responsibility, incumbent on all Jews, to assure the freedom of fellow Jews. Synagogue members in Sefarad observed this through special collections for this purpose, augmenting the benevolence of wealthy brethren.³⁶ Samuel and Benvenida Abravanel, son and daughter-in-law of Isaac Abravanel, were particularly recognized among those of great wealth who paid the ransom of many a Jew held in captivity.³⁷

Earlier, we described commercial activities where Jews, Christians and Muslims were involved with each other, even occasionally in joint ventures, despite the prevalence of laws limiting such contact. Now we'll examine the broader picture of social and secular relationships. Followers of the three religions were prevented legally from socializing with, and living near, each other. Specific needs and tasks, however, resulted in frequent defiance of this law. The prosperous and successful or those in court or other high positions could win exemptions from living in their local *juderías* or *calls*, as we learned in Chapter Six.

Important Jewish thinkers of the fifteenth century showed the influence of Christian philosophers and theologians in their work. Isaac Abravanel was one of these, his writing including references to Thomas Aquinas and Saint Jerome, as well as other non–Jewish writers and thinkers. Two centuries earlier, Maimonides, in prose, and Judah Halevi, in poetry, presented tolerant views of Christianity and Islam, calling attention to the oneness of humanity in the family of believers in God.[38] One tends to find Jews returning experiences of respect and pleasant intercourse with Christians in like manner, while invoking contempt and withdrawal when meeting with degradation and persecution.[39]

What did Jews do for fun? How did they amuse themselves and spend what leisure time they had? Here the Sabbath loomed large. After morning prayer and midday meal, there were visits back and forth among families and friends, with refreshments at every home and families and friends resting and relaxing. Following evening prayers and *havdalah*, the ritual that recognizes the end of the Sabbath when the first stars of nightfall make a bridge with a new week, there was more pleasant interchange.[40] Two proscriptions limited what could and could not be done for enjoyment. Gambling and pastimes which allowed free interaction between men and women were prohibited. Chess and games of chance, such as cards, were frowned on by rabbinical authorities, although they were permitted if not played for money. Another activity looked down on, but not forbidden, was hunting. In addition to the general concern to prevent cruelty to animals, a major reason was the prohibition against carrying arms, decreed in the Ordinances of Cifuentes in 1412. These declared that Jews may not "carry swords, daggers, or similar arms in the cities, towns, and places of my kingdoms." Varieties of this prohibition appeared from time to time in different regions. Another reason was that the requirement to own and ride horses, if one was to participate in the hunt, often put hunting outside the lifestyle and pocketbook of the average Jewish city or town dweller. Finally, Jews were prevented from eating meat resulting from a hunt, due to dietary restrictions regarding animals not ritually slaughtered.[41]

Foot races and ball games were often played separately by both men and women. Dancing was also popular, although the sexes could not dance together — with some exceptions. Mothers could dance with sons, fathers with daughters and brothers with sisters. Otherwise, dancing took place in separate groups of males and females, largely for the entertainment of onlookers. There were often active performances with leaping and hopping and women joined in line or circle dances, a leader setting the style, followed by the rest playing cymbals.[42]

Enjoyment of wine often added to observances. Participants in a Passover seder enjoyed four or more glasses of wine, written into the body of the service. Like today, one was supposed to enjoy enough wine on Purim for players to confuse "Cursed be Haman" from "Blessed be Mordechai."

Games of the mind also enjoyed popularity. *Gemetría*, an ancient intellectual game found in the Talmud, took advantage of the fact that Hebrew letters have numerical equivalents. Players created sentences or phrases with moral or humorous messages and word and number relationships. Numerical analysis of each phrase revealed they share the value of 502. In a game, players guessed the connection between the words and the numbers, and the grand point of it all. *Gemetría* was particularly popular among rabbis and scholars in the fifteenth century.

Less demanding were the games of *Samach* and *Pe*, named after two letters used frequently as markers in the Bible. Each of the two persons playing chose a letter, then opened the book and counted the number of each letter appearing on each spread. Other popular games of the mind were riddles and puzzles, often enjoyed at the family dinner tables or at gatherings on *Shabbat*, holidays and feast days.[43]

Games enjoyed by children included Blind Man's Buff, along with other competitive activities, where each team tried to capture the members of the other.[44] Another type of sport, taking place between the seventeenth of Tammuz and the ninth of Ab, allowed boys to parody ordinarily sacred subjects, such as the rabbi, his voice and manner, and even the prayer book.[45]

The last two chapters focused on life in Sephardic homes and communities a few months before the issuing of the Alhambra Decree which would set the terms of expulsion for all unconverted Jews from Spain. In November of 1491, the order, issued the following March 31, was undoubtedly already an option, perhaps even a plan, in the minds of the sovereigns, Church officials, members of the nobility and *Cortés* representatives. There were different motivations: ridding the recently unified country of the spiritual distractions practicing Jews were said to create for the tens of thousands of New Christians, lust for the wealth resulting from abandoned property and possessions, elimination of competition in commerce and business and ending the influence and close relations with royalty by a powerful minority. There were ample models in history, chief among them England in 1290 and France in 1306. Surely this option existed in the thoughts of the king and queen, but it was kept on hold, even as they used the generous loans from Jews and *conversos* to great benefit in the final battles with the Muslims. While the siege of Granada was underway, Jewish donors for the war effort were still very much needed. In four months, the war would have been won, the sovereigns comfortably holding court in Granada, and Jewish contributions thought to be no longer needed. On March 31, 1492, the estimated 100,000 to 200,000 Jews still observing the laws of Moses would learn that their days in Sefarad were over — a final solution for the fifteenth century. Within the next four months, they would find themselves saying farewell to family homes and ancestral burial sites, making their way on the high road with other coreligionists to points of crossing and embarkation and an uncertain future.

EIGHT

Resilience and Recovery: Turkey and Brazil, Two Diaspora Communities

When it became clear, that fateful spring in 1492, that appeals to reason and common sense, as well as offers of money, were ineffective in deterring the Catholic Majesties from expelling all Jews from Spain, Don Isaac Abravanel was reported by sixteenth century historian Eliahu Capsali to have penned the monarchs a stern letter. He warned of dire consequences for their actions, and pointed to the capacity for the Jewish people of the past to survive long after their persecutors had lost power or become pages in history. When Spain would no longer be a world power because of her unwise policies, he predicted that Jews would still be a modern, as well as historical, presence.[1]

History shows that, indeed, expulsion was not the end for the Sephardic Jews, as it hadn't been for their brethren in France and England centuries before. Certainly the wrenching and devastating exile forced upon them was to take a heavy toll through loss of life and property. Their experiences in the early days of the diaspora were rarely encouraging, with few states or principalities offering an unqualified welcome. Many of the exiles were poor, having arrived at potential places of settlement with few possessions and no connections. Still, most who had survived the exodus would become part of new communities in new environments. The passage of time would see many a descendant continue the family lines of the survivors over the centuries, with blood lines existing to this day. The exiled Sephardim established footholds in fresh earth, establishing synagogues, schools and burial sites. They continued practice of their customs to care for the poor, the sick, the infirm, the wayfarer. These could be observed in the centuries that followed in all parts of the globe.[2]

Was Isaac Abravanel correct? He appeared to be expressing continuity for all Jews, in addition to his Sephardic brethren. What does hindsight show us, five hundred years later, about Abravanel's declaration of the eternality of Judaism? This chapter focuses on the experiences of Sephardim in two of the destinations where they settled in the fifteenth through the eighteenth centuries: the Ottoman Empire, its possessions in Europe, Africa and Asia, and the colony of Brazil in the Americas, under both Dutch and Portuguese rule. This will give a picture of the various situations in which exiles found themselves, depending on the particular political entity or territory. The following chapter will view nineteenth century historical events and movements and see how they affected the continuity and expression of Judaism, exploring the fears and realities of today's Jews as they affect religious and social identities and see if Abravanel's prediction can be validated.

There were two major periods of emigration for the Sephardim. The first was triggered by the expulsion of observant Jews in 1492 from Spain and in 1496–7 from Portugal.[3] The map shown on page 164 indicates the destinations that were open for these exiles as they crossed national borders on overland or sea routes, to points in Southern Europe, North Africa, the Ottoman Empire and the Middle East.

The second major exodus for Sephardim began in 1500 and continued for three centuries. The exiles were New Christians, seeking to escape the grasp of the Inquisition, the clean blood laws and other restrictions. There had been fresh outbreaks of violence early in the sixteenth century, such as the Lisbon riots of 1506, where thousands of *conversos* were set upon and massacred.[4] The map shown on page 165 indicates that the possible destinations had considerably expanded, when compared to those open for Jews of the earlier period. This was due in part to changing religious, political and economic realities, brought about by events and movements such as the spread of Protestantism, the defeat of the Spanish Armada, the emergence of England as a sea power and the prosperity and competition of European nations with overseas colonies and settlements. The Christian identity of the exiles allowed them to enter countries forbidden to professing Jews. For example, they could settle in England and France — albeit with great care — where Jews were still banned since their expulsions from England in 1290 and France in 1406. In a few places, such as Amsterdam, with its tolerant Dutch views toward religious freedom, and Ferrara, where Duke Ercole understood what such a population would add to his economy, *conversos* could return to the practice of Judaism without penalty. As the map shows, the second wave of exiles streamed farther out on the north and the east, even beyond Western Europe to Austria and Poland. One arrow, scarcely as dramatic looking as the passage it indicates, points west, across the Atlantic. This was the direction

Eight. Resilience and Recovery

of those who boarded ships to reach the Spanish and Portuguese colonies in the Caribbean — those who traveled to New Spain, Peru and Brazil, finding ways, somehow, to evade the laws against New Christian travel or settlement.

The receptions they received varied from place to place. Chapter Four describes the plight of most of the 100,000 to 200,000 Sephardim who crossed the Spanish border into Portugal in 1492, were permitted haven in that country for eight months only, and then declared slaves if they could not meet the required payment of a fee. Then, five years later, all who had entered in 1492, unable to leave when facing an expulsion order, were forcibly converted to Catholicism. We read of Abraham Zacuto, determined to avoid conversion, who left with his son in 1497, and how their ship, headed for Tunis, was captured by pirates, the prisoners held for several years.

Chapter Two records how emigrant ships, sailing in 1492 from Valencia, on Spain's east coast, were refused entry along the western Italian peninsula, Naples the lone exception. Even those who found haven there, such as the Abravanel family, were forced to move on over a period of three decades, due to alternate efforts by France and Spain to capture the Italian port.

In the north of Spain, exiles had fled in the direction of Navarra, an independent kingdom not subject to the expulsion decree, but soon that state succumbed to pressures from its powerful southern neighbor and from the Vatican, and expelled Jews as well. The scenario was similar for the exiles heading for North Africa. At first, they found refuge among Jewish populations already resident in Tunis, for example, but were jeopardized again when Spain was to spread her control and with it, her policies.

As the experiences of Isaac Abravanel and Gracia Nasi show, many found temporary respite in the Italian states of Ferrara, Ancona and the Venetian Republic, but with it came the possibility of papal interference in local policies and of popular opinion turning to mob action.

One destination, however, could be counted on to provide haven, even encouragement and support from its leaders. That was the Ottoman Empire. With territories spread across three continents, the Empire controlled parts of Europe and North Africa, including the Balkans and Greece, and the old Byzantine Empire and the Middle East, including the Holy Land. The cities of Constantinople and Salonika glittered like gems from the eastern edge of Europe to those about to be exiled in 1492 from Spain. They were particularly attractive to those with sufficient funds to afford the combination of land and water passage required to reach them. The emigrants knew of the welcome Sultan Bayazid II had declared, as he ridiculed the wisdom of Spain's Catholic monarchs, sending the message that the way was clear for expelled and endangered Jews to settle in his Empire. He further instructed adminis-

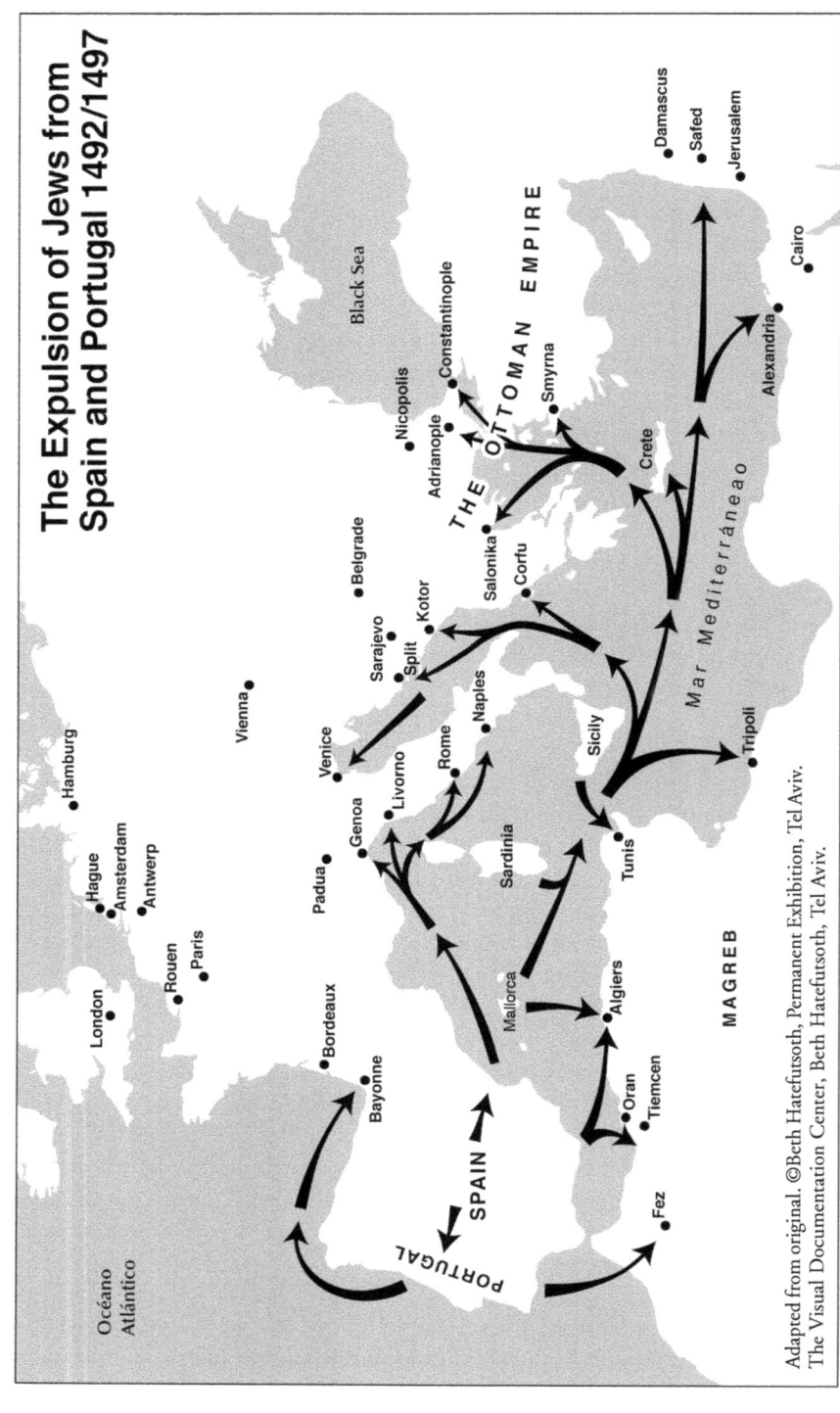

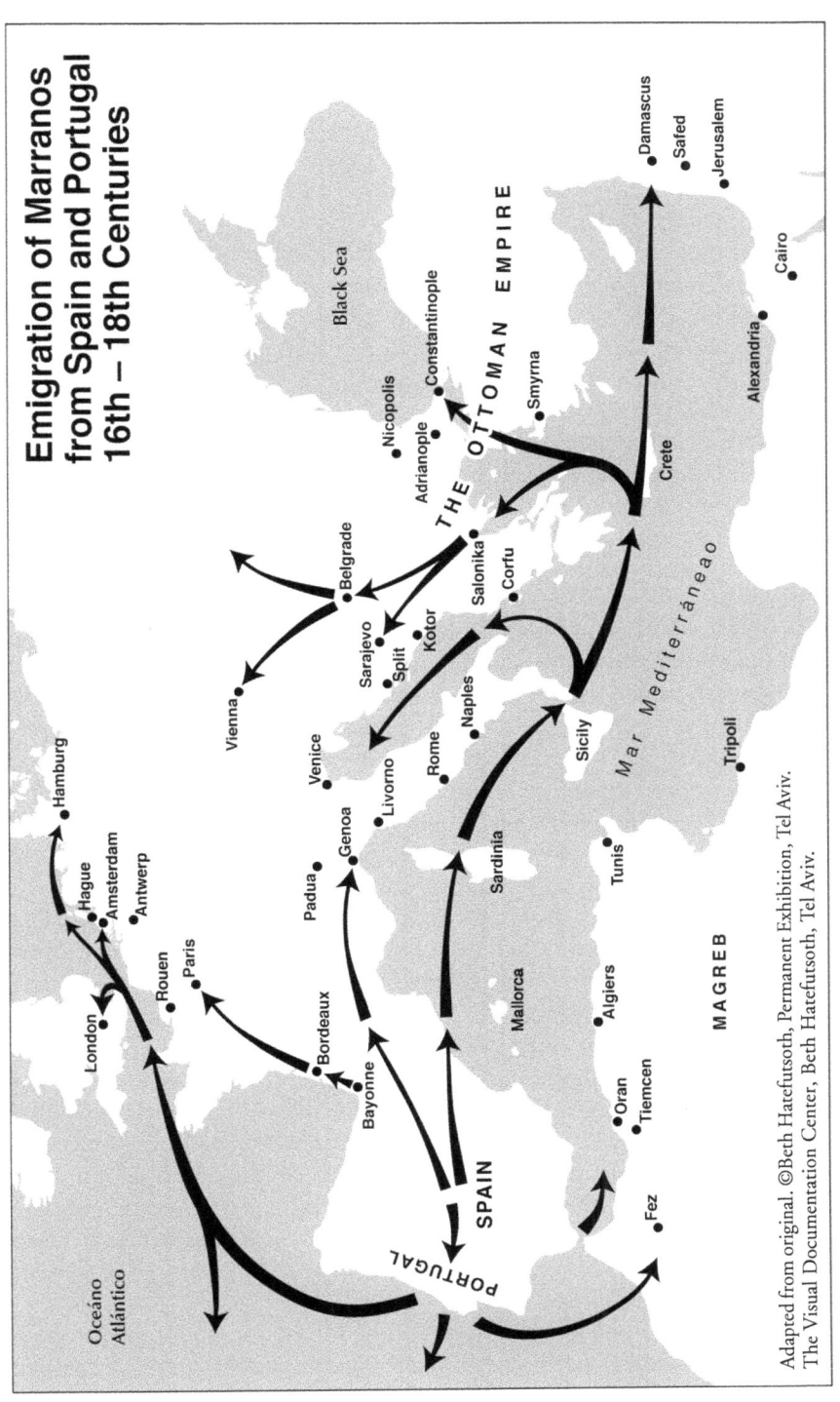

trators throughout the vast territories to protect the newcomers, and enacted penalties for those violating his orders.[5]

There are countless examples of how the Sephardic Jews were able to establish a vibrant religious and cultural presence in the Ottoman Empire after being uprooted from two millennia of life in Iberia. Two of the notables written about previously, Abraham Zacuto and Gracia Nasi, found respite there, as did descendants of Isaac Abravanel. In attempting to know how well the newcomers adapted to the new land and circumstances, it would be helpful to call attention to five Sephardic individuals who appear in the records as exiles in the Empire. As with the four notables from the expulsion era highlighted earlier, they represent the spectrum of talent and achievement of their coreligionists in Ottoman lands, and their life stories parallel the experiences of Jews and *conversos* elsewhere, under similar conditions.

They include two physicians, Moses Hamon, body physician to three sultans and patriarch of a family dynasty in medicine, who came to Constantinople as a young child, and the distinguished Amatus Lusitanus, known throughout Europe before his arrival in Salonika, his last place of residence before his death. Two of the individuals were literary figures: Samuel Usque, author of the acclaimed *Consolation for the Tribulations of Israel*, which would continue to inspire disheartened Jews, and Saadiah Longo, poet and member of the Salonika literary circle, called on frequently to eulogize prominent persons. The fifth individual is Moses Almosnino, rabbi, scholar and author, scion of two respected émigré families, and head of a Salonika synagogue and *yeshiva* for Portuguese *marranos*.

Of the five, some were relatively early arrivals, coming soon after the establishment of the Spanish Inquisition at the end of the fifteenth century, while others had passed from city to city in the Lowlands and the Italian states before arriving in the Empire. Some brought with them major accomplishments, while others were celebrated because of achievements made on Turkish or Greek soil after arrival. The five individuals attained varying degrees of distinction and represented the range of background and endeavor of the thousands of Sephardim streaming through the points of entry to swell Jewish populations in Constantinople, Salonika and throughout the Empire. History takes note of them, but relegates most to a relatively few lines, sometimes only a footnote, compared to the notables described earlier. Yet each was acknowledged within their communities as a person of significance. We take note of them because they give examples of how the resilient Sephardic exiles transplanted themselves in new, relatively hospitable but culturally different, soil, and created family and community.

Turning to Moses Hamon and Amatus Lusitanus, it will be seen how they present differing perspectives of the significant role played by Jewish

Eight. Resilience and Recovery

physicians in the early Renaissance. Moses Hamon was born in Granada just before the Andalusian state fell to the Catholic Majesties in 1491. His father Joseph had been court physician for the vanquished Muslim rulers. Forced to flee soon after by the expulsion, Joseph brought his family to Constantinople, where he was appointed physician to Bayazid II. He also served under Selim II, dying in the winter of 1517–18 when returning from a military campaign with the sultan. His son Moses, who had studied medicine also, then assumed the position of court physician.[6]

Moses Hamon and Jewish physicians of the Ottoman Empire are thought to have inspired this engraving. (Henri Bonnart, *Juif de la Terre sainte* [Paris, ca. 1680] B3.31.1a. Courtesy of the Library of the Jewish Theological Seminary.)

The decline of Ottoman medicine had opened opportunities at court for Sephardic practitioners. Uriel Heyd writes how

> Jewish physicians, especially refugees from Spain, Portugal and Italy, found in the Ottoman capital a wide scope for their activities. Many of them had studied at the famous universities of Christian Europe ... and brought with them extensive knowledge of both Eastern and Western Medical science.... Jewish and crypto–Jewish (*marrano*) physicians in the Iberian peninsula and Italy had excelled as practitioners, scholars and translators of the Greek and Arabic classics. Quite a number of them had also published important works on philosophy, astronomy and other natural sciences.[7]

Jewish physicians at court "regarded it as a moral obligation to use their influential position for the promotion of Jewish learning and the protection of their coreligionists."[8] Moses Hamon illustrated this in 1549, when he persuaded Sultan Suleiman to send a representative to Venice to win the release of Gracia Nasi and her daughter, Reyna, as citizens in intent of the Empire. The two women were permitted to leave, stopping in Ferrara, and eventually entering Constantinople four years later. A subsequent rumor had Reyna promised in marriage to Hamon's son, Joseph, also a physician, but we saw in Chapter Five that she wed cousin Joseph Nasi soon after their arrival in Constantinople.

Another intercession by Hamon on behalf of Jewish welfare concerned blood libel accusations, where Jews would be accused of murdering Christians to use their blood for religious rituals. These charges were not uncommon in the Middle Ages. Hamon won a ruling from the sultan that any such charge made against Jews in the future would be considered in royal courts only, where it would be easier to defend against them. His advocacy came after a supposed victim of such an act was found alive after several Jews had been falsely accused, tried and executed for his presumed ritual murder.

In addition to his medical skills, Hamon was known as a scholar and linguist, with knowledge of Turkish, Persian and Arabic. He was founder of a *yeshiva* and supported the publishing of books in Hebrew for the growing number of returning Jews who were learning that language in their new land. He continued to be vigilant with regard to his coreligionists' needs until his death around 1567.[9] His sons also became court physicians, continuing the family's medical dynasty and tradition of service.

The background of fellow physician Amatus Lusitanus and the trajectory of his life varied considerably from that of Moses Hamon. Born in 1511 in Castelo-Branco, Portugal, after all Jews had been forcibly converted to Catholicism, he was first called João Rodrigues de Castelo-Branco, after the town in the Serra de Mogadouro of the country's mountainous northwest. It is believed that the family's name had been Haviv, which means lovable or likable in Hebrew.[10]

Eight. Resilience and Recovery

He pursued a career as physician, studying medicine and botany at the University of Salamanca, then began his practice in Portugal. Identifying secretly with Judaism and wary of the Inquisition, he left for Antwerp in 1533. The city in the Lowlands had a vital Portuguese *marrano* population, and was a likely site for a young *converso* physician to pursue his career. There he continued his studies in botany and the uses of herbs and plants in medicine, writing *Index Dioscorides*, a commentary on the studies of the botanist Dioscorides of ancient Greece.[11]

His skills and knowledge were much sought after, and his patients included the mayor of Antwerp, the Portuguese consul and the family of Doña Gracia Nasi. In fact, his diaspora mirrored the path of *La Señora*, for, like her, he eventually left Antwerp for Ferrara, arriving there around 1533. It was there that he changed his name to the Latin Amatus, which had the same meaning in translation as his reputed Hebrew family name, Haviv, and Lusitanus, of Portugal [12]

In Ferrara, he joined the faculty of the university, teaching medicine. Some have attributed the discovery of the presence of valves in veins to Amatus while he was at the university, but the credit for this has often been given to the anatomist Canano, who was watching him from the audience at the time. Hashavit describes Amatus' account of the experiment performed before scholars at the university:

> He blew air into the lower part of the azygos, and showed that the vena cava would not be inflated. It was not possible for the air to escape because of the valve or operculum mentioned. When it is clear that if air cannot pass out of the azygos into the vena cava, it is all the more certain that blood, much thicker than air, could [sic] not flow through.[13]

Amatus left Ferrara in 1556, probably for the same reasons as the Nasis and Abravanels, spending the next three years in the Ragusan Republic, now Dubrovnik, as a respected physician. The sixth part of his monumental work, *Curationum Medicinallium Centuriae Septem*, reviewed one hundred cases that he treated during his stay there. Several of these *Centuriae* were published throughout his career, each giving attention to one hundred different cases and their treatments.

He next moved on to Ancona, where he continued treating prominent individuals, such as Pope Julius III, Emperor Charles V and the Duke of Tuscany, Cosimo de Medici. Forced to flee for his life as one of the New Christians arrested and charged with *judaizante* in 1555, he made his way first to Pesaro, then to Salonika, where he spent the last years of his life writing and practicing, dying in 1568 during an outbreak of the plague.[14] Among his works is an oath that he published in 1559 or 1561, consisting of an ethical statement about the practice of medicine. In it, he states "that I have ever striven

Curationum Medicinalium
AMATI LVSITANI
MEDICI PHYSICI
PRAESTANTISSIMI

CENTVRIAE DVAE,
Quinta videlicet ac Sexta,
In quarum vltima Curatione continetur
Colloquium eruditiſsimum, in quo doctiſsime
diſputatur, & agitur de curandis
capitis vulneribus:

Cum Indice omnium curationum quæ ipſis Centurijs continentur.
omnia nunc primum in lucem ædita.

Cum Priuilegio Illuſtriſs. Senatus Veneti.

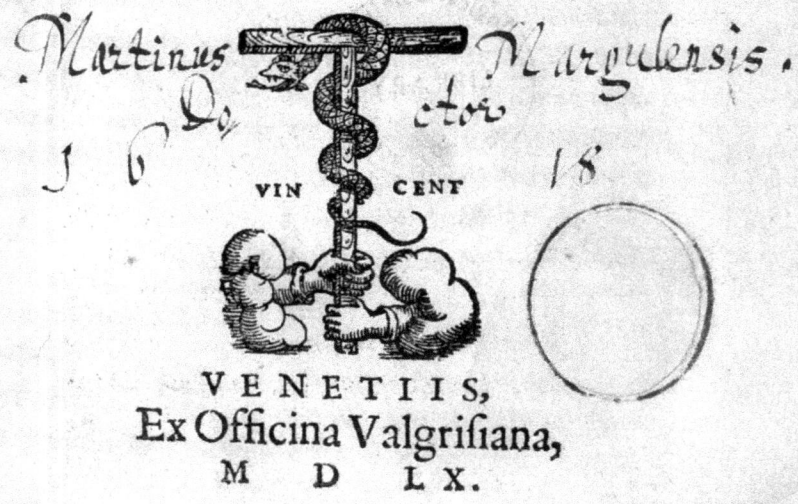

VENETIIS,
Ex Officina Valgriſiana,
M D LX.

In the 1560 edition of *Curationum medicinalium*, one of several works by Amatus Lusitanus, the *marrano* physician describes various cases and their treatments. (Amati Lusitani. *Curationum medicinalium* [Venice: 1560], RB446:24, fol. 1r. Courtesy of the Library of the Jewish Theological Seminary.)

that benefit might accrue to mankind," and that "I have done nothing which might be considered unbecoming to an honorable and distinguished physician having always held Hippocrates and Galen before me as examples worthy of imitation and not having scorned the precepts of many other excellent practitioners of our art."[15]

Looking next at the two Sephardim in the literary arts, respected for their creative use of both prose and poetry in the spoken and written word, one sees that Samuel Usque and Saadiah Longo were both active in literary circles in both Constantinople and Salonika. Each appeared earlier in Chapter Five, Usque as the writer whose epic work was published thanks to the patronage of Doña Gracia, Longo as the eulogist whose words paid tribute at her memorial service.

There is little historical material recorded about either of these writers. In the case of Usque, however, scholars have been able to infer biographical information from analyzing his epic work, *Consolation for the Tribulations of Israel*. Cohen believes that "The lack of precise data about his life turns Usque, as it were, into a symbol of the composite personality of the Portuguese *marrano* and his biography into the epic of his suffering people."[16] In his major work, Usque wrote that his family had crossed into Portugal at the time of the expulsion. Cohen deducts, from descriptions in *Consolation*, that Usque had actually observed some of the harrowing experiences of *marranos* taking place during his time there, such as the exportation of children to the island of São Tomé. He surmises that Usque left Portugal after 1531, the Inquisition to be established a few years hence.[17]

Records show him in Naples soon after, where he established a close relationship with Samuel and Benvenida Abravanel, son and daughter-in-law of Don Isaac. His reasons for leaving the Italian state are not known, but the danger was great, as France and Spain took turns invading the small state, and then fought each other for primacy. Increased persecution of Jews may have also played a part in his decision. After Naples, he traveled in the Ottoman Empire, staying first in Constantinople and then in Salonika. His ties with the literary circles in both cities may have begun at that time. Cohen describes him next traveling to the Holy Land, where he was reported participating with those who predicted 1550 as the year when the Ten Lost Tribes would return.

He next passed through Europe, making his way to Ferrara, where he found the Abravanels again. It is there that Gracia Nasi sponsored the printing of his epic work, which was published in 1553.[18] In the "Prologue," Usque explains the decision to write the work in Portuguese, rather than Spanish, the preferred tongue for the Iberian diaspora.

> My primary intention was to speak to the Portuguese, to describe the record of our diaspora, and by many sometimes circuitous means, to see some relief from

the hardships we have been enduring. It would therefore have been inappropriate for me to shun my mother tongue and to seek a borrowed language in which to speak to my countrymen. And though at one time there were many among us from the diaspora of Castilla — my own forebears came from there — it seems more proper for me to consider the majority of our people today.[19]

Cohen calls attention to the "profound knowledge of religious and classical disciplines which characterized the well-bred man in the Iberian Peninsula in the middle years of the sixteenth century," and surmises that "the range of Usque's learning ... suggests a regimen of studies at a university."[20] Preto-Rodas writes that "Few sixteenth century prose writers in Portugal match his graceful use of the vernacular, and his literary prowess is remarkable. Especially noteworthy is Usque's success in wedding a major cultural convention..., the pastoral perspective, with a passionate commitment to consoling his people during a time of extreme hardship."[21] The work was published and read widely in the Sephardic diaspora. Writing in 1948, Roth reported that it was still being read by Portuguese schoolchildren because of its skillful use of the pastoral form.[22]

Following the paths of Doña Gracia and of Samuel and Benvenida Abravanel, Usque left Ferrara, which was growing unsafe even under Duke Ercole, for Constantinople, then Salonika. It is pleasant to think of him in contact with the writers in that city during this sunset period of his life, especially with Saadiah Longo, who is covered next, although no evidence appears to authenticate it. The date and place of his death is unknown, although Cohen hypothesizes the possibility of a second trip to the Holy Land.[23]

There is even less information available on the life and work of Saadiah Longo than there is for Usque, his fellow writer and contemporary. Born in Turkey in the early part of the sixteenth century, one generation after his family's exodus from Sefarad, Saadiah ben Abraham Longo was connected, religiously and emotionally, to the large population of Jews who had come to Turkey as New Christians, returning to Judaism in the new setting.

Brooks reports him taking part as a lay reader for Moses Hamon, in the physician's private *midrash* in Constantinople, and that he was employed later in various synagogues in Salonika.[24] It was as poet and eulogist, however, that he became well known in both cities. He was affiliated with *Hakhmei ha–Shir*, or Scholars of Poetry, whose patron was Gedaliah ibn Yahya of Salonika. His work of elegiac poems, *Shivrei Huhot*, containing dirges and laments, was published in Salonika in 1594.[25]

Roth calls him the "poet in-ordinary ... who kept the spark of the Hispano-Jewish school of singers alive in a remote land." Known among his coreligionists for his eloquence, Longo was called upon frequently to provide elegies upon the death of prominent persons. In his elegy for Doña Gracia in

1569, "he laments how every mother-town in Israel weeps for the fate of those in anguish left" because she is no longer alive to defend them.[26]

Likewise, Longo's elegy in 1579 for Don Joseph Nasi tells of his "mourning in a bitter cry," his expression of loss for *La Senora's nephew* not restrained.[27]

Longo accompanied his book of dirges with *Seder Zemannim*, an account of Jewish literary figures of the day and their works.[28] Other poems commented on friendship. Members of the poetry circle would meet to hear each others work and debate the conventions of poetry. Sometimes the writers would critique each others work harshly, and Longo's poetry was no exception from the practice. This would lead to spirited and sometimes rancorous gatherings.[29]

Longo's reputation as a writer and his eloquence in memorializing the deceased brought him into contact with the well-to-do and influential. One of these was the esteemed rabbi of *Livyat Hen*, the synagogue that had been built in Salonika by Doña Gracia in 1560. We move now to that personage, Moses ben Baruch Almosnino, who had been rabbi at *Neveh Shalom* of Salonika when he was chosen by *La Señora* to head the congregation and *yeshiva* at the newly-established *Livyat Hen*, to serve recently arrived *marranos* from Portugal who were returning to Judaism.[30]

Like Saadiah Longo, Moses Almosnino was born in the Ottoman Empire in the early sixteenth century. He was of the second generation native to Turkey. Both sides of his family had been leaders of the Jewish community in their native Huesca, their destinies linked in the last century in Sefarad, when his maternal and paternal great-grandfathers, Abraham Almosnino and Isaac Cocumbriel, perished in 1489 in the flames of the Inquisition. Their sons were able to escape to Salonika, where the long established custom of linking the families in marriage was continued.[31]

Almosnino's interests ranged from philosophy and science to literary expression and *halakhah*. His rabbinic scholarship and writings on moral and theological issues were highly thought of, with prominent *halakhic* scholars choosing to publish some of his *responsas* with their own work.[32]

In 1566–67, he represented the Jewish community of Salonika at the sultan's court in Constantinople. The undertaking had been made difficult by the absence, and then the death, of Suleiman early in the pleading. Then followed a long wait for Selim, the new sultan, to arrive at the Sublime Porte and ascend his throne. The process of appeal and rejection took almost two years, but finally concluded with a new charter confirming the civil rights of his community. In the sermon delivered on his victorious return to Salonika, he paid tribute to those who had been of support, primarily "the Prince, the Lord Don Joseph Nasi, the Duke (may his might increase!) who helped us

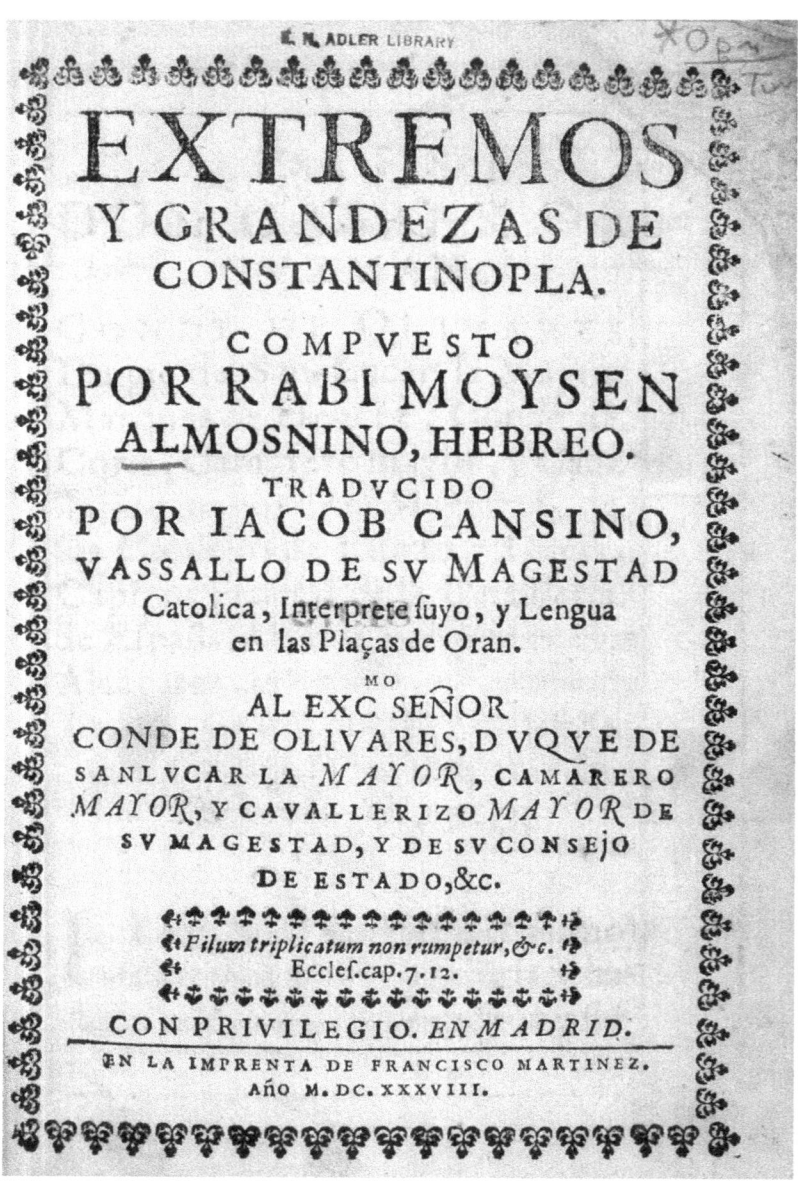

Moses Almosnino, rabbi and scholar, headed the congregation and *yeshiva* of Livyat Hen, founded by Gracia Nasi in Salonika in 1560, for Portuguese *conversos* returning to Judaism. *Extremos y Grandezas de Constantinopla*, describing the political situation and lifestyles of the Ottoman city, was written in 1555–56 while its author waited to petition the sultan on behalf of his city's Jewish community. (Moses Ben Baruch Almosnino. *Extremos y Grandezas de Constantinopla* [Madrid: Francisco Martínez, 1638], title page, DR424.A5 1638, 1r. Courtesy of the Library of the Jewish Theological Seminary.)

from the time we went to him ... from the beginning to the end." He had stayed at Belvedere, Don Joseph's palace, during the process. He had also received support from Joseph Hamon, who had succeeded his father as body physician to the sultan, and from the Grand Mufti, Abu Saud el Amadi, whom he had met on an earlier journey, and with whom he had enjoyed discourses on Aristotle and Galen.

During the long wait for his audiences with vizier and sultan, Almosnino authored a work on the Ottoman capital, *Extremos y Grandezas de Constantinopla*. The book is a record of the political situation and lifestyles of the day. In addition, he contributed a chapter on "Dreams, Their Origin and True Nature" to a book on spiritual issues, when requested by Joseph Nasi.[33]

In addition to the five notables just surveyed, one comes across, during the century after the expulsion in the Ottoman Empire, others whose surnames are found among the learned and the distinguished of pre-expulsion Spain. Francisco Coronel, for example, was a direct descendent of Abraham Seneor, once the most powerful Jewish courtier in Spain. It was Seneor who had accompanied Isaac Abravanel when they intensified their efforts, that fateful spring of 1492, to dissuade the Catholic Majesties from carrying out the edict of expulsion. Having failed, and with the deadline for exile imminent, Seneor had surrendered to pressures from the monarchs and converted to Catholicism, taking the name Fernando Pérez Coronel, with Fernando and Isabel as godparents.

His descendants were able to maintain high status as Christians, although some held secretly to Jewish loyalty. One of them, Solomon Coronel, had become the leading assistant of Joseph Nasi in Constantinople. His son, Francisco, a doctor of law, remained a nominal Christian. Don Joseph chose Francisco to serve as Lieutenant Governor of Naxos, administering the island for him. Coronel's rule was said to be wise and tolerant, maintaining equality among Muslims, Christians and Jews and respecting the customs and laws that had been in effect since antiquity. His Christian identity facilitated the trust he received from those whose ancestors had been residents of the island in ancient times.[34]

Descendants of Abraham Zacuto also found their way to the safety of the Ottoman Empire,[35] joining the many who emigrated for the reasons enumerated by Samuel Usque about "the great nation of Turkey" in his *Consolation*: "This country is like a broad and expansive sea which our Lord has opened with the rod of His Mercy.... Here the gates of liberty are always wide open for you that you may fully practice your Judaism; they are never closed."[36]

We take up again the questions posed early in the chapter about the predictions of Don Isaac of the survival of the Sephardim in particular and Jews

Nineteenth-century worshippers in the Portuguese Synagogue in Amsterdam hear a sermon by David de Jahocob Lopez Cardozo, the famous Talmudist. The architecturally notable building had frequent non–Jewish visitors, who viewed with respect the well dressed, formal congregation, most of them *marranos* returning to Judaism or their descendants. (Jacques-Emile-Edouard Brandon. *Sermon of Jeune d'Av*, oil on canvas [Amsterdam: 1867], RF1116. Photograph: Herve Lewandowski, D.94.511, Louvre, Paris, France. Réunion des Musées Nationaux/Art Resource, New York.)

in general. It is seen that those reaching the Ottoman Empire as Jews were able to practice in relative freedom, while those considered *anusim*— the forced ones who had converted — were welcomed back to the ancestral religion. Their descendants in what is now Turkey have continued to flourish for more than five centuries, to this day. What about some other examples of the diaspora experience after the exodus?

Certainly Amsterdam, where Portuguese *marranos* could go to return to Judaism, stood out as a vindication of Abravanel's optimism, as did the England of Oliver Cromwell, which opened the doors to Jews for the first time since the thirteenth century.

In the space of this book, however, it is possible to describe only a few of the destinations for the exiles. In addition to the Ottoman Empire, we have chosen to look westward to the Americas and the Spanish and Portuguese colonies, reached by those wanting safety from the Inquisition and able to find a way to avoid the prohibition against New Christians emigrating to the New World.

From Portugal, *conversos* seeking refuge made their way to Brazil. The colony had its beginnings in 1500, when Pedro Alvares Cabral touched ground, his ship off course for an eastern destination. With him was Gaspar da Gama, originally a Jew, adopted son of Vasco da Gama, who had been taken by force and forcibly converted when found by the discoverer on his epic voyage.

The New Christian population grew exponentially in the century that followed, estimated at a considerable percentage of the 50,000 who had emigrated there during this period.[37] Jews, as *conversos*, were part of the earliest settlements, present among the expedition of Tomé de Sousa, first governor of the colony. Simms writes that "Even in the original band of six Jesuits led by Manoel da Nóbrega, the majority were former Jews.... In subsequent years, an extraordinary number of the intellectual founders of Brazilian civilization proved to be New Christians...."[38] Novinsky estimates that thirty percent of those arriving in the early days were converted Jews.[39]

In the middle of the sixteenth century, the Inquisition tribunals made deportation to Brazil one of the penalties for prisoners who had been convicted but were "penitent," or had confessed to *judaizante* and sworn to maintain Christian loyalty. Roth writes that "Hence Brazil became filled with New Christians, of doubtful orthodoxy. Indeed, even before this date, the settlement had been considerable. The colony thus harbored an increasingly high proportion of secret Jews."[40]

Outwardly, converts continued, as they had in Portugal, to maintain Christian identity. That changed when the Dutch were successful in 1630 in their efforts to seize part of Brazil, establishing New Holland in the northeast. This was followed by New Christian emigration from Portuguese held territory into regions near Recife and Pernumbuco. Simms estimates that "At the height of this Dutch enclave's power, some 2,000 kilometres of coastline and hinterland, there were between 1,500 and 5,000 Jews living free of Portuguese interference."[41] Many of these returned to the open practice of Judaism, building synagogues, such as *Kahal Zur* in Recife, still standing today as the oldest structure of its kind in the Americas. Jews were numbered as 1,500, or half of the total population at the time. When the Portuguese managed to overwhelm the Dutch colony in 1654, their persecution of Jews led to a large emigration, with new Jewish centers subsequently founded in New York and Curacao.[42]

How well did the New Christians, former Sephardic Jews from Spain and Portugal, fare economically in their settlements in Brazil? Among the immigrants who had been deported from Portugal for *judaizante*, many were well-educated professionals. Some were quite wealthy. These individuals had a good start in the new land, as they took part in the economic development connected with businesses such as the lucrative sugar enterprises.[43] Indeed, the involvement of Jews and New Christians in the sugar industry was so predominant, that their persecution and large-scale emigration later, following takeover of New Holland, seriously threatened the processing and export of this product.[44]

A large percent of Jews were involved in commerce and other industries, with some scholars claiming their pre-eminence in finance, the retail trades and commerce with other nations. Simms does point out, however, that not all Sephardim in the Portuguese colony shared in this prosperity. He quotes Sedycias that "many ... achieved only a modest competence ... while some others remained in abject poverty.[45]

In 1658, twenty-three Jews aboard a ship fleeing from Brazil found themselves moored outside the Dutch colony of New Amsterdam. They were able to come ashore and settle, thanks to their coreligionists' influence in Amsterdam in the Dutch East India Company. They were the founders of a congregation of Sephardic Jews in New York, *Shearith Israel* which is vibrant and flourishing today.

But these were not the first Jews on American soil, as has been so often claimed. More will follow in the next chapter about the Spanish New Christians who followed the Rio Grande in 1598 into what is now northern New Mexico, seeking freedom from the Inquisition. They are part of the story of Sephardic recovery from the harshness of uprooting and homelessness, a partial corroboration of Don Isaac's claim of Jewish survival despite the efforts of their enemies. As we move forward through the centuries, is there more to support this?

You shall go to the valley of Josafath
And you shall meet a lion;
If he asks you for meat, give him bread;
If he asks you for the password,
give him money;
If he asks of what Law you are,
Answer, of Moses's Law.
May he let you pass
Free and unharmed,
Wherever God lets you,
Wherever God sends you.
If he asks you who made you,
Tell him it was a Hebrew woman,
Who stays on in this world.
Who did for you what she knew,
Who did not for you what she should have.

— *New Christian burial prayer,*
Belmonte, Portugal*

*Anita Novinsky and Amilcar Paulo. "The Last *Marranos*." *Commentary*, Vol. 43 No. 5 (New York: American Jewish Committee, May 1967), 79.

ꙭ NINE ꙭ

Endurance, Persistence and Identity: Insights from the Sephardic Experience

We have reviewed the adventures and achievements, facts and foibles of four notable Sephardic individuals in the fifteenth and sixteenth centuries. We have also looked at the lives and times of the average Jewish man and woman from the streets, villages and urban centers of the period just before their expulsion from Spain. Then we examined the experiences of Sephardic exiles in the diaspora, focusing particularly on Constantinople and Salonika in the Ottoman Empire and Brazil in the New World. What can we learn from this overview that has relevance to Don Isaac's prediction and the debate today on the lasting nature of Judaism? Are there insights to apply to continuing arguments, dialogues and debates about Jewish survival? Are Jews here to stay, long after those who have tried to destroy them have become insignificant, or have even disappeared? Or is Judaism in jeopardy as a result of assimilation and intermarriage, as many fear? Does our exploration of Sephardic culture in medieval Spain and Portugal help us to answer these questions?

As it has been seen, the experiences were varied for those who became exiles after the expulsions and forcible conversions, depending on the policies of the states where they settled. Loss of Iberian roots did not signify the end of their identity as Jews from Sefarad or as keepers of the covenant.

In the centuries that followed, Jews everywhere faced increasing varieties of discrimination — many were herded into ghettos, restricted in livelihoods, forced into dress codes, or subjected to violence. Then came the nineteenth century, with encouraging accounts of the American experience across the sea. Napoleon's armies were carrying democratic ideals with them as they moved across Europe. Ghetto walls were coming down and Inquisition trials were no more. Diaspora Jews in Europe found themselves relatively free, compared to prior centuries of oppression and restriction. For the first time, Jews could be citizens of some of the countries in which they lived, and were, more and more, embracing their identities as English, French, German, American. This encouraged wide scale emigration from the lands of Eastern Europe and Russia and immigration to nations offering more opportunity and liberty.

With less need to beware of danger from the outside, one issue, long smoldering, began to surface among Jewish populations, particularly in England, Germany and the United States. It concerned the relevance of the old ways of doing things. Increasing opportunities for secular education meant a wider world view, and a growing middle class meant more leisure time to study, assess and evaluate. This led some to examine the way religious life was organized and practiced. There was growing pressure for Jewish women to have more of a role in religious aspects of synagogue life and for religious education for girls as well as boys. The tree of Judaism sprouted its new branches of Conservative and Reform Judaism in the nineteenth century and of Reconstruction and Jewish Renewal in the twentieth.

Then, the unthinkable occurred. Hitler's hordes and the explosion of repressed anti–Semitism saw millions of European Jews murdered in a technologically engineered way that present generations call genocide, and in even more contemporary terms, ethnic cleansing. This destroyed the Jewish communities of Central and Eastern Europe, the Balkans and old Russia, with remnants of the latter already secularized by the anti-religious policies of Soviet communism.

In postwar years, Jews living in England, the United States and other democratic nations, feeling more secure, could explore the majority culture around them — spiritual, religious, intellectual. Some were actually thinking and living a new definition of identity, trying out ways to observe their religious views in concert with like-minded men and women from other backgrounds who shared the same values. They visited, sometimes affiliated, with transdenominational, non–Christian, religious institutions, such as Unitarian-Universalism, Unity, and Religious Science. Some looked eastward to Buddhism for spiritual renewal. Most did not feel they were giving up Judaism by this behavior, but rather bringing it with them to the particular group of their choice, which served as an umbrella over worshippers from different backgrounds. Many would continue observing Jewish holidays such as Rosh Hashanah and Yom Kippur, Passover and Hanukah, but were not seen on synagogue membership rosters or at *Shabbat* services. They continued identifying as ethnic Jews, with little practice of the rituals and observances of their ancestors.

In this environment of increased secularization, and with vastly enlarged professional and work environments, many met and married or coupled with non-Jews. While some of these chose to raise their children in Judaism, others did not, except to acknowledge the children's right to choose which parent's practices to follow later on. And some saw their children raised in other religions brought to the family by their mates.

With the establishment of the state of Israel in 1948 and the subsequent immigration policies of the new nation, discussion focused even more on the age old question, "What is a Jew?" and the more present-day one, "Will current trends result in the end of Judaism?" Debate rages on among Jews everywhere on these issues. It takes place in synagogues, courtrooms and universities, in print and electronic media. It is common in Jewish community settings, meaning anywhere two or more Jews gather and discuss issues they consider important. Significantly, it also rages in cyberspace, that vast planetary phenomenon touching the millions who log on to the debate through keynote search and surfing synchronicity.

Which brings us back to Isaac Abravanel's prediction of the eternality of Judaism and the question we raised earlier: how valid is the assumption that the ancient persuasion, in its present religious and cultural forms, will last forever? What have we learned from our exploration of Sephardic culture and the people who created and lived it that can contribute to this discussion? Are there other forces influencing this? Can, will, Judaism come to an end?

Let's begin by clarifying the positions in the debate. On one side, there is the belief that Jews, living peacefully and securely without discrimination and with lots of opportunity, will blend with the dominant "outside" culture. There, they will be exposed to the temptations that go with assimilation. These include a world view and philosophies that are cosmopolitan, or feeling "at home ... in many spheres of interest," as *The American Heritage Dictionary* defines it.[1] At the very least, the argument continues, the comfortable interaction with Christians will increase possibilities for marriage across religious borders. Once wed to a non-Jew, the Jewish partner may go with the flow of the dominant Christian religious majority, and not assure that offspring be raised in his or her ancestral environment or traditions. Worse yet, the parent may drop any vestige of Jewish family practice; even neglect the minimum observance of Passover, Hanukah and/or the High Holidays, usually the last Judaic hold-outs for iconoclastic and secular Jews. He or she may slide into Christian customs, such as Christmas trees, lights and presents, even Easter eggs.

The fears of those dreading assimilation continue, with their projection that the children of these "mixed" marriages will tend toward Christianity themselves, as they explore the relative advantages of each parent's background. Certainly, open identity with the religion of the Christian American majority population brings more acceptance and opportunity than with a minority cultural and belief system regarded negatively since ancient times. As this continues through the generations, the argument concludes, Judaism will disappear.[2]

Now, let's look at the other side, those who believe that Judaism is expressing itself in new, as well as old, ways, and has resources that continue to nourish its existence. They point to history from ancient times to today, citing the research and interest in crypto Judaism, and examples of outwardly non–Jewish people observing Jewish practices or customs in secret. These practices are found in Spain and Portugal and regions where people from those nations explored and settled from the sixteenth century onward, including North and South America, the Philippines, European and Asian countries from the old Ottoman Empire and North Africa. Further, they cite examples of tribes and groups in the least likely places, such as Africa, India and China, who insist to this day that they have descended directly from Jewish peoples in biblical Israel and other related sites. Moreover, those who hold that Judaism's survival is far from threatened present as additional evidence the cultural and tribal groups who, despite no apparent Hebrew roots, have chosen to convert to Judaism as their religion of choice. Finally, they cite the cultural loyalty of many who have little or no synagogue affiliation, yet identify themselves with the customs and traditions that came with the Jewish families they were born into. And they include those who, despite no attention to any Jewish manifestations, report identity with Judaism.[3]

Let's examine these arguments in turn, beginning with a look at crypto Judaism. In the twelfth and thirteenth centuries, the peak of the Sephardic Golden Age, there were approximately 250 Jewish communities of various sizes in Sefarad. Yet, by the last days before the expulsion in 1492, persecution, conversion pressures and violent attacks had greatly diminished this number. The estimated number of Jews leaving Spain in August, 1492 ranges from a low of 40,000 to Isaac Abravanel's figure of 200,000.[4] Of these, the largest group fled across the border into Portugal, where, three years later, they were forcibly baptized and declared Christian. We have seen how only a very few could manage to leave that country before the mass conversion of 1497. Jews who stayed behind had no resources to help them practice their ancestral religion in secret. There were no rabbis, Torahs, prayer books, bibles, *yeshivas* or formal religious study opportunities. There could be no open observance of *Shabbat*, including washing of self, cleaning of household and abstention from work. Even not eating pork held one up to the possibility of servants or neighbors reporting *judaizante* behavior to the authorities.

Across the border in Spain, thousands of New Christians faced the same kind of reality, forcing them to end customary Jewish practices or observe them in secret. As the centuries passed, *halahka,* or observing Judaism as interpreted by the prophets and sages, disappeared, due to the lack of nurturing resources. What survived was passed along through the generations by word of mouth, and became more and more syncretic, blending influences from the Christian environment with the traditional practices of Sephardic Judaism.

David Gitlitz's monumental study, *Secrecy and Deceit,* reveals the ingenuity of secret Jews, who were outwardly Christian, in maintaining even a slight emotional or spiritual connection with their ancestral religion.[5] In *Hidden Heritage: The Legacy of the Crypto-Jews,* Sociologist Janet Jacobs tells us how women helped preserve what practices and prayers survived for over five hundred years, although these differed from their original forms.[6] Other scholars present recent research from the American Southwest, particularly Stanley M. Hordes.[7]

Benito Garzon, former Chief Rabbi of Spain, reports coming across the phenomenon described when he tried to purchase some land in his country. The seller, whom the rabbi presumed to be Christian, told him that there were specific dates in the fall of that year when he would not be available to schedule an appointment to arrange the sale. The rabbi asked why, and was told that the seller took part in a customary card game with his friends on those days. Rabbi Garzon checked his calendar and found that the dates were the same as Rosh Hashanah and Yom Kippur, the Jewish New Year and Day of Atonement. He then asked the seller on what dates they had observed this custom the previous year, and found them also corresponding with the Jewish high holidays. The tradition, found to this day throughout the Spanish-speaking world where crypto Jews settled, allows men to observe these days secretly. They keep prayer books open on their laps while appearing to play, so that passersby, such as police, servants or neighbors, assume they are engrossed in friendly games. The practice has also been reported in Mexico. And it continues well past the prohibition of Jewish practice.[8]

To this day, Spanish-speaking people in Northern New Mexico, many of whom descend from sixteenth and seventeenth century New Christians, call cards *barajas,* instead of *naipe* or *cartas.* In a letter to the editor of the *Chronicle,* publication of the Jewish Historical Society of Southern Arizona, writer and researcher Emma Moya comments on a talk given by historian Arthur Benveniste. Rabbi Garzon had related the story of the cards to Benveniste, who had passed it on in his talk.

> Mr. Benveniste refers to Sephardic families playing cards while deterring away any suspicion of their practice of hidden Judaism. In Nuevo Mexico, cards are called BA_RA_JAS. In other southwestern areas, the cards are referred to as

Nine. Endurance, Persistence and Identity 185

In Sandoval County, New Mexico, a grave is marked by a wooden cross and a six-pointed star. It is believed that many Spanish settlers from the late fifteenth century were *conversos*, moving into the northern reaches of New Spain, now New Mexico, to put distance between themselves and the Inquisition. (©2003 Cary Herz. *New Mexico's Crypto Jews: Image and Memory* [Albuquerque: University of New Mexico Press, 2007], 85.

> CARTAS. Our Academia Hebraeica, in Alburquerque, had researched and recorded the following information.... The word BARAHA or BARAJA alludes to the word BARAHAH (prayer). Our ancestors, including our Sephardic grandparents, cleverly hid their home prayers, away from the Catholic Church, and its members.

This would seem to indicate some ancestral Jewish connection, however distant, for the players.[9]

In *The Mezuzah in the Madonna's Foot,* Trudi Alexy writes of encounters with hidden Jews, some of them Catholic priests prominent in Spanish and Latin American society, who are, for all intents and purposes, devout Christians.[10] In *The Marrano Legacy,* she publishes her letters with a South American Catholic priest whose family had long practiced Judaism in secret, and had entered the priesthood in the *converso* tradition. It has been the practice for many New Christian families to give a son to the church to divert attention from their hidden observances or away from anything "suspicious" in family behavior.[11]

One can go online for instant retrieval of more anecdotes and vignettes by those of Christian background searching for possible Jewish roots and how they first suspected they might have this ancestry. At *http://www.cryptojews.com*, one finds an archive of articles that have been published since 1997, in the quarterly publication *HaLapid,* The Torch, of the Society for Crypto-Judaic Studies. Some are first person accounts from individuals of Hispanic background who discovered their Jewish roots. Others are reports from scholars such as historians, anthropologists, sociologists and folklorists of contemporary research in the field.[12]

Http://www.saudades.com is a website about Portuguese crypto Jews throughout the world, where one can read their stories of searching, discovery and decision making. Subscribing to *http://www.saudades-sefarad@yahoogroups.com* will bring daily email on the subject from other subscribers.[13] On *http://www.sephardim.com,* one finds lists of Sephardic names culled from archives, research and cemeteries, which searchers use to help determine the origin of family names.[14]

Many of the individuals who find clues indicating that they have Jewish roots will insist that no one in their families had told them, or even hinted, about the ancestry they now suspect. Some assert that "I always knew" or "Now I know what I was seeking all this time." Others report a personal history of choosing mostly Jewish friends, long before their discovery. One may ask how the "knowing" of Jewish roots could have lasted over five hundred years, in environments swept clean of rabbis, synagogues, Jewish education, without bibles or prayer books, prayer shawls, *kippahs* or *yarmulkes,* where Jewish holidays have not been observed openly and where many of the individuals claim no prior knowledge of Jewish ancestors.

These are the people whose primogenitors "lost" their link with the ancestral religion through the centuries and who have connected once again despite tangible evidence, with logic to the contrary. They are found wherever the exiles from expulsion and Inquisition found their way. And they are found even in Spain and Portugal. As early as 1917, a Polish engineer working for the Portuguese government stopped in the village of Belmonte during his travels in the mountainous north. Through a series of happenstance coincidences, Samuel Schwarz discovered that New Christians there had been practicing Judaism secretly for over five hundred years, since the forced conversions of their ancestors in 1497. Later he published an account of his findings in *Os Cristãos Novos no Século XX,* New Christians of the Twentieth Century. In November, 1965, Brazilian researcher Anita Novinsky and Portuguese researcher-writer Amilcar Paolo visited Belmonte. Their observations were published in the article, "The Last *Marranos,*" in *Commentary.*[15] There have been other scholars and observers, who have visited the small community in northern Portugal, and chronicled the return to observant Judaism by

In the northern Portuguese village of Belmonte, a community of New Christians continued to observe Judaism in secret for over 500 years, holding hidden Sabbath and holiday services until returning to the open practice of their ancestral religion in the last half of the twentieth century. In December, 1996, the community dedicated Synagogue Beth Eliahu and a Jewish cemetery. A museum has also been established to mark the continuity of Judaic practice. (©1994 Cary Herz.)

the Belmonte New Christians following the demise of the Salazar government, their interactions with rabbis, the building of a synagogue and museum, and the effects on them and their community.

Belmonte is only one of the places in Portugal where Jews are emerging into recognition of their identity. In Lisbon, a community of crypto Jews has found a spiritual home in Ohel Yaacov, the tent of Jacob, a synagogue that had been established after World War I by German and Polish refugees and was no longer active. Under their leadership, the energetic congregation has affiliated with the Conservative movement. In the city of Porto, Ladina, "a Portuguese based registered non-profit society dedicated to rescuing the memory and culture of the Portuguese Jewish people," holds regular seminars on cultural and historical subjects and has an active website.[16]

On a cold December night in 1996, a program at Lisbon's grand Teatro Nacional D. Maria II attempted to come to terms with the historical fact of the expulsion. In the very building that once held prisoners of the Inquisition, a musical and literary program titled *Memoría e Reencontro* observed the 500th anniversary of the edict expelling the Jews from Portugal. The program was funded by a local bank and an electric utility company.[17]

In neighboring Spain, as well, there is growing awareness of the Jewish ancestry in much of the population. The Spanish tourism office is paying increased attention to directing visitors to sites with Jewish history, along with guidebooks for background.[18] And, on March 31, 1991, King Juan Carlos cancelled the Edict of Expulsion on the 500-year anniversary of its existence.[19]

Meanwhile, in the American southwest, growing interest in the subject was given special attention in the 1990s by a series of radio documentaries titled "The Hidden Jews of New Mexico."[20] Aired on National Public Radio, the programs, along with conferences and feature stories in the press, helped fuel the emergence of individuals with Hispanic backgrounds, many with ancestors who came to the region as early as the late sixteenth century, suspecting or claiming to have Jewish roots. As reported earlier, *HaLapid*, quarterly publication of the Society for Crypto-Judaic Studies, has published personal accounts of individual experiences, also available on the Society's website.[21] The Society was founded in 1991.

We have been reviewing the phenomenon of crypto–Judaism in communities with Hispanic background. Now we will learn how, much as Samuel Schwarz "discovered" the hidden Jewish Belmonte community in 1917, scholars and others have, by coincidence or academic search, come upon non–Hispanic groups far afield who claim descendency from ancient peoples of Israel. These communities have a long oral tradition of Jewish belief and practice. Their conscious Judaism is a continuous stream, which appears to flow directly from the Babylonian exile in the first century CE or the Roman diaspora after that. Among these, the Lemba people of South Africa, Zimbabwe and Mozambique are better known than others because of contemporary media attention to their genealogy. For thousands of years, tribal members, who number between 50,000 and 70,000, have maintained that the tribe was led out of ancient Judea to Yemen. In a magazine interview, Matshaya Mathivha, immediate past president of the Lemba Cultural Association, now deceased, described how they made their way south through Africa.

> One group went to Ethiopia, and others moved down the east coast, between Tanzania and Malawi, to become the ancestors of today's Lemba. We ritually slaughter our cattle, we only eat fish with scales, we do not mix meat with milk.

"But unfortunately, during colonial times," continued Professor Mathivha, in an interview in *The Scribe—Journal of Babylonian Jewry*, "the missionaries in Africa forced many to learn the New Testament, as the only way to receive an education was in their schools."

Throughout the apartheid years, when people of color were separated from whites in South Africa, the Lemba bore double persecution as blacks and coloreds and for calling themselves Jews. Now they have a synagogue in the community of Louis Trichardt near the border with Zimbabwe.

"Whether we are accepted or not, Israel is our ancestral home and the Jewish people are our brothers," Mathivha said, adding that he and others would, if necessary, accept the need for formal conversion to Judaism. "It would confirm what our forefathers had said."

The Lemba became international news when DNA testing showed them having the same markers as Cohanim, descendents of the priestly tribe of Israel, strengthening their claim of Jewish ancestry. Before this, they were rejected by most Jewish congregations in their region.[22]

In India, a subcontinent away from the Lemba, the Bnei Menashe, claiming Jewish direct descent as a lost tribe of Israel, have impressed Western visitors with their commitment to Judaism. They live in the northeastern Indian states of Mizoram and Manipur, with a smaller number in Assam and Myanmar. In 2002, an Israeli team of rabbis visited the community in Mizoram, joining one hundred members of the congregation of Aizawl in prayer, led by the group's chief cantor, Eliezer Sela.

Five of Sela's nine children now live in Israel, and the patriarch hopes to join them. "I can't wait to go to Israel, the land of my forefathers," he says. "We pray for its well-being every day."

There are an estimated 4,500 Bnei Menashe living in the four Indian states. They belong to the Mizo and Kuki tribes, and have preserved belief of descent from the lost Israelite tribe of Manasseh, exiled by the Assyrians in

723 BCE. Their tradition holds that they migrated to China, then Burma, and finally into northeast India. In the nineteenth century, they were converted by Christian missionaries, who were astonished to discover their belief in one god.

In the 1970s, some of them expressed a desire to return to their ancestral religion, and began to live according to *halakha*, following Judaic practice in as strict a way as possible. They have been in communication with Rabbi Eliyahu Avichail, former Director of Amishav, an Israeli organization that supports returnees to Judaism. He believes that the Bnei Menashe's origins are authentically Jewish. "As I studied the community and learned about its ancient beliefs, I could not help but conclude that they are in fact descended from the tribe of Menashe," he says. "They have ancient songs and chants with words from the bible. For centuries their children have been taught to sing, *Litenten Zion*, which means "Let Us Go to Zion," even though they had no idea what Zion was.

"There is simply too much similarity between their customs and ours for it to be coincidental," he adds, citing as examples a lunar calendar, rites of mourning and laws of family purity. The rabbi reports on an interview he and a colleague, Rabbi Shlomo Riskin, had with a 65-year-old Bnei Menashe named Yossi Hualngo. The latter chanted songs he learned from his uncle, who sang them long ago during sacrificial ceremonies. The listening rabbis were astonished to hear the words of one song refer to Shiloh, the capital of the twelve Israeli tribes before their conquest by the Assyrians.

"If anyone doubts the tremendous power of the Jewish soul, if anyone questions the magnificent strength of Jewish traditions, if anyone for one moment would question the eternity of the Jewish people, this proves its strength," the amazed Rabbi Riskin declared. "For me, it is surrealistic.... I am in India, near the Burmese border, ... and here are what appears [sic] to be contented Jews living a very Jewish life and having one real hope and dream: to come to Israel as soon as possible and rejoin their people."[23]

The Bnei Menashe and the Lemba are but two examples of emerging "lost" Jews. In Kaifeng, China, a Jewish community was established over 1,000 years ago. There, a synagogue, begun in 1163, stood for 700 years. Unlike diaspora tales elsewhere, the Jews in China met with no discrimination, became prosperous and soon rose to high positions in civil service, trade and positions. They erected stone monuments in Kaifeng on which were inscribed their history. Two of these are on display in the city's Municipal Museum.

The Kaifeng Jews embody a cautionary tale that holds promise. Successful and accepted as residents, they intermarried with the local population and were assimilated, abandoned Judaic practice, and seemed to forget their customs and history. Shi Lei, a descendant who is attempting to learn about his culture, reports that a present-day study by the Kaifeng museum discovered 300 residents who identified themselves as Jewish. He is quick to point out, however, that there is nothing like a Jewish community existing at present, as connections have been lost over the centuries: "Every Jewish family in Kaifeng, every family is an orphan, an island in a lake, so this family has no connection with that family and they don't know each other," he explains, telling how people from his clan, the Shi, visit his grandparents to meet each other. "So you can see it is only about individuals." He stresses the influence of foreign Jewish visitors in bringing together representatives from different families. "So through this, we get to know more and more Jewish descendants in the city."[24]

In Uganda, in west central Africa, a different scenario is unfolding, unlike that of the Lemba and Bnei Menashe who trace their ancestry to biblical era Hebrews, or the Kaifeng Jews whose origins are documented. The Abayudaya have no historical roots in Judaism, yet in February 2002, more than 300 members, or over one-half of the tribe, converted. Abayudaya means People of Judah. They have been practicing as Jews since about 1919, when their leader, Semei Kakungulu, was inspired by biblical studies and meditation to lead his people into their new religion. At first, they observed the laws as written in the bible, later adding some *halahkic* rituals learned from visiting Jews.

The Abayudaya, then, are modern converts, beginning their Jewish observance in the twentieth century. But like the Lemba, they have been persecuted for their pursuit of Judaism. They suffered during the dictatorship of Idi Amin in the 1970's, during which Judaism was banned. They were able to resume open practice when Amin's regime ended.

In February 1999, the tribe was converted by a visiting *beit din* of four rabbis from the Conservative movement of the United States and Israel. This followed conversion in the United States of Abayudaya leaders Gershom Sizomu and JJ Keki, after a semester of studies at Hebrew Union College. A rabbi at the tribal conversion, Howard Gorin of Tikvat Congregation, Rockville, MD, reports he is "incredibly impressed that people in the middle of Third World poverty still maintain their Judaism to the extent that they do." And, like the Lemba, they have done so in spite of hostile treatment as recently as the 1980's from established Ugandan Jewish congregations, as well as from Christians and Muslims.[25]

Many thousands of miles away from Africa, in Tijuana, Mexico, is a related example of a congregation where most are converts to Judaism with no Hebraic roots, reports Hilda M. Nuñez, in the *Los Angeles Times*.

Carlos Samuel Salas is religious leader of Congregación Hebrea de Baja California, a synagogue made up of converts to Judaism, only 12 to 14 percent of whom are descendents of *anusim*, or Jews forced to convert to Christianity. He founded the synagogue in 1975, thirteen years after his formal conversion at the University of Judaism in 1962. In the interim, he had moved to Tijuana and was offering bible study classes. When his students desired conversion, it was carried out in the United States at American Jewish University, which the University of Judaism is now called. In 1984, twenty-two individuals were converted, followed by two more groups in the early 90's. Subsequent conversions have been conducted in the Tijuana synagogue, housed in its own building near the Mexican–U.S. border, and carried out by a *beit din* of three rabbis from Los Angeles. Salas' classes in theology are based mainly on the bible, emphasizing the first five books, which constitute the Torah, Judaism's religious foundation. He reports how "eager" students are "to learn about the bible."

"They never studied the bible in the Catholic religion. They started to develop an interest to learn Judaism as I started to offer courses." Salas, often addressed as Rabbi although not formally ordained, denies that he is proselytizing, a taboo in Judaism.

"I don't believe in going out into the streets and seeking students and members," he says. "If people are sincere and they want to learn, we open our doors."

His approach is supported by Rabbi Mimi Weisel, assistant dean of the Ziegler School of Rabbinic Studies at American Jewish University. "It is creating an awareness in the community. Anyone is welcome to learn about another culture — about another way of living in the world," she believes.

More than one hundred thirty families, converted during the past twenty years, observe their faith in the synagogue, built with Salas' personal funds. Owner of a newspaper, *La Opinión de Baja California,* and a successful businessman, he continues to support the congregation financially, with no fees required for services or classes, although a donation box is present.

"What he's doing is very good for people who join his congregation," according to Rabbi Edward M. Tenenbaum, Chairman of Los Angeles' Westside Rabbinical Assembly, and member of the *beit din* that converted members of the Tijuana temple. "These are people who didn't have a spiritual home and they found a home in Judaism."

Temple member Francisco Madero attributes Salas' classes with meeting his need for knowledge in his spiritual search: "I felt a restlessness," explains Madero, who was once a Catholic altar boy in Nayarit. "It was that same restlessness that led me to study various religions. In Judaism, I found the root of the religions and I found myself."[26]

Communities like Rabbi Salas' and the Abayudaya go largely unreported and are scarcely known to the general public. Some other examples of congregations where members are largely converted Jews without Hebrew roots

Nine. Endurance, Persistence and Identity 193

exist in Vera Cruz, Mexico and in Peru. Rabbi Samuel Lehrer of San Antonio, Texas, now deceased, provided religious instruction and the conversion process for those wanting it, in the city on Mexico's east coast, where a synagogue bears his name. Formerly rabbi of an English-speaking Mexico City congregation, he visited frequently, also conducting *bar* and *bat mitzvah* for congregational members. Likewise, American Rabbi Jacques Cukerkorn has conducted conversions for congregations in Peru and Brazil, where many members are not returning Jews.[27] These are Jews by choice, not by bloodline legacy. They have elected to cast their religious identities with a minority religion which is scorned at the very least, persecuted and massacred at the very worst. To become Jews, they study the fundamentals and *halakha* of Judaism, and in almost all cases, undergo conversion by a *beit din*. They take observance seriously, unlike many coreligionists who elect a more casual, informal approach.

In a *Los Angeles Times* article, Daniel J. Wakin reports on varying estimates on the numbers of American Jews. The National Jewish Population Survey, conducted by the United Jewish Communities in 2002, found the number of Jews to be 5.2 million, declining 300,000 from the previous decade, and aging, with women bearing children at later ages. UJC is an umbrella group of Jewish communities and federations.

The survey met with criticism from others who also study U.S. Jewish populations. One of these is the Institute for Jewish and Community Research in San Francisco, whose Director, Gary Tobin, characterized the report as "utter nonsense." He believes that the UJC survey failed to take into account those who decline to say they are Jewish from fear of anti–Semitism. He points out that those who live on the West coast and immigrant Jews were not included in the sample. His survey claims there are 6.7 million American Jews, or 1.5 million more than UJC's survey claims.[28]

Another study, released around the same time by the Glenmary Research Center, estimates the number of Jews at 6.1 million, which, while 600,000 fewer than Tobin's survey, was almost one million more than UJC's. The figure is based on estimates from community leaders throughout the country, and the Center credits the UJC study with being more scientific.[29]

The different figures arrived at by the three organizations, and their varied approaches, is illuminating, going right to the heart of this chapter's core question: Who and what is a Jew? Dr. Tobin's definition includes those who listed no religion but said they had ethnic or cultural roots in Judaism, and those who listed no religion but said they had a Jewish upbringing, a Jewish parent, or had previously observed Judaism. The UJC survey included those with a Jewish parent or upbringing who did not list themselves as Jews, but not the other categories in the Tobin or Glenmary studies. The surveys with the most liberal definitions of Jewishness arrived at the highest population figures.

Is the label of "Jew" only to be applied to those who are in the orthodox category of conversion and observance? Does it mean all those with synagogue membership and those without, who attend services occasionally and during high holidays? Or is it a term of ethnic origin, which clings to the individual like a chronic condition, regardless of his or her conscious self description? How we answer this will influence how we answer the larger question driving this chapter: Is Judaism here to stay, or is it disappearing?

In *Saving Remnants, Feeling Jewish in America,* authors Sara Bershtel and Allen Graubard quote first person accounts from individuals who, despite either indifference to, or ignorance of, their Jewish past, acknowledge how it influences their daily lives and is still a part of who they are. These are people of accomplishment — writers, businesspersons, educators, etc. They have been totally immersed in the American landscape of opportunity, have made the most of possibilities for achievement, and move comfortably among the non–Jewish establishment today. Yet their first person accounts tell us of Judaic remnants that just won't go away, no matter how much they present themselves to the outer world as not Jewish. For them, Judaism is a chronic condition.

The authors examine the concept of assimilation, putting it in a historic context. They describe it as taking place mostly among second generation Jewish Americans. Their children, the third generation, are the inheritors of that decision, not its initiators. Many of the parents of today's adults, the first generation of American-born Jews, were raised in Orthodox homes and were forced to attend Hebrew and Sunday School, which most of them did not enjoy. They vowed not to repeat that with their children, the young and not-so-young adults of today, who have inherited their parents' decision to assimilate.

The second and subsequent generations, therefore, know they are ethnically Jews, but have neither the training nor knowledge to tie themselves to the ancestral faith. So they explore, ask questions. They have choices about what paths to take. Do they fit the definition of Jews? Are they included in the population for Jewish census polls? Should they be considered Jews? This brings us back to the question raised earlier about who is a Jew and whether active observance is the touchstone.

This is not to deny some of the problematic aspects of assimilation, among them loss of a meaningful connection to community and all that means. It is observed, however, that even among the assimilated — those absorbed into the dominant culture with little or no awareness of seasonal markers or issues — stirs a Jewish consciousness, however much submerged. Bershtel and Graubard tell us that

The episodic but intense involvement with Jewishness and Jewish identification found among the unaffiliated is at odds with the traditional paradigm of assimilation, which emphasizes the abandonment of identification and repression of Jewish connection ... the traditional "either-or" construction does not capture the contemporary nature of either assimilation or identification today....

Currently, the millions of unaffiliated Jewish-Americans, along with other hyphenated Americans, find themselves in a historically unprecedented situation, where nostalgia for a lost world coexists easily with integration into the larger culture, and where feeling ethnic requires no communal affiliation.[30]

There appears to be a stubborn persistence of the Jewish connection. Although threatened by intermarriage and assimilation, and shadowed by the common memory of persecution, massacre, expulsion and holocaust, Judaism seems determined to surface again and again, within the old structures as well as from unsuspected sources outside. This is supported by the emergence of more and more individuals world-wide, previously hidden as crypto Jews, the persistence of self-identification among populations claiming descent from lost tribes of Israel, and the conversion of groups with no Jewish roots but with serious commitment to Jewish spiritual life.

"It's hogwash to lament the demise of the Jewish people when there may be millions of people who want 'in' and we refuse to deal with them," claims Rabbi Moshe Cotel, who was part of the *beit din* that converted the Abayudaya.[31] Since the conversions were conducted by Conservative rabbis, the Orthodox rabbinate denies their validity, as it does the conversion of the Tijuana congregation members, also beneficiaries of Conservative conversions.

In an article in *The New York Jewish Week,* Gary Rosenblatt writes that the Arab population of Israel, "now about 20 percent, is increasing more rapidly than its Jewish numbers." He asks, "...why do we and the rest of the Jewish world, consumed as we are with bolstering our numbers, turn a deaf ear to the tens of thousands of people — maybe far more — in India, Peru, Africa, Japan, Spain, Burma and other exotic places who claim to be part of our people and long to settle in Israel?"[32] Following in that vein, Eliahu Salpeter, writing in *Haaretz,* English-language Israeli newspaper, warns that "The Jewish demographic future in Israel, as well in the United States and the former Soviet Union, largely depends on how the community chooses to deal with the hundreds of thousands of people who are not Jewish by *halakha* but who have linked their destiny to the Jewish peoples through marriage or immigration."[33]

More recent testimony to the seemingly countless ways individuals identify themselves with Judaism can be found in *I Am Jewish: Personal Reflections Inspired by the Last Words of Daniel Pearl.* Pearl was kidnapped and murdered by a terrorist organization in Pakistan while on the job as a reporter for *The Wall Street Journal*. His final words, captured on a video made by his captors before his death, were "My father is Jewish, my mother is Jewish, I am Jewish." His parents, Judea and Ruth Pearl, gathered responses from almost 150 individuals of Jewish background to the question "What do you mean when you say 'I am Jewish?'" Respondents were prominent individuals, including, but not limited to United States Supreme Court Justices and the Lord Chief Justice of England and Wales; U.S. Senators and university presidents and professors; TV personalities, film directors, actors and comedians; theologians and rabbis; architects and engineers; CEOs and bankers; community organizers and service leaders; and musicians, composers and artists of varied genres. Widely recognized names pop up from the pages, such as Larry King, Mike Wallace, Ruth Bader Ginsburg, Kirk Douglas, Peter Yarrow, Natan Sharansky, Nadine Gordimer, Vidal Sasoon and Jackie Mason. Also represented throughout are youth from ages ten to eighteen.[34]

The replies seem almost as varied as the almost one hundred fifty indi-

The caretaker of Museo Luso-Hebraico in Tomar, Portugal, shows a visitor the remains of a fifteenth-century *mikveh*, or ceremonial bath, next to an ancient synagogue now housing the museum. After the forced conversion of Jews in 1497, synagogues were given to Catholic organizations or churches and many passed into private hands. Some are being restored today as historic sites. (©Beth Hatefutsoth, Photo Archive, Tel Aviv. Visual Documentation Center, Beth Hatefutsoth, Tel Aviv. Courtesy of Isaac Ike Bitton, U.S.A.)

The medieval synagogue in Tomar, Portugal has been restored and now marks the Jewish presence in the region as Museo Luso-Hebraico. (©1994 Cary Herz.)

viduals featured. The editors organized them by five categories: Identity; Heritage; Covenant, Chosenness and Faith; Humanity and Ethnicity; and *Tikkun Olam* (Repairing the World) and Justice.[35] Only one — Covenant, Chosenness and Faith — falls under what one respondent called "the holy traditions of Judaism," or religious belief relating to Jewish texts, performance of *halahka*, and relations with God.[36] The editors describe this section as covering "Our relationship to God, our understanding of the relationship between God and the Jewish people, and our understanding of Judaism as a religion."[37] Only thirty-five persons out of one hundred forty-nine, or a little less than one fourth, of those questioned, related their sense of Jewishness directly to religious observance or theology. The rest presented themselves in more secular and cultural terms, such as involvement with, and concern for, fellow humans; issues of belonging to and inheriting tradition, culture and ethnicity; and questions of inner life and values. There were one hundred forty-nine differing views of who and what is a Jew. The answers reveal a resiliency in Judaism that helps it survive because those claiming it declare their ownership, no matter how much their definitions of it may differ or others try to deny them a place in the tent.[38]

Returning, then, to the issue framed in the early pages of this chapter, one asks again if the current concern about the endurance of Judaism, debated so hotly, is a crisis or a challenge. Surely, the Spanish and Portuguese Sephardic Jews in fifteenth and sixteenth century Spain and Portugal were a people whose religion and traditions were in crisis. Their communities dismembered, themselves dispersed and largely impoverished by expulsion or decimated and terrified by the Inquisition, the challenge was to survive. Studies of Sephardim in the post-expulsion diaspora reveal that they did, indeed survive, although fewer in numbers and scattered. Clearly, the oil lamps and candles, some kindled in secret, cast a strong light and protective shadow through the centuries. So does the insistence of those such as today's Lemba and Abayudaya, who, threatened by apartheid and persecution, have also kept the flame burning. Returning to Isaac Abravanel's predictions of the eternality of the Jew and the diminution of those who persecute him and her, we take to heart words on that subject by non–Jewish writer Mark Twain, published in *Harper's* in 1899, over a century ago.

> He [the Jew] has made a marvelous fight in this world in all the ages, and has done it with his hands tied behind him. He could be vain of himself and be excused for it. The Egyptians, the Babylonians, and the Persians rose, filled the planet with sound and splendor, and faded to dream stuff and passed away.
> The Greeks and the Romans followed and made a vast noise and they are gone. Other peoples have sprung up and held their torch high for a time. But it burned out, and they sit in twilight now, or have vanished. The Jew saw them

all. Beat them all, and is now what he always was, exhibiting no decadence, no infirmities of age, no weakening of his parts, no slowing of his energies, no dulling of his alert and aggressive mind.

Twain ends his article with a timeless quote, bolstering what is epitomized by today's Sephardim, the crypto Jews, the Lemba, and other ethnic, tribal or national groups, whose *neshama,* or Jewish soul, emerges from the ashes or from seemingly nowhere. This appears to validate Abravanel and others that Judaism is not about to pass away. Mark Twain has the final word: "All things are mortal but the Jew. All other forces pass, but he remains."[39]

Appendix: Judah Abravanel to His Son

Judah, Isaac Abravanel's son, fled to Naples with his father and other members of the family at the time of the expulsion. He became known as Leone Ebreo, respected physician, philosopher and poet and author of *Dialoghi di Amore*, Dialogues on Love, published in Venice in 1545 (see Chapter Two).

In the poem that follows, Judah Abravanel mourns the loss of his young son, whom he had sent to Portugal in 1492 to avoid kidnapping by agents of the king. Fernando had hoped that taking the youngster would force Judah and Don Isaac to convert and remain in the country so he could continue to benefit from their services. In Portugal, the child was swept up in the efforts by João and Manoel to convert all Jews to Catholicism (see Chapter Two). Judah knew who was caring for the youngster in the following years, and this letter may have actually been sent to him.

The following translation by Raymond P. Scheindlin, professor of medieval Hebrew literature, Jewish Theological Seminary of America (copyright 2007), was made from the Hebrew text published in *Mivhar hashira ha'ivrit b'italya* by Hayim Schirmann (Berlin, 1934), pages 216–222. It appeared in "Judah Abravanel to His Son," an article by Dr. Scheindlin in *Judaism*, Vol. 41 (1992), pages 190–99.

> Time with his pointed shafts has hit my heart
> and split my gut, laid open my entrails,
> landed me a blow that will not heal,
> knocked me down, left me in lasting pain.
> Time wounded me, wasted away my flesh,
> used up my blood and fat in suffering,
> ground my bones to meal, and rampaged, leapt,
> attacked me like a lion in his rage.

He did not stop at whirling me around,
exiling me while yet my days were green,
sending me stumbling, drunk, to roam the world,
spinning me dizzy round about its edge —
so that I've spent two decades on the move
without my horses ever catching breath —
so that my palms have measured oceans,
weighed the dust of continents —
so that my spring is spent —
no, that was not enough:
He chased my friends from me, exiled
my age-mates, sent my family far
so that I never see a face I know —
father, mother, brothers, or a friend.
He scattered everyone I care for northward,
eastward, or to the west, so that
I have no rest from constant thinking, planning —
and never a moment's peace, for all my plans.
Now that I see my future in the East,
their separation clutches at my heels.
My foot is turned to go, but my heart's at sea;
I can't tell forward from behind.
Yes, Time —
my bear, my wolf! — ate up my heart,
cleft it in two and cut it into bits,
so that it aches with groaning, panic, plunder,
confiscation, loss, captivity.
But even this was not enough for him; he also seeks
to snuff my spark, exterminate my line.

Two sons were born to me, two splendid sons,
two precious, noble, handsome boys.
The younger I named Samuel. Time,
my watchful overseer, confiscated him,
struck him down, just five years old,
and all that grew from him was misery.
The elder I called Isaac Abravanel,
after the quarry where I myself was hewn,
after one of Israel's greats, his grandfather,
a man a match for David, Lamp unto the West.
At birth I saw that he was good,
his heart a fitting site for wisdom, apt
repository for the goods
his forebears handed down through me.
He was just one year old — alas! — when Time,
the enemy ever at my heels, took him away.

Judah Abravanel to His Son

The day the King of Spain expelled the Jews
he ordered that a watch be set for me
so that I not slip away through mountain passes,
and that my child, still nursing, should be seized
and brought into his faith on his behalf.
A good man got word to me in time, a friend;
I sent him with his wet-nurse in the dark
of midnight — just like smuggled goods! —
to Portugal, then ruled by a wicked king
who earlier had nearly ruined me.
For in his father's time — a worthy king! —
my father had achieved success and wealth.
Then this one followed him, a grasping thing,
a man but with the cravings of a dog.
His courtiers and his brother schemed revolt.
He thwarted them and killed his brother; then,
alleging that my father was with them,
he tried to kill him too! But God,
the Rider of the clouds, preserved his life.
My father fled to Castile, home of my ancestors,
my family's source. But as for me,
The King seized all my gold and silver,
took as forfeit everything I owned.

Now, seeing that my child was in his land,
and learning that I planned
to join my father's house in Italy,
the King detained my child and gave command
that none should send my stray lamb back to me.
After he died a foolish king arose,
fanatical and hollow in head,
who violated all the House of Jacob,
turned my noble people to his faith.
Many killed themselves, rather than
Transgress the Law of God, our help in need.
My darling boy was taken, and his good name,
the name of the rock from which I was hewn, changed!
He's twelve years old; I haven't seen him since —
so are my sins repaid!
I rage, but only at myself;
there's no one else but me to bear the blame.
I chased him from mere troubles to a trap,
I drove him from mere sparks into a flame.
I hope to see him, heartsick with my endless hope.

O dear gazelle! What makes you tarry so?
Why do you thus crush a father's heart?
Why do you aim your arrows at my inmost parts?

Why do you dim the light by sending clouds
and make the shining seem like night to me?
The moon is always darkened in my sight,
my star is blotted out by clouds;
no sun's ray ever penetrates my home,
or crosses my doorsill to reach my beams.
My roses never bloom on Sharon's plain,
my grasses never feel the driving rain.
You steal my very sleep with the thought of you —
am I sleeping or awake? I cannot tell.
I cannot touch my food, for even honey stings,
and sweets taste venomous to me.
Miserably I nibble coal-burnt crusts,
moistening with tears my dried-out bread.
My only drink is water mixed with tears;
the blood of grapes does not come near my mouth.
I'm drunk with nothing more than water,
like a Nazirite or one of Rechab's sons.

But when I dream of your return, and when
I picture in my mind's eye how you look,
how good my fortune seems! The rose returns
to dress my cheek in sanguine once again.
I sleep and find sleep sweet; I wake
refreshed, delighting in your lingering image.
The water that I drink is sweet, and even earth
tastes sweet when I imagine you are here.
But when I think about our separation,
heat blasts my heart, a desert wind within.
I seem like one dismayed or in a faint,
diminished somehow and reduced in size.
The thought of you is joy to me and pain,
tonic and torment are from you, balm and bane.
I have your image graven on my heart,
but also our separation in my core,
and any joy your image brings to me
cannot outweigh the reproach your absence speaks.
Your absence frustrates all my plans,
your exile blocks, diverts my roads.
For you my pride is humbled and my
dignity has fled. I who was a cypress
now am overtopped by sycamores,
and hyssops rise above my cedar trees;
Bats fly higher than my hawks;
far above my eagles soars the fly;
My arms and legs are weaker than a boy's;
a lamb can throw my lions easily.

I've even turned on poetry, smashed
my lute and hung my lyre upon the willow boughs.
My song has turned to mourning and my flute
moans like an echo from within the tomb.
My swallows hoot like owls, my turtledoves
howl like jackals, and my pigeons crow.
I cannot bear the palaces of kings;
I only yearn to be a hermit in the wild.
My son! Your banishment has breached me, broken me.
It crushes me and blocks me from all sides.
It fills my heart with faintness, fills my thoughts
with rage, fills my bones with rot!
And every day I have to hear your mother
wailing, crying, "Darling, tender sprout!
Who was the man who stole you from my breast,
who made a foundling of my body's fruit?"

When I could not bear it any more,
or hide the suffering that plagued me too,
I left her and went off to serve my king
whom God had made my benefactor.
And so I shift and wander, so I roam
among the Edomites, nation of the flames,
never finding healing for my hurt.
For who can turn Time just,
Time, who makes me roam the world in shame.
I cannot bear my futile days and nights;
Death would be my choice, if choice were mine.
Life lies heavy on me: days weigh
like sacks of sea-sand on my back.
What profit is there in my wretched life?
Why wait out the time alotted me?
To a bitter man, life itself is death.
I've had enough; this little is too much!
Why should I hope for length of life and years of joy,
when Time is lurking, raging like a cub-reft bear?
The days are arrows, and the Bow on high
is in the hands of Time, that master archer;
the target is myself. The wheel
on which Time turns has me as pole.

Let me go back to speaking to my boy,
for that will make him leave off hurting me.
Now pay attention, son: Know that you
descend from scholars, men with minds
developed to the point of prophecy.
Wisdom is your heritage, so do not waste
your boyhood, precious boy.

Think of your studies as pleasure: learning Scripture,
conning the commentators, memorizing *Mishna*,
reasoning out the Talmud with the Thirteen Principles,
guided by the glosses of the ancient Schools...
— But how can I control myself when *he* is lost?
That is the thought that sickens, strangles, slashes
me; that is the razor, sharper than any barber's
blade, that rips the membrane of my aching heart,
that brings into my miserable heart
into my very gut the flaming sword:
To whom will I hand on my scholarship?
To whom can I pour the nectar from my vines?
Who will taste and eat the fruit of all my learning,
of my books, when I am gone?
Who will penetrate the mysteries
my father put into his sacred books?
Who will slake his thirst at my father's well?
Who will drink at all in this time of drought?
Who will pluck the blooms of my own garden,
hew and harvest my own wisdom's tree?
Who will take my undone works in hand?
Who will weave my writings' woof and warp?
Who will wear the emblem of my faith
when once I die?
Who will mount my mule or ride my coach? —
Only you, my soul's delight, my heir,
the pledge for everything I owe to God.

For you, my son, my heart is thirsting, burning;
in you I quell my hunger and my thirst.
My splendid skills are yours by right, my knowledge,
and the science that has gotten fame for me.
Some of it my mentor, my own father
bequeathed to me — a scholars' scholar he;
the rest I gained by struggling on my own,
subduing wisdom with my bow and sword,
plumbing it with my mind. Christian scholars
are grasshoppers next to me. I've seen their colleges —
they've no one who can best me in the duel of words.
I beat down any man who stands against me,
crush and hush my opponent, prove him wrong.
Who but I would dare to tell the mysteries
of the Creation, of the Chariot, of its Rider?
My soul excels, surpasses all the souls
of my contemporaries in this wretched age.
My Form is fortified by God, my Rock,
locked, imprisoned in my body's cage.

Judah Abravanel to His Son

It yearns for you to surpass my degree;
I always hoped that you would outdo me.
Dear one, what keeps you with an unclean folk,
an apple tree alone amid the carobs,
a pure soul lost among the nations,
a rose among the desert thorns and weeds?
Set out upon the road to me, my dear.
Fly, bound like a fawn or a gazelle,
and make your way to your father's house, who sired you
(may God protect you, Who protected me!).
May the Lord give you smooth roads to travel,
lift you out of straits to my ample court,
heap upon your head my forefathers' bounty,
besides my father's and my grandfather's wealth.
Then He will light my spirit in its darkness,
and redirect my footsteps to the plain.

I now commend my son to God, my shepherd,
and cast my burden on my Highest Father.
He will bring my dear son to my presence:
When I call, my darling boy will hear.
Then I will sing a love-song to my Maker,
hymning my passion to Him while I live,
bringing my offering, setting my gift before Him.
My song it is that binds me to my Holy One.
The best of me is in it: my heart and eyes.
O may it please Him like the Temple rams;
my hymn, my words, like bulls upon His altar.
And may He show me Zion in her splendor,
the royal city of my anointed king,
and over it, two luminaries, equals:
Messiah, son of David, and Elijah.
May never enemy again divide her,
or nomad pitch his tent in her again.

Chapter Notes

Preface

1. To this day, family members call one who does not help oneself by the name of a person in the village who acted likewise.
2. Madeline Brandeis, *The Little Spanish Dancer* (New York: Grossett and Dunlap, 1936), 86–7.
3. Edwin B. Williams, *The Bantam New College Spanish & English Dictionary* (New York: Bantam Books, 1981); Smith, C. C., G. A. Davies and H. B. Hall, *Langenscheidt's Standard Dictionary of the English and Spanish Languages* (Berlin/Munich/Zurich: Langenscheidt, 1966).
4. Jane S. Gerber, *The Jews of Spain, A History of the Sephardic Experience* (New York: The Free Press, 1992), 2.
5. I. L. Peretz, "On History," in *I. L. Peretz: Selected Stories*, ed. trans. Eli Katz (New York: Zhitlowsky Foundation for Jewish Culture, 1991), 332–50.
6. Cecil Roth, *The House of Nasi, Doña Gracia* (Philadelphia: Jewish Publication Society, 1948), 31. Roth writes of Bomberg: "In Venice, for example, the underground agency was managed by the former Antwerp burgher, Daniel Bomberg, who in addition to his great work as a printer of Hebrew books (there is no Christian to whom Jewish scholarship is under a greater debt) received the property transmitted by the Mendes bank for Marranos settled in Italy, and reconsigned it to the owners." Roth's reference is Goris, J. A., *Les colonies marchandes méridionales à Anvers* (Louvain, 1925), 566.
7. Examples are available from The Jewish Foundation for the Righteous, 305 Seventh Avenue, 19th Floor, New York, NY 10001-6008, *jfr@jfr.org*, http//:www.jfr.org.
8. This is documented in notes for Chapter Nine, when these communities are referred to.

Chapter One

1. Sources differ on the number of observant Jews living in Spain at the time of the expulsion, the number of those who left, and where they were headed. Baer and Gerber are favored in selecting figures for this work (citations follow). See Yitzhak Baer, *A History of the Jews in Christian Spain*, Vol. 2. (Philadelphia: Jewish Publication Society, 1992), 510, where he cites Abravanel's estimate that 300,000 Jews were living in Spain in 1492. Of these, Baer estimates that there were "about 6,000 families" in Aragón and 30,000 families in Castilla (245–6). He cites Bernáldez, saying that 93,000 left for Portugal and 2,000 for Navarra, and that "300 families sailed from the port of Laredo (Vizcaya) … and 8,000 families sailed from Cádiz" (511). Baer favors Zacuto's estimate of "more than 120,000 souls" leaving for Portugal (510). Also utilizing Zacuto's estimate is Jane S. Gerber in *The Jews of Spain, A History of the Sephardic Experience* (New York: Free Press, 1994), 139.
2. Andrés Bernáldez, "History of the Catholic Kings Don Fernando and Doña Isabel," in *Expulsion 1492 Chronicles*, ed. David T. Raphael (North Hollywood, CA: Carmi House Press, 1992), 73.
3. B. Netanyahu, *Don Isaac Abravanel, Statesman & Philosopher* (Philadelphia: Jewish Publication Society, 1968), 5.
4. M. Kayserling, *Christopher Columbus and the Participation of the Jews in the Span-*

ish and Portuguese Discoveries, trans. Charles Gross (New York: Trow Press, 1907), 70. Kayserling writes of Santángel: "He was a favorite of King Fernando, enjoyed the latter's complete confidence, knew all his secrets.... The king held him in high esteem for his fidelity, his sagacity, his extraordinary industry and administrative talent, his sterling integrity and his complete devotion to the crown; whenever Fernando wrote to him, he called him 'the good Aragonese, excellent, well-beloved councillor.'"

5. Miguel Angel Ladero Quesada, Presidencia de la Generalitat Valenciana, "Luís de Santángel en la corte de Castilla," in *Lluís de Santángel y Su Época: Un Nuevo Hombre, Un Mundo Nuevo*, (Valencia: Comisión Valenciana de la Expo-92, Comisión del V Centenario del Descubrimiento de América: Encuentro de dos mundos, 1991), 246, 256.

6. Netanyahu, *Don Isaac Abravanel*, 59–60. See also the mournful poem by the child's father, who became known in latter years as Leone Ebreo, in the Appendix of this work.

7. Trudi Alexy, *The Mezuzah in the Madonna's Foot, Marranos and Other Secret Jews* (San Francisco: HarperSanFrancisco, 1994), 273–80.

8. Gerber, *The Jews of Spain*, 151.

9. Francisco Cantera Burgos, *Abraham Zacut* (Madrid: M. Aguilar, 1935), 29. See also pages 35–7 about use of the astrolabe and almanac by Vasco da Gama.

10. Kayserling, *Christopher Columbus*, 47.

11. Cecil Roth, *The House of Nasi, Doña Gracia* (Philadelphia: Jewish Publication Society, 1948), 10–20.

Chapter Two

1. Elijah Capsali, "Seder Eliyahu Zuta," in David T. Raphael, *Expulsion 1492 Chronicles* (North Hollywood, CA: Carmi House Press, 1992), 16. See note 17, below.

2. B. Netanyahu, *Don Isaac Abravanel, Statesman & Philosopher* (Philadelphia: Jewish Publication Society, 1968), 3. This study, with its detailed attention to his biography and works, is the major source in English for Abravanel's life chronology. Other primary sources are Lipiner, Trend and Loewe, and Kellner (citations below).

3. Netanyahu, *Don Isaac Abravanel*, 5. See also 266–7, footnote 12.

4. Elias Lipiner, *Two Portuguese Exiles in Castile, Dom David Negro and Dom Isaac Abravanel* (Jerusalem: Magnes Press, Hebrew University, 1997), 52.

5. *Ibid.*, 57. Lipiner writes: "Abravanel pours out his feelings in language borrowed from the Bible...," 55. Lipiner's bracketed inserts of biblical references have been eliminated.

6. *Ibid.*, 63.

7. *Ibid.*, 77.

8. *Ibid.*, 55–6.

9. *Ibid.*, 73.

10. Netanyahu, *Don Isaac Abravanel*, 47–50.

11. *Ibid.*, 50–2.

12. Paul Goodman, "Introduction," in eds. J. B. Trend and H. Loewe, *Isaac Abravanel, Six Lectures* (London: Cambridge University Press, 1937), 8.

13. See M. Kayserling, *Christopher Columbus and the Participation of the Jews in the Spanish and Portuguese Discoveries*, trans. Charles Gross (New York: Trow Press, 1907) and Simon Wiesenthal, *Sails of Hope: The Secret Mission of Christopher Columbus* (New York: Macmillan, 1973).

14. Netanyahu, *Don Isaac Abravanel*, 53–4.

15. Goodman, in Trend and Loewe, *Isaac Abravanel*, 9.

16. Netanyahu, *Don Isaac Abravanel*, 55–6.

17. Capsali in Raphael, *Expulsion 1492 Chronicles*, 16. Raphael's translation reads "Thus Don Isaac Abravanel sent a letter to Queen Isabel, in which he chastised her mercilessly and showed no respect for her rank.... [H]e had written that God would avenge the Jews from [sic] her and her household.... He also reminded her that all those who had been bad to the Jews had ultimately perished." Capsali is also Netanyahu's resource for the account of Abravanel's admonitions to the queen, 55–6. Elijah Capsali (Raphael's spelling), or Kapsali (Netanyahu's spelling), (c. 1483–1555) was Rabbi of the island of Crete, which was under the dominion of the Ottoman Empire. Raphael reports that his well-established Romaniote family was active in helping the Sephardic Jews who were leaving Iberia for the Ottoman Empire. In his 1988 novel, *The Alhambra Decree*, Raphael constructs wording for Abravanel's confrontation with Isabel. Circulated online, the fictionalized text of his words has been mistakenly presented as the statesman's literal words.

18. The child's father, Judah Abravanel, left Spain at the time of the expulsion, eventually settling in Venice, where he became

known as Leone Ebreo, famous for his writings in poetry and philosophy. His mournful poem on the loss of his son can be read in the Appendix.

19. Capsali, in Raphael, *Expulsion 1492 Chronicles*, 17.
20. See Chapter One, note 1. These numbers are estimated from the variety of figures cited in numerous sources for this work.
21. Capsali, in Raphael, *Expulsion 1492 Chronicles*, 53.
22. Netanyahu, *Don Isaac Abravanel*, 59.
23. *Ibid.*, 61–81.
24. For extended analysis and commentary of Abravanel's literary work, see Netanyahu, *Don Isaac Abravanel*, Part Two and Trend and Loewe, Ch III-VI.
25. Netanyahu, *Don Isaac Abravanel*, 69.
26. See L. Rabinowitz, "Abravanel as Exegete," 75–92, and L. Strauss, "On Abravanel's Philosophical Tendency and Political Teaching," 93–130, in Trend and Loewe, on Abravanel's philosophy and writings on messianism.
27. H. Loewe, "Isaac Abravanel and His Age," in Trend and Loewe, *Isaac Abravanel*, xxvi-ii.
28. Netanyahu, *Don Isaac Abravanel*, 88–91.
29. *Ibid.*, 255–56.
30. *The Abravanel Family Newsletter*, ed. Allan R. Abravanel, No. 23 (Portland, OR: June 1998).

Chapter Three

1. Francisco Cantera Burgos, *Abraham Zacut* (Madrid: M. Aguilar, 1935), 29, 35–7; M. Kayserling, *Christopher Columbus and the Participation of the Jews in the Spanish and Portuguese Discoveries*, trans. Charles Gross (New York: Trow Press, 1907), 48–51, 113; "Zacuto, Abraham Ben Samuel," *Encyclopedia Judaica*, 1973, in http://www.zacutohistory.com/docu3z.htm.
2. "The Discovery of North America by Leif Ericsson, c. 1000," from *The Saga of Eric the Red*, 1387," *Flateyar-bok*, compiler Jon Thordharson, 1387, trans. A. M. Reeves; original source *American Historical Documents, 1000–1904: with introductions and notes* (New York: P. F. Collier, 1910). The Harvard classics v. 43. Reproduced in *Internet Modern History Sourcebook* (New York: Fordham University Center for Medieval Studies), http://www.fordham.edu/halsall/mod/1000Vinland.htm, December 10, 2006.
3. Museu da Marinha, (Lisbon: June 15, 2002). The reader's attention is called to the gallery of the museum's entry, with statues and descriptions of the explorers' voyages and their impact on Portuguese life and empire.
4. Howard M. Sacher, *Farewell España: The World of the Sephardim Remembered* (New York: Vintage Books, 1994), 330–1.
5. *Ibid.*, 331–2. Mallorca was also noted for its respected school for Jews studying medicine.
6. B. Netanyahu, *Don Isaac Abravanel, Statesman & Philosopher* (Philadelphia: Jewish Publication Society, 1968), 82–5.
7. Sacher, *Farewell España*, 332.
8. Cantera Burgos, *Abraham Zacut*, 33–5.
9. *Ibid.*, 29–30.
10. *Ibid.*, 34.
11. Abraham Haim Freimann, "Introduction to the Complete Book of Yohassin," in Abraham b. Samuel Zacuto, *Sefer Yohassin or Book of Lineage*, ed. Joseph Kaplan, trans. Israel Shamir, in *Sephardic Sages Past and Present*, 1999, p. 6, http://home.flash.net/~mdccull/Census/Rabbi%20Abraham%20Zacuto,%20by%20Francisco%20Cantera%20y%20Burgos.pdf. The title of this work is transliterated as *Séfer Yujasin* by Cantera Burgos in *Abraham Zacut* and as *Sefer Yuhasin* by David T. Raphael in *Expulsion 1492 Chronicles* (North Hollywood, CA: Carmi House Press), 1992.
12. "Zacuto, Abraham Ben Samuel," in *Encyclopedia Judaica* Vol. 2 (Jerusalem: Macmillan, 1971), 94.
13. Cantera Burgos, *Abraham Zacut*. Other Sephardim who excelled in Jewish studies and world affairs included Don Isaac Abravanel and the Rambam, Moses Maimonides.
14. Marcelin Defourneaux, *Daily Life in Spain in the Golden Age* (Palo Alto, CA: Stanford University Press, 1979), 163.
15. Cantera Burgos, *Abraham Zacut*, 24–6.
16. Defourneaux, *Daily Life in Spain*, 165–7.
17. *Ibid.*, 165.
18. "Zacuto, Abraham Ben Samuel," in *Encyclopedia Judaica*, http://www.zacutohistory.com/docu3z.htm, August 15, 2007, 1.
19. Cantera Burgos, *Abraham Zacut*, 33.
20. Kayserling, *Christopher Columbus*, 48–9.
21. Cantera Burgos, *Abraham Zacut*, 104–9.
22. *Ibid.*
23. Jane S. Gerber, *The Jews of Spain, A History of the Sephardic Experience* (New York: Free Press, 1994), 79–80.

24. Cantera Burgos, *Abraham Zacut*, 78–9.
25. *Ibid.*, 27.
26. *Ibid.*, 28.
27. *Ibid.*, 48.
28. Kayserling, *Christopher Columbus*, 14, 113.
29. Cantera Burgos, *Abraham Zacut*, 30.
30. *Ibid.*, 33.
31. *Ibid.*, 36–7.
32. Jerónimo Osório, "Of the Life and Deeds of King Manuel," in ed. David T. Raphael, *Expulsion 1492 Chronicles* (North Hollywood, CA: Carmi House Press, 1992), 160.
33. Gerber, *Jews of Spain*, 141–2; see also Samuel Usque, "Portugal 5257 [1497] When They Were Made Christians by Force," in trans. Martin A. Cohen, *Samuel Usque's Consolation for the Tribulations of Israel* (Philadelphia: Jewish Publication Society, 1965), 202–4.
34. Cantera Burgos, *Abraham Zacut*, 37–8.
35. "Zacuto, Abraham Ben Samuel" in *Encylopedia Judaica,* Vol. 2 (Detroit: Thomson Gale, 2007), 94.
36. Cantera Burgos, *Abraham Zacut*, 87–8.
37. *Ibid.*, 38.
38. *Ibid.*, 42–3.
39. *Ibid.*, 75–7.
40. *Ibid.*, 42.
41. *Ibid.*, 38–9.
42. *Ibid.*, 39.
43. "Zacuto, Abraham Ben Samuel," in *Encyclopedia Judaica,* 94.
44. Cantera Burgos, *Abraham Zacut*, 87–8.

Chapter Four

1. Peter Cole, *The Dream of the Poem* (Princeton, NJ and Oxford, UK: Princeton University Press, 2007), 37, 62.
2. Cecil Roth, *A History of the Marranos* (Philadelphia: Jewish Publication Society, 1941), 49–51.
3. Yitzhak Baer, *A History of the Jews in Christian Spain*, Vol. 2, 2nd Ed., (Philadelphia: Jewish Publication Society, 1992), 370.
4. Miguel Angel Motis Dolader, "Lineage of the Santángel Family in Aragon: Intellectual Life and Socioeconomic Structure," paper presented at *Santángel 98, The Life and Times of Luís de Santángel*, International Symposium. (River Forest, IL: Dominican University, August 25, 1998). Motis Dolader describes how the name Santángel appears in 1413 and 1414 among unrelated New Christians baptized en masse by Cardinal Santángel following the Disputation at Tortosa, giving them his name as godfather.
5. Baer, *History of the Jews*, 321–2.
6. *Ibid.*, 170–4.
7. Roth, *History of the Marranos*, 17–18.
8. M. Kayserling, *Christopher Columbus and the Participation of the Jews in the Spanish and Portuguese Discoveries,* trans. Charles Gross (New York, Trow Press, 1907), 61–6.
9. Rafael Benitez Sánchez-Blanco, "El Valenciano Luis de Santángel," in *Lluís de Santángel y Su Época: Un Nuevo Hombre, Un Mundo Nuevo.* (Valencia: Comisión del V Centenario del Descubrimiento de América: Encuentro de dos mundos, 1991), 221–30.
10. *Ibid.*, 237–8.
11. Kayserling, *Christopher Columbus*, 70.
12. Miguel Angel Ladero Quesada, "Luís de Santángel en la Corte de Castilla," in *Lluís de Santángel y Su Época: Un Nuevo Hombre, Un Mundo Nuevo.* (Valencia: Comisión del V Centenario del Descubrimiento de América: Encuentro de dos mundos, 1991), 243–259.
13. Kayserling, *Christopher Columbus*, 71–3.
14. *Ibid.*, 73–9.
15. *Ibid.*, 100. See also only known copy of the Barcelona printing of the Columbus Letter to Santángel, Rare Books and Manuscripts Division, Center for the Humanities, New York Public Library.
16. *Ibid.*, 101–2.
17. *Ibid.*, 123–4.
18. *Ibid.*, 124–5.
19. Yitzchak Kerem, "The Jewish Identity of Santángel and His Descendants, A Genealogical Query," paper presented at *Santángel 98, The Life and Times of Luís de Santángel*, International Symposium (River Forest, IL: Dominican University, August 24, 1998).
20. B. Netanyahu, *The Origins of the Inquisition in Fifteenth Century Spain* (New York: Random House, 1995), 1170.
21. Sánchez-Blanco, "El Valenciano Luís de Santángel," 231. The word "*marrano(a)*" presents various meanings in this context. Dictionary searches reveal the animals pig, hog, and sow and the pejoratives filthy person, slattern, slut, base, vile, dirty, sloppy. It came to be used as a popular slur of contempt for Jewish converts to Christianity. See "Glossary" in Appendix.
22. *Ibid.*, 232.
23. Kayserling, *Christopher Columbus*, 69.
24. On how *conversa* women kept Jewish traditions alive in their families, the reader is

referred to Janet Liebman Jacobs, *Hidden Heritage: The Legacy of the Crypto-Jews* (Berkeley: University of California Press, 2002) and Renée Levine Melammed, *Heretics or Daughters of Israel? The Crypto-Jewish Women of Castile* (Oxford: Oxford University Press, 1999).

25. Henry Kamen, *The Spanish Inquisition* (London: The Folio Society, 1998), 57.
26. Netanyahu, *Origins of the Inquisition*, 217–53.
27. Jane S. Gerber, *The Jews of Spain, A History of the Sephardic Experience* (New York: Free Press, 1994), xix-xx.
28. Ladero Quesada, "Luís de Santángel," 256–8; Elliott, J. H. *Imperial Spain 1469–1716* (London: Penguin Books, 1963), 135–7.
29. Kayserling, *Christopher Columbus*, 125.
30. Gerber, *Jews of Spain*, 127.
31. Kerem, *Jewish Identity of Santángel*.
32. Sánchez-Blanco, "El Valenciano," 227.
33. Octavio Paz, *The Labyrinth of Solitude*, quoted in Harold R. Isaacs, *Idols of the Tribe: Group Identity and Political Change* (Cambridge, MA: Harvard University Press, 1975), 120.
34. Sánchez-Blanco, "El Valenciano," 228
35. Baer, *History of the Jews*, 328.
36. Kayserling, *Christopher Columbus*, 71.
37. *Meditations for the High Holydays*. (Los Angeles: Makom Ohr Shalom, 1999/5760), 46–7.

Chapter Five

1. Joshua Soncino, *Nahala li-yehoshua* (Constantinople: 1731), referred to in Andrée Aelion Brooks, *The Woman Who Defied Kings* (St. Paul, MN: Paragon House, 2002), 469, 557.
2. Cecil Roth, *The House of Nasi, Doña Gracia* (Philadelphia: Jewish Publication Society, 1948), xii.
3. *Ibid.*, xi.
4. Brooks, *Woman Who Defied Kings*, 24–5. For differing accounts of family names and their origins, see also Roth, *Doña Gracia*, 12–13, 17–20 and Marianna D. Birnbaum, *The Long Journey of Gracia Mendes* (Budapest/ New York: Central European University Press, 2003), 1–4.
5. *Ibid.* He is called Agostinho in Roth, *Doña Gracia*, and Birnbaum, *Long Journey*, and Aries in Brooks, *Woman Who Defied Kings*.
6. Examples are found throughout David M. Gitlitz, *Secrecy and Deceit: The Religion of the Crypto-Jews* (Philadelphia and Jerusalem: Jewish Publication Society, 1996).
7. Juan Blasquéz Miguel, *Historia del Toledo Judío* (Toledo: Arcano, 1989). Quoted in Gitlitz, *Secrecy*, 41.
8. Brooks, *Woman Who Defied Kings*, 44.
9. Roth, *Doña Gracia*, 12.
10. Brooks, *Woman Who Defied Kings*, 50.
11. Roth, *Doña Gracia*, 19.
12. *Ibid.*, 20.
13. *Ibid.*, 29–31.
14. Roth calls her Brianda, 14; Brooks calls her Ana, 95.
15. Roth, *Doña Gracia*, 16.
16. *Ibid.*, 28.
17. *Ibid.*, 54–5; Birnbaum, *Long Journey*, 43–4.
18. Brooks, *Woman Who Defied Kings*, 230–2.
19. Roth, *Doña Gracia*, 61.
20. *Ibid.*, 63–4.
21. *Ibid.*, 72–4. The relative laxity of the Holy Office in approving a book which praises, and is sponsored by, a known judaizer seems harmonious with the relatively tolerant policies of the Duchy of Este toward *conversos* and Jews. It also suggests flexibility surrounding the enforcement of edicts or laws, with those in charge of nations, states or other organizations sometimes able to negotiate their own interpretations of rulings, probably for a price.
22. *Ibid.*, 74–3.
23. *Ibid.*, 71–2. The image on the medal has been mistakenly identified, from time to time, as that of the aunt, Doña Gracia.
24. *Ibid.*, 86–7. Roth calls Salonika "a microcosm of the entire Jewish world. There were Jews from France, Italy, Germany, Hungary, Calabria, Apulia, Sicily and every province of Spain. Every ship that arrived from the West and every mule-train that came from the north brought a fresh contingent of Portuguese Marranos. Jews constituted the majority of the population."
25. *Ibid.*, 90.
26. Roth. *The House of Nasi: The Duke of Naxos* (Philadelphia: Jewish Publication Society, 1948), 9.
27. Roth, *Doña Gracia*, 173. Ch VII, "The Ancona Boycott," cites Doña Gracia repeatedly for her leadership and steadfastness in the effort. Roth's judgment is representative of a group of post-holocaust writers who condemned the lack of Jewish support for what Roth calls "direct action" against their enemies. See especially, 162: "She and her son-in-law, in advance of their age, realized the

possibility of ameliorating the position of the Jews throughout the world, not by the twin traditional methods, of prayer and payment, but by direct political and economic action." See also in Netanyahu, B. *Don Isaac Abravanel, Statesman and Philosopher* (Philadelphia: Jewish Publication Society, 1968), 256, the negative comparison of Isaac Abravanel to Joseph Nasi: "Abravanel's maxim that the Jews can and should do nothing for their salvation ... destroyed the influence of Don Joseph Nasi," who had tried and failed to attract Jews to his settlement in Palestine. "The Jews of his time were accustomed to thinking of redemption in a supernatural way. They were infatuated with the predictions of Abravanel and the miraculous messianic powers which could effect their deliverance at one fell swoop."

28. Roth, *Doña Gracia*, 174.
29. Gad Nassi and Rebecca Toueg, *Doña Gracia Nasi* (Tel-Aviv: Women's International Zionist Organization, 1991), 22.
30. Dahlia Gottan, "Foreword," in Nassi and Toueg, *Doña Gracia Nasi*, 3.
31. Roth, *Doña Gracia*, 133.
32. Brooks, *Woman Who Defied Kings*, xiii.
33. Montague Frank Modder, *The Jew in the Literature of England* (New York: Meridian Books and Philadelphia: Jewish Publication Society, 1960), 19–21.
34. Ludwig Lewisohn, *The Last Days of Shylock* (New York/London: Harper & Brothers, 1931).
35. Emilie Roi and Rochelle Furstenberg, *Doña Gracia of the House of Nasi,* unpublished film script, (Jerusalem: 1987).
36. Naomi Ragen, *The Ghost of Hannah Mendes* (New York: Simon & Schuster, 1998).

Chapter Six

1. Foremost sources for this subject are the studies of Spanish Jewish communities by the following scholars from the Hebrew University of Jerusalem, who have published detailed studies of pre-expulsion communities: Yom Tov Assis, Haim Beinart, J. Doñate Sebastia, J. R. Magdalena Nom de Deu and José Hinojosa Montalvo. The works of Israel Abrahams and Yitzhak Baer are also helpful for this area of study. Specific references to their works follow in the notes below.
2. George B. R. de Brigard, ed., *Let's Go, Spain & Portugal Including Morocco 2002* (New York: St. Martin's, 2002), 181; Penelope Casas, *Discovering Spain, An Uncommon Guide* (New York: Knopf, 2000), 184; Darwin Porter, *Frommer's Comprehensive Travel Guide, Spain,* 16th Ed. (New York: Macmillan Travel, 1995), 248.
3. Brigard, *Let's Go,* 180–5; Casas, *Discovering Spain,* 184, 192; Porter, *Frommer's Spain,* 248, 252.
4. José Luís Lacave, trans. Celer, *Viaje por la España Judía, A Trip Through Jewish Spain* (Madrid: Subdirección General de Medios de Promoción, Turespaña, Secretaria General de Turismo), 53–4. Spanish tourism officials have developed *Red de Sefarad*, a recommended route for travelers to visit sites of Jewish quarters and cultural centers.
5. Haim Beinart, *Trujillo, a Jewish Community in Extremadura on the Eve of the Expulsion from Spain* (Jerusalem: Magnes Press, Hebrew University, 1980), 1–2.
6. *Ibid.*, 102.
7. *Ibid.*, 35.
8. B. Netanyahu, *Don Isaac Abravanel, Statesman & Philosopher,* 2nd Ed. (Philadelphia: Jewish Publication Society of America, 1968), 48–9.
9. Jane Gerber, *The Jews of Spain, A History of the Sephardic Experience* (New York: Free Press, 1992, 113–4; Abram Leon Sachar, *A History of the Jews,* 5th Ed. (New York, Knopf, 1967), 204.
10. Gerber, *Jews of Spain,* 103
11. Beinart, *Trujillo,* 4.
12. Tortosa was to be host city from 1413–14 for a disputation in which Catholic and Jewish representatives were obliged to debate and was designed to favor the Christian view. Important Jewish community leaders were commanded to attend. See Baer, Vol. 2, 174–6. Upon conclusion, many converted under pressure. Jewish residents of Tortosa were especially vulnerable thereafter to conversionary pressures because of their proximity to the site of the disputation. The number of converts from that community and nearby Tarragona was at its highest in 1422, following anti–Jewish sermons by a local priest. These were stopped by Queen María because she feared their inflammatory nature might result in wide scale violence. See Yom Tov Assis, ed., *The Jews of Tortosa 1373–1492, Regesta of Documents from the Archivo Histórico de Protocolos de Tarragon, Sources for the History of the Jews in Spain-3* (Jerusalem: Hebrew University of Jerusalem, Henk Schusshiem Memorial Series, 1991), VII.
13. Beinart, *Trujillo,* 10–12.

14. *Ibid.*, 5.
15. *Ibid.*, 6–8.
16. *Ibid.*, 10–12.
17. José Hinojosa Montalvo, *The Jews of the Kingdom of Valencia, from Persecution to Expulsion, 1391-1492* (Jerusalem: Magnes Press, Hebrew University, 1991), 80–82; J. Doñate Sebastia and J. R. Magdalena Nom de Dieu, *Three Jewish Communities in Medieval Valencia, Castellon de la Plana, Burriana, Villareal* (Jerusalem: Magnes Press, Hebrew University, 1990), 179–80.
18. Assis, *Tortosa*, X.
19. Hinojosa Montalvo, *Valencia*, 80–7.
20. *Ibid.*, 82–3
21. Sebastia and Nom de Dieu, *Three Jewish Communities*, 181.
22. Beinart, *Trujillo*, 28–33.
23. *Ibid.*, 11–12.
24. *Ibid.*, 13–19.
25. Assis, *Tortosa*, X.
26. Hinojosa Montalvo, *Valencia*, 106–9; Abrahams, 1, 4.
27. Hinojosa Montalvo, *Valencia*, 108–9.
28. Israel Abrahams, *Jewish Life in the Middle Ages* (Philadelphia: Jewish Publication Society, 1896), 27.
29. Sebastia and Nom de Dieu, *Three Jewish Communities*, 183; Hinojosa Montalvo, *Valencia*, 112.
30. Abrahams, *Jewish Life*, 4.
31. Hinojosa Montalvo, *Valencia*, 113–14.
32. *Ibid.*, 114.
33. Abrahams, *Jewish Life*, 15.
34. *Ibid.*, 25.
35. *Ibid.*, 346.
36. On how *conversa* women kept Jewish traditions alive in their families, the reader is again referred to Janet Liebman Jacobs, *Hidden Heritage: The Legacy of the Crypto-Jews.* (Berkeley: University of California Press, 2002) and Renée Levine Melammed, (*Heretics or Daughters of Israel? The Crypto-Jewish Women of Castile.* Oxford: Oxford University Press), 1999.
37. Hinojosa Montalvo, *Valencia*, 35.
38. Netanyahu, *Isaac Abravanel*, 52; Francisco Cantera Burgos, *Abraham Zacut, Siglo XV* (Madrid: M. Aguilar, Ed., 1935), 12.
39. Abrahams, *Jewish Life*, 13–14.
40. Netanyahu, *Isaac Abravanel*, 255–6, Cecil Roth, *The House of Nasi, Doña Gracia* (Philadelphia: Jewish Publication Society, 1947), 173–4.
41. Beinart, *Trujillo*, 18.
42. Assis, *Tortosa*, VIII.
43. Abraham, *Jewish Life*, 87–8.
44. *Ibid.*, 166.
45. *Ibid.*, 90, 175.
46. *Ibid.*, 185.
47. *Ibid.*, 192–3.
48. *Ibid.*, 188.
49. Yitzhak Baer, *A History of the Jews in Christian Spain,* Vol. 2 (Philadelphia: Jewish Publication Society, 1992), 261–2.
50. Abrahams, *Jewish Life,* 353.
51. Judah Ibn Tibbon, quoted in Abraham, *Jewish Life,* 354.

Chapter Seven

1. Haim Beinart, *Trujillo, A Jewish Community in Extremadura on the Eve of the Expulsion from Spain* (Jerusalem: Magnes Press, Hebrew University, 1980), 35.
2. Yom Tov Assis, ed., *The Jews of Tortosa 1373-1492, Regesta of Documents from the Archivo Histórico de Protocolos de Tarragon* (Jerusalem: Hebrew University of Jerusalem, Henk Schussheim Memorial Series, 1991), XIX.
3. José Hinojosa Montalvo, *The Jews of the Kingdom of Valencia, from Persecution to Expulsion* (Jerusalem: Magnes Press, Hebrew University, 1991), 213.
4. *Ibid.*
5. Isaac Abrahams, *Jewish Life in the Middle Ages* (Philadelphia: Jewish Publication Society, 1896), 222.
6. J. Doñate Sebastia and Magdalena Nom de Déu, *Three Jewish Communities in Medieval Valencia* (Jerusalem: Magnes Press, The Hebrew University, 1990), 281.
7. Assis, *Tortosa*, XIX.
8. *Ibid.*
9. Hinojosa Montalvo, *Jews of Valencia*, 183.
10. Yitzhak Baer, *A History of the Jews in Christian Spain,* Vol. 1 (Philadelphia: Jewish Publication Society, 1992) 205–6, 426n20. See also Hinojosa Montalvo, *Jews of Valencia,* 183.
11. Assis, *Tortosa*, XVII-XIX.
12. Beinart, *Trujillo*, 39–47.
13. Hinojosa Montalvo, *Jews of Valencia*,183–4.
14. Beinart, *Trujillo*, 10–11.
15. *Ibid.*, 10.
16. Abrahams, *Jewish Life,* 227–8.
17. Assis, *Tortosa*, XIII.
18. Hinojosa Montalvo, *Jews of Valencia,* 184–5.
19. Assis, *Tortosa*, XVII-XVIII.

20. *Ibid.* For a comprehensive picture of money lending during this period, see also Hinojosa Montalvo, *Jews of Valencia*, 184–92; Beinart, *Trujillo*, 39–40; Sebastia and Nom de Déu, *Three Jewish Communities*, 95–7, 283–4.
21. Abrahams, *Jewish Life*, 295–6.
22. Baer, *History of the Jews*, 160.
23. Abrahams, *Jewish Life*, 302, 305.
24. *Ibid.*, 313.
25. *Ibid.*, footnote 1, quoting *Authorized Hebrew Prayer-book*, 5.
26. Leviticus, 19:9.
27. *Ibid.*, 19:33.
28. Proverbs 31:8–9.
29. Abrahams, *Jewish Life*, 318–19.
30. *Ibid.*, 319–1.
31. *Ibid.*, 320–1.
32. *Ibid.*, 307–11.
33. *Ibid.*, 311.
34. *Ibid.*, 336.
35. *Ibid.*, Ch XVII-XVIII, 307–35. The reader's attention is drawn to this particularly rich description of Jewish practices in the Middle Ages with regard to charity and the relief of the poor and the sick. Particular references for notes 22–24, 26, and 28–33, above, are found within these chapters.
36. *Ibid.*, 335–9.
37. *Ibid.*, 414–15.
38. Samuel Usque, *Consolation for the Tribulations of Israel*, trans. Martin A. Cohen, *Samuel Usque's Consolation for the Tribulations of Israel* (Philadelphia: Jewish Publication Society, 1965), 209–10.
39. Abrahams, *Jewish Life*, 410.
40. *Ibid.*, 373–4.
41. *Ibid.*, 375–8.
42. *Ibid.*, 379–81.
43. *Ibid.*, 381–2.
44. *Ibid.*, 379.
45. *Ibid.*, 382–3.

Chapter Eight

1. Elija Capsali, *Seder Eliyahu Zuta*, "The Minor Order of Elijah" in ed. David T. Raphael, *Expulsion 1492 Chronicles* (North Hollywood, CA: Carmi House Press, 1992), 16.
2. Howard M. Sachar, *Farewell España, The World of the Sephardim Remembered* (New York: Vintage, 1995). Chapters IV-XVII, 74–386, describe post-expulsion life in the various cities and states of the diaspora.
3. See Chapters One through Four and notes.
4. See Chapter Five and notes.
5. Jane S. Gerber, *The Jews of Spain, A History of the Sephardic Experience* (New York: Free Press,1991), 150–1.
6. Uriel Heyd, "Moses Hamon, Chief Jewish Physician to Sultan Süleyman the Magnificent," *Oriens*, vol. 16 (12/31/63), 155. http://links.jstor.org/sici?sici=0078-6527% 2819631231%2916%3C152%3AMHCJPT%3 E2.0.CO%3B2-T.
7. *Ibid.*, 152.
8. *Ibid.*, 152–3.
9. Gotthard Deutsch and Meyer Kayserling, "Hamon," www.JewishEncyclopedia.com, 2002. http://www.jewishencyclopedia.com/view_friendly.jsp?artid=188&letter=H.
10. David Hashavit, "Amatus Lusitanus Discovered Valves in Veins and Arteries," in *HaLapid*, Vol. XIII Issue 1, (Winter 2006), 1. Also available on http://www.cryptojews.com.
11. "Noteworthy Sephardim," American Sephardi Federation, 2000–2005, http://www.americansephardifederation.org/PDF/sources/ASF_Bios.pdf, 1/10/08.
12. Cecil Roth, *The House of Nasi, Doña Gracia* (Philadelphia: Jewish Publication Society, 1948), 27; Andrée Aelion Brooks, *The Woman Who Defied Kings* (St. Paul, MN: Paragon House, 2002), 140–1.
13. Hashavit, "Amatus Lusitanus Discovered Valves," 10.
14. Brooks, *The Woman Who Defied Kings*, 475.
15. "Oath of Amatus Lusitanus," *HaLapid*, Vol. XIII. Issue 1 (Winter 2006), 13.
16. Martin A. Cohen, "Introduction," in trans. Martin A. Cohen, *Samuel Usque's Consolation for the Tribulations of Israel* (Philadelphia: Jewish Publication Society, 1964), 12.
17. *Ibid.*, 12–13.
18. *Ibid.*, 13–14.
19. Samuel Usque. "Prologue." *Consolation for the Tribulations of Israel* in trans. Martin A. Cohen, *Samuel Usque's Consolation for the Tribulations of Israel* (Philadelphia: Jewish Publication Society, 1964), 40.
20. Cohen, "Introduction," 12–13.
21. Richard A. Preto-Rodas. "Samuel Usque's *Consolação às Tribulaçõs de Israel* as Pastoral Literature Engagée," *Hispania*, Vol. 73, Number 1. Biblioteca Virtual Miguel D. Cervantes, March 1990, http://www.cervantesvirtual.com/servlet/SirveObras/01482074901275970760035/p00000.
22. Roth, *Doña Gracia*, 75.
23. Cohen, "Introduction," *Samuel Usque's Consolation*, 16–17.

24. Brooks, *The Woman Who Defied Kings*, 466.
25. "Longo, Saadiah." *Encyclopedia Judaica*, Vol. 13 (Detroit: Thomson Gale, 2007) 187.
26. Roth, *Doña Gracia*, 183.
27. Roth, *The House of Nasi: The Duke of Naxos* (Philadelphia: Jewish Publication Society, 1948) 192.
28. "Longo, Saadia Ben Abraham," http://jewishencyclopedia.com/view_friendly.jsp?artid=538&letter=L, 5/02/06.
29. "Longo, Saadiah," *Encyclopedia Judaica*, Vol. 13, 187.
30. "Moses Ben Baruch Almosnino." *Encyclopedia Judaica*, Vol. 1, 685.
31. *Ibid.*
32. "Almosnino." *The Jewish Encyclopedia* (New York/London: Funk and Wagnalls Company, 1912), 484.
33. *Ibid.*
34. Roth, *The Duke of Naxos*, 86–8.
35. Nina Rebecca Zacuto, "The Descendants Abraham Zacuto." *FamilyTreeMaker.com User Home Pages*, http://www.familytreemaker.com/users/z/a/c/Nina-Rebecca-Zacuto/index.html, 11/23/00.
36. Samuel Usque, in Cohen, 231.
37. Alden Oreck, "The Virtual Jewish History Tour." American-Israeli Cooperative: 2008, http://www.jewishvirtuallibrary.org/jsource/vjw/Brazil.html.
38. Norman Simms, "Being Crypto-Jewish in Colonial Brazil (1500–1822): Brushing History Against the Grain," in *Journal of Religious History*, Vol. 31, No. 4. (December 2007), 421–2.
39. Michael Kepp, "Documentary Looks at Brazilians Rediscovering Their Jewish Roots" (Rio de Janeiro: JTA and United Jewish Communities), http://www.ujc.org/page.html?ArticleID=74955.
40. Cecil Roth, *History of the Marranos* (Philadelphia: Jewish Publication Society, 1932), 283–4.
41. Simms, "Being Crypto-Jewish...," 431.
42. Oreck, *Virtual Jewish History Tour*.
43. Roth, *History of the Marranos*, 283–4.
44. Oreck, *Virtual Jewish History Tour*.
45. Simms, "Being Crypto-Jewish...," 424; also 433, quoting João Sedycias, "Straddling Two Worlds: The Sephardic Presence in Northern Brazil," paper presented at Modern Language Association Convention (Chicago: Modern Language Association, December 1990). http://home.yawl.com.br/hp/sedycias/Sepharad.

Chapter Nine

1. *The American Heritage Dictionary of the English Language*, New College Edition (Boston: Houghton Mifflin, 1978), 301.
2. Expositions of this viewpoint can be found regularly in articles and in Letters to the Editor sections of weekly newspapers published for Jewish readers.
3. Expositions of this viewpoint will be found later in this chapter.
4. Yitzhak Baer, *A History of the Jews in Christian Spain*, 2nd Ed, Vol. 2. (Philadelphia: Jewish Publication Society, 1992), 510–11. This very long note by Baer testifies to the wide variety of statistics on population.
5. David M. Gitlitz, *Secrecy and Deceit: The Religion of the Crypto-Jews* (Philadelphia and Jerusalem: Jewish Publication Society, 1996).
6. Janet Liebman Jacobs, *Hidden Heritage: The Legacy of the Crypto-Jews* (Berkeley: University of California Press), 2002. See also Jacobs, "Women, Ritual and Secrecy: The Creation of Crypto-Jewish Culture." *HaLapid*, Vol. VIII Issue 2 (Spring 2000), 1–2, 6–9.
7. Stanley M. Hordes, *To the Ends of the Earth, A History of the Crypto-Jews of New Mexico* (New York: Columbia University Press, 2005).
8. Arthur Benveniste, Conversation with Rabbi Benito Garzon in 1992 (Los Angeles: Interview with author, 2003).
9. Emma Moya, "Letter to Editor," *Jewish Historical Society of Southern Arizona* (Tucson, July 16, 1999). Ms. Moya uses the original spelling of "Alburquerque" for the New Mexico city.
10. Trudi Alexy, *The Mezuzah in the Madonna's Foot, Marranos and Other Secret Jews* (San Francisco: HarperCollins, 1994), 255–7, 261.
11. Trudi Alexy, *The Marrano Legacy, A Contemporary Crypto-Jewish Priest Reveals Secrets of His Double Life* (Albuquerque, NM: University of New Mexico Press, 2003), 11–13.
12. http://www.cryptojews.com (Los Angeles: Society for Crypto-Judaic Studies, 1997-present).
13. http://www.saudades.com (Johannesburg: Bernadetti Silva Mausenbaum, 1997–present).
14. http://www.sephardim.com (Tucson, AZ: Harry Stein, 1/01/01-present).
15. Anita Novinsky and Paulo Amilcar, "The Last Marranos," in *Commentary*, Vol.

43 No. 5, (American Jewish Committee, May 1967, 76–81; also see Kitty Teltsch, "Belmonte: A Reporter Revisits an Anusim Community," in *HaLapid* Vol. X Issue 1 (Los Angeles: Society for Crypto-Judaic Studies, Winter 2003), 1, 4–5.

16. Ladina, http://ladina.blogspot.com. This site stays current with events in Portugal concerning crypto Jews.

17. *Memória e Reencontro*, Teatro Nacional D. Maria II, December 4, 1996. The program included two pieces, *Da Expulsão à Diáspora* (From Expulsion to Diaspora) and *Oração de compromisso, hoje* (Oration of Promise and Hope), with presentation of Sephardic songs. The program noted that, while memories of the past are sad, presenters hope present day Portugal will see harmony among its cultures. Funders were Banco Espirito Santo and Portugal Telecom.

18. José Luís Lacave, trans. Celer, *Viaje por la España Judía, A Trip Through Jewish Spain* (Madrid: Subdirección General de Medios de Promoción, Turespaña, Secretaria General de Turismo, 2002).

19. "Spain to Reverse Historic Decree" *Vista* (Coral Gables, FL: *Vista*, date unknown), 4.

20. Nan Rubin, *The Hidden Jews of New Mexico: Return to Iberia* (New York: Nan Rubin), http://nanrubin.com/.

21. *HaLapid* (Los Angeles: Society for Crypto-Judaic Studies, 1997–present), http://www.cryptojews.com.

22. Rufina Bernardetti Silva Mausenbaum, "Article in 'The Scribe' on the Lemba," saudades-sefarad@yahoogroups.com, 11/13/99.

23. Michael Freund, "4 Rabbis Visit Bnei Menashe in India," in *Kulanu*, Vol. 9 No. 1 (New York: Kulanu, Spring 2002), 1, 16–17.

24. Michael Freund, "A Jewish Spark Rekindled in China," in *Kulanu*, Vol. 8 No. 4 (New York: Kulanu, Winter 2001–02), 3, 13.

25. Karen Primack, "Profile of a Leader: J. J. Keki," in *Kulanu*, Vol. 6 No. 1 (New York: Kulanu, Spring 1999), 1, 12.

26. Muñoz, Hilda M., "A Twist of Faith," in *Los Angeles Times, Westside Weekly* (Los Angeles: Times Mirror Corporation, July 6, 2001), 1, 6.

27. Kitty Teltsch, "2003 San Antonio Conference Highlights, Members Hear Research, Personal Stories; Lavender Elected President with New Board," in *HaLapid* Vol. X Issue 3 (Los Angeles: Society for Crypto-Judaic Studies, Fall 2003, 1; can also be read on http://www.cryptojews.com).

28. Daniel J. Wakin, "A Count of U.S. Jews Sees a Dip; Others Demur," in *The New York Times* (New York: The New York Times, October 9, 2002), A1, A17.

29. Teresa Watanabe, "A Clouded View of U.S. Jews," in *Los Angeles Times* (Los Angeles: Times Mirror Corporation, October 9, 2002), A1, A18.

30. Sara Bershtel and Allen Graubard, *Saving Remnants, Feeling Jewish in America* (Berkeley/Los Angeles: University of California Press, 1993), 43–44.

31. Gary Rosenblatt, "Lost Jews Find New Friends," *New York Jewish Week* (New York: New York Jewish Week, October 4, 2002).

32. *Ibid.*

33. Eliahu Salpeter, "There Is No Need to Fear Intermarriage," in *Ha'aretz*. Israel: *Ha'aretz*, July 10, 2002).

34. Judea Pearl and Ruth Pearl eds., *I Am Jewish, Personal Reflections Inspired by the Last Words of Daniel Pearl* (Woodstock, VT: Jewish Lights, 2005), 138.

35. *Ibid.*, xvii.

36. *Ibid.*, xvi.

37. *Ibid.*

38. *Ibid.*

39. Mark Twain, "Concerning the Jew," in *The Complete Essays of Mark Twain*, ed. Charles Neider (Garden City, NY: Doubleday & Company, 1963), 249; from *Harper's*, September 1899.

Bibliographical Sources

"Abraham ben Samuel Zacuto & Vasco de Gama." Valencia, Spain: Comisión Valenciana de la Expo-92, Comisión del V Centenario del Descubrimiento de América: Encuentro de dos mundos, 1992.

Abrahams, Israel. *Jewish Life in the Middle Ages.* Philadelphia: Jewish Publication Society, 1896.

Abravanel, Allan R., ed. *The Abravanel Family Newsletter,* No. 23 (June 1998).

Alexy, Trudi. *The Mezuzah in the Madonna's Foot, Marranos and Other Secret Jews.* San Francisco: HarperCollins, 1994.

_____. *The Marrano Legacy, A Contemporary Crypto-Jewish Priest Reveals Secrets of His Double Life.* Albuquerque: University of New Mexico Press, 2003.

American Sephardi Federation. "Noteworthy Sephardim." New York: American Sephardi Federation, 2000–2005, http://www.americansephardifederation.org/PDF/sources/ASF_Bios.pdf.

Assis, Yom Tov, ed. *The Jews of Tortosa 1373–1492: Regesta of Documents from the Archivo Histórico de Protocolos de Tarragona.* Henk Schussheim Memorial Series. Jerusalem: Hebrew University, 1991.

Baer, Yitzhak. *A History of the Jews in Christian Spain,* Vol. 1 and 2. Louis Schoffman, trans. Philadelphia: Jewish Publication Society, 1992.

Bedini, Silvio A., ed. *Christopher Columbus and the Age of Exploration: An Encyclopedia.* New York: Da Capo Press, 1998.

Beinart, Haim. *Trujillo: A Jewish Community in Extremadura on the Eve of the Expulsion from Spain.* Jerusalem: Magnes Press, Hebrew University, 1980.

Benveniste, Arthur. Conversation with Rabbi Benito Garzon, 1992. Los Angeles: Interview, 2003.

_____. "A Jewish Community in Tomar, Portugal." http://home.earthlink.net/-benven/tomar.htm.

Bernáldez, Andrés. *Memorias del Reinado de los Reyes Católicos.* Madrid: Real Academía de la Historia, 1962.

Bershtel, Sara, and Allen Graubard. *Saving Remnants: Feeling Jewish in America.* Berkeley/ Los Angeles: University of California Press, 1993.

Birnbaum, Marianna D. *The Long Journey of Gracia Mendes.* Budapest and New York: Central European University Press, 2003.

Brooks, Andrée Aelion. *The Woman Who Defied Kings.* St. Paul, MN: Paragon House, 2002.

Camões, Luís Vaz de. *The Lusíads.* Landeg White, trans. Oxford/New York: Oxford University Press, 1997.

Canelo, David Augusto. *Belmonte, Judaísmo e Criptojudaísmo, Estudos de História.* Belmonte, Portugal: Câmera Municipal de Belmonte, 2001.

_____. *The Last Crypto-Jews of Portugal.* Joshua Stampfer, ed. Werner Talmon-l'Armee, trans. Portland, OR: 1990.

Cantera Burgos, Francisco. *Abraham Zacut: Siglo XV.* Madrid: M. Aguilar, 1935.

Capsali, Elijah. *Seder Eliyahu Zuta,* The Minor Order of Elijah. Shmuel Himmelstein, trans. Quoted in David Raphael, ed., *The Expulsion Chronicles.* North Hollywood, CA: Carmi Press, 1992.

Chazan, Robert, ed. *Church, State, and Jew in the Middle Ages.* New York: Behrman House, 1980.

Cohen, Martin A., ed. and trans. *Samuel Usque's Consolation for the Tribulations of Israel.* Philadelphia: Jewish Publication Society, 1965.

Cole, Peter, ed. and trans. *The Dream of the Poem: Hebrew Poetry from Muslim and Christian Spain 950–1492.* Princeton and Oxford: Princeton University Press, 2007.

Defourneaux, Marcelin. *Daily Life in Spain in the Golden Age.* Palo Alto, CA: Stanford University Press, 1979.

Deutsch, Gotthard and Meyer Kayserling. "Hamon." www.*JewishEncyclopedia.com*, 2002. http://www.jewishencyclopedia.com/view_friendly.jsp?artid=188&letter=H.

Duran Guidiol, Antonio. *La Judería de Huesca.* Zaragoza: Guara Editorial, 1984.

Elliott, J. H. *Imperial Spain 1469–1716.* London: Penguin Books, 1963.

Finkelstein, Norman H. *The Other 1492.* New York: Scribners, 1989.

Freimann, Abraham Haim. "Introduction to the Complete Book of Yohassin." In Abraham b. Samuel Zacuto, *Sefer Yohassin or Book of Lineage,* Joseph Kaplan, ed., Israel Shamir, trans. On *Sephardic Sages Past and Present,* 1999, 6, http://home.flash.net/~mdccull/ Census/Rabbi%20Abraham%20Zacuto,%20by%20Francisco%20Cantera%20y%20 Burgos.pdf.

Freund, Michael. "4 Rabbis Visit Bnei Menashe in India." *Kulanu,* Vol. 9 No. 1 (Spring 2002).

_____. "A Jewish Spark Rekindled in China." *Kulanu,* Vol. 8 No. 4 (Winter 2001–02).

Gerber, Jane S. *The Jews of Spain: A History of the Sephardic Experience.* New York: The Free Press, 1994.

Gitlitz, David M. *Secrecy and Deceit: The Religion of the Crypto-Jews.* Philadelphia and Jerusalem: Jewish Publication Society, 1996.

Gottan, Dahlia. "Foreword." In Gad Nassi and Rebecca Toueg. *Doña Gracia Nasi.* Tel Aviv: Women's International Zionist Organization, 1962.

Greenleaf, Richard E. *The Mexican Inquisition of the Sixteenth Century.* Albuquerque: University of New Mexico Press, 1969.

HaLapid. Marina del Rey: Society for Crypto-Judaic Studies, 1998–2007, http://www.cryptojews.com.

HaLevy, Schulamith, ed. "Crypto-Judaism," *Shofar,* Vol. 18 No.1 (Fall 1999).

Hashavit, David. "Amatus Lusitanus Discovered Valves in Veins and Arteries." *HaLapid,* Winter 2006. Marina del Rey, CA: Society for Crypto-Judaic Studies; also on http://www.cryptojews.com.

Heschel, Abraham Joshua. *Maimonides.* Joachim Neugroschel, trans. New York: Farrar Straus Giroux, 1983.

Heyd, Uriel. "Moses Hamon, Chief Jewish Physician to Sultan Süleymān the Magnificent," *Oriens,* Vol. 16 (12/31/63): 155. http://links.jstor.org/sici?sici=0078-6527%2819631231%2916%3C152%3AMHCJPT%3E2.0.CO%3B2-T.

Hinojosa Montalvo, José. *The Jews of the Kingdom of Valencia from Persecution to Expulsion, 1391–1492.* Jerusalem: Magnes Press, Hebrew University, 1993.

Hordes, Stanley M. *To the Ends of the Earth, A History of the Crypto-Jews of New Mexico.* New York: Columbia University Press, 2005.

Husik, Isaac. *A History of Medieval Jewish Philosophy.* Mineola, NY: Dover Publications, 2002.

Isaacs, Harold R. *Idols of the Tribe: Group Identity and Political Change.* Cambridge, MA: Harvard University Press, 1975.
Jacobs, Janet Liebman. *Hidden Heritage: The Legacy of the Crypto-Jews.* Berkeley: University of California Press, 2002.
———. "Women, Ritual and Secrecy: The Creation of Crypto-Jewish Culture." *HaLapid,* Vol. VIII Issue 2 (Spring 2000).
Kamen, Henry. *The Spanish Inquisition.* London: The Folio Society, 1998.
Kayserling, M. *Christopher Columbus and the Participation of the Jews in the Spanish and Portuguese Discoveries.* Translated by Charles Gross. New York: Trow Press, 1907.
Kedourie, Elie, ed. *Spain and the Jews, The Sephardic Experience, 1492 and After.* London: Thames and Hudson, 1992.
Kepp, Michael. "Documentary Looks at Brazilians Rediscovering Their Jewish Roots." Rio de Janeiro: JTA and United Jewish Communities, http://www.ujc.org/page.html?ArticleID=74955.
Kerem, Yitzchak. "The Jewish Identity of Santángel and His Descendants, a Genealogical Query." Paper presented at *Santángel 98,* International Symposium. Park Forest, IL: Dominican University, August 25, 1998.
Lacave, José Luís. *A Trip Through Jewish Spain.* Celer, trans. Madrid: Subdirección General de Medios de Promoción, Turespaña, Sectretaria General de Turismo.
Lamsa, George M., trans. "Leviticus 19:9–10." *Holy Bible.* New York: HarperSanFrancisco, 1968.
LeMieux, Kathleen E., *comisaria* (ed.). *Luís de Santángel: Primer Financiero de América.* Valencia, Spain: Generalitat Valenciana, 2008.
Lewisohn, Ludwig. *The Last Days of Shylock.* Arthur Szyk, illustrations. New York: Harper & Brothers, 1931.
Lipiner, Elias. *Two Portuguese Exiles in Castile, Dom David Negro and Dom Isaac Abravanel.* Jerusalem: Magnes Press, Hebrew University, 1997.
Loewe, H. "Isaac Abravanel and His Age." J. B. Trend and H. Loewe, eds. *Isaac Abravanel, Six Lectures.* London: Cambridge University Press, 1937.
"Longo, Saadia Ben Abraham." *www.JewishEncyclopedia.com.* 2002. http://jewishencyclopedia.com/view_friendly.jsp?artid=538&letter=L, 5/02/06.
"Longo, Saadiah." *Encyclopedia Judaica.* Jerusalem: MacMillan, 1971.
Mann, Vivian B., Thomas F. Glick, and Jerrilynn D. Dodds, eds. *Convivencia, Jews, Muslims and Christians in Medieval Spain.* New York: George Braziller in association with The Jewish Museum, 1992.
Marcus, Jacob R. *The Jew in the Medieval World.* New York: Athenaeum, 1977.
Mausenbaum, Rufina Bernardetti Silva. "Article in 'The Scribe' on the Lemba." saudadessefarad@yahoogroups.com, 11/13/99.
Melammed, Renée Levine. *Heretics or Daughters of Israel? The Crypto-Jewish Women of Castile.* Oxford: Oxford University Press, 1999.
Memória e Reencontro. Teatro Naciónal D. Maria II. December 4, 1996.
Modder, Montagu Frank. *The Jew in the Literature of England.* New York: Meridian Books and Philadelphia: Jewish Publication Society, 1960.
Moore, Kenneth. *Those of the Street, the Catholic Jews of Mallorca.* Notre Dame, IN: University of Notre Dame Press, 1976.
Morris, William, ed. *The American Heritage Dictionary of the English Language,* New College Edition. Boston: Houghton Mifflin, 301.
"Moses Ben Baruch Almosnino." *Encyclopedia Judaica.* Jerusalem: Macmillan, 1971.
Moya, Emma. "Letter to Editor." *Jewish Historical Society of Southern Arizona.* Tucson, AZ July 16, 1999.
Muñoz, Hilda M. "A Twist of Faith," *Los Angeles Times, Westside Weekly* (July 6, 2001).

Nassi, Gad, and Rebecca Toueg. *Doña Gracia Nasi*. Tel-Aviv: Women's International Zionist Organization, 1991.

Ne'eman, Yuval. "Astronomy in Sefarad." In *The Nearest Active Galaxies*. J. Beckman, L. Colina and H. Netzer, eds. "Nueva Tendencias" series. Madrid: Consejo Superior de Investigaciones Científicas, 1993. Reissued as brochure at the inauguration of The Raymond and Beverly Sackler Institute of Astronomy, December 1, 1994.

Netanyahu, B. *Don Isaac Abravanel, Statesman and Philosopher*, 2nd Ed. Philadelphia: Jewish Publication Society, 1968.

_____. *The Origins of the Inquisition in Fifteenth Century Spain*. New York: Random House, 1995.

Novinsky, Anita, and Amilcar Paulo. "The Last Marranos." *Commentary* Vol. 43 No.5 (May 1967).

Oreck, Alden. "The Virtual Jewish History Tour." American-Israeli Cooperative Enterprise: 2008, http://www.jewishvirtuallibrary.org/jsource/vjw/Brazil.html.

Paz, Octavio. *The Labyrinth of Silence*. Lysander Kemp and Yara Milos, trans. New York: Grove Press, 1994.

Pearl, Judea, and Ruth Pearl, eds. *I Am Jewish, Personal Reflections Inspired by the Last Words of Daniel Pearl*. Woodstock, VT: Jewish Lights, 2005.

Perera, Victor. *The Cross and the Pear Tree: A Sephardic Journey*. New York: Alfred A. Knopf, 1995.

Pérez, Roberto Ferrando. "The Santángel Family in the Royal Court." Paper presented at *Santángel 98,* International Symposium. Park Forest, IL: Dominican University, August 25, 1998.

Presidencia de la Generalitat Valenciana, *Lluís de Santángel y Su Época: Un Nuevo Hombre, Un Mundo Nuevo*. Valencia: Comisión Valenciana de la Expo-92, Comisión del V Centenario del Descubrimiento de América: Encuentro de dos mundos, 1991.

Preto-Rodas, Richard A. "Samuel Usque's *Consolação às Tribulaçõs de Israel* as Pastoral Literature Engagée." *Hispania*, Vol. 73, Number 1. Biblioteca Virtual Miguel D. Cervantes (March 1990). http://www.cervantesvirtual.com/servlet.SirveObras/01482074901275970760035/p00000.

Primack, Karen. "Profile of a Leader: J. J. Keki." *Kulanu* Vol. 6 No. 1 (Spring 1999).

Promoción del Turismo y La Artesanía, Cáceres. *Routes of Sepharad*. Salamanca: Kadmos.

"Rabbi Abraham Ben Samuel Zacuto III 1452–1525," http://www.zacutohistory.com/az.htm, August 15, 2007.

Rabinowitz, L. "Abravanel As Exegete." In *Isaac Abravanel, Six Lectures*. J. B. Trend and H. Loewe, eds. London: Cambridge University Press, 1937.

Raphael, David, ed. *The Expulsion Chronicles*. North Hollywood, CA: Carmi House Press, 1992.

Ragen, Naomi. *The Ghost of Hannah Mendes*. New York: Simon & Schuster, 1998.

Roi, Emilie, and Rochelle Furstenberg. *Doña Gracia of the House of Nasi*, unpublished film script. Jerusalem: 1987.

Rosenblatt, Gary. "Lost Jews Find New Friends." *New York Jewish Week*. New York: New York Jewish Week (October 4, 2002).

Rosenblatt, Norman. *Joseph Nasi, Court Favorite of Selim II: A Dissertation in History*. University of Pennsylvania: 1957.

Roth, Cecil. *A History of the Marranos*. Philadelphia: Jewish Publication Society, 1941.

_____. *The House of Nasi: Doña Gracia*. Philadelphia: Jewish Publication Society, 1948.

_____. *The House of Nasi: The Duke of Naxos*. Philadelphia: Jewish Publication Society, 1948.

Rubin, Nan. *The Hidden Jews of New Mexico: Return to Iberia*. New York: Nan Rubin, http://nanrubin.com/.

Sachar, Abram Leon. *A History of the Jews,* 5th Ed. New York: Knopf, 1967.
Sachar, Howard M. *Farewell España: The World of the Sephardim Remembered.* New York: Vintage Books, 1994.
Salpeter, Eliahu. "There Is No Need to Fear Intermarriage." *Ha'aretz.* Israel: *Ha'aretz* (July 10, 2002).
Sebastia, J. Doñate, and J. R. Magdalena Nom de Deu. *Three Jewish Communities in Medieval Valencia, Castellon del la Plana, Burriana, Villarreal.* Jerusalem: Magnes Press, Hebrew University, 1990.
"Sephardi and Mizrahi Women Write About Their Lives." *Bridges,* Vol. 7 No. 1 (Winter 5758/1997–98).
Simms, Norman. "Being Crypto-Jewish in Colonial Brazil (1500–1822): Brushing History against the Grain." *Journal of Religious History,* Vol. 31 No. 4 (December 2007).
"Spain to Reverse Historic Decree." *Vista.* Coral Gables, FL: *Vista,* date unknown.
Strauss, L. "On Abravanel's Philosophical Tendency and Political Teaching." In *Isaac Abravanel, Six Lectures.* J. B. Trend and H. Loewe, eds. London: Cambridge University Press, 1937.
Teltsch, Kitty. "Belmonte: A Reporter Revisits an Anusim Community." *HaLapid.* Society for Crypto Judaic Studies, Vol. X Issue 1; can also be read on http://www.cryptojews.com.
_____. "2003 San Antonio Conference Highlights, Members Hear Research, Personal Stories; Lavender Elected President with New Board." *HaLapid.* Society for Crypto-Judaic Studies, Vol. X Issue 3 (Fall 2003); also available on http://www. cryptojews.com.
The Jewish Encyclopedia. New York/London: Funk and Wagnalls, 1912.
Trend, J. B., and H. Loewe, eds. *Isaac Abravanel: Six Lectures.* London: Cambridge University Press, 1937.
Twain, Mark. "Concerning the Jew." In *The Complete Essays of Mark Twain.* Charles Neider, ed. Garden City, NY: Doubleday, 1963; from *Harper's,* September 1899.
The Universal Jewish Encyclopedia. New York: Universal Jewish Encyclopedia, Inc., 1943.
Usque, Samuel. *Consolation for the Tribulations of Israel.* Martin A. Cohen, trans. *Samuel Usque's Consolation for the Tribulations of Israel.* Philadelphia: Jewish Publication Society, 1965.
Wakin, Daniel J. "A Count of U.S. Jews Sees a Dip; Others Demur." *The New York Times* (October 9, 2002): A1 & A17.
Watanabe, Teresa. "A Clouded View of U.S. Jews." *Los Angeles Times* (October 9, 2002): A1, A18.
Wiesenthal, Simon. *Sails of Hope: The Secret Mission of Christopher Columbus.* New York: Macmillan, 1973.
Zacuto, Abraham b. Samuel. *Sefer Yohassin or Book of Lineage.* Joseph Kaplan, ed., Israel Shamir, trans. Zacuto Foundation, 2005. On *Sephardic Sages Past and Present* (1999): 6. http://home.flash.net/~mdccull/Census/Rabbi%20Abraham%20Zacuto, %20by%20Francisco%20Cantera%20y%20Burgos.pdf.
"Zacuto, Abraham Ben Samuel." *Encyclopedia Judaica.* New York: Macmillan, 1973.
Zacuto, Nina Rebecca. "The Descendants Abraham Zacuto." *www.FamilyTreeMaker.com User Home Pages,* 9/05/00. http://www.familytreemaker.com/users/z/a/c/Nina-Rebecca-Zacuto/index.html, 11/23/00.

Websites and Electronic Sources

http://www.saudades.org/: about Portuguese crypto Jews, world-wide.
http://www.sephardim.com/: lists of Sephardic names from archives and cemeteries.
http://www.cryptojews.com/: articles from *HaLapid,* quarterly publication.

Documents, Exhibits

Berger, Natalia, ed. *Jews and Medicine: Religion, Culture, Science*, Tel Aviv: Beth Hatefutsoth, Museum of the Jewish Diaspora, exhibit.

Entry hall exhibit of explorers. Lisbon: Museu da Marinha.

Letter of Columbus to Luís de Santángel. New York: New York Public Library, Center for the Humanities, Rare Books and Manuscripts Division.

Comments on Sources

For the reader who wants to further explore the subjects covered, we present notes about primary sources — print, electronic and cyber — that supported the preparation of this work. Complete citations are found in the Bibliography. Sources referred to are in English, unless otherwise stated. Readers of other languages can undoubtedly find rich references through independent research.

The reader is referred at the outset to the museums and special libraries with extensive material on the subject. Examples are Beth Hatefutsoth, the Nahum Goldmann Museum of the Jewish Diaspora in Tel Aviv; the Library of the Jewish Theological Seminary; and Museu da Marinha, the Maritime Museum, in Lisbon.

Chapter One. On the Eve of Expulsion

This chapter is an orientation to the era, places and events unfolding in the pages ahead. The resources cited are utilized in greater depth in the chapters to follow. They include studies of history particular to Spain and related regions, as well as works which focus on particular individuals or events.

Of the first type, generalized histories covering several centuries and periods, we have been supported, in great measure, by Jane S. Gerber's comprehensive *The Jews of Spain* and Yitzak Baer's complete two-volume *History of the Jews in Christian Spain*. We direct the reader to Gerber's user-friendly section in her Appendix, "A Note on Further Reading," which details and describes a myriad of sources on the subjects covered.

One must also single out David Raphael's *The Expulsion 1492 Chronicles,* a valuable sourcebook of documents from the period covered, by historians, scribes and personages of the day.

As this chapter provides an introduction to the notables to be covered in the work, resources about individuals will be described in the chapter which portrays the specific personage. Many of the following studies referred to are out of print. Most can be found through university research libraries, using inter-library exchange privileges when not in the local collection.

Chapter Two. Isaac Abravanel

Benzion Netanyahu's *Don Isaac Abravanel, Statesman and Philosopher* provides detailed attention to Don Isaac's biography and critical analysis of his philosophy, writings, and influence on successive generations. One is also referred to Elias Lipiner's *Two Portuguese Exiles in Castile, Dom David Negro and Dom Isaac Abravanel*, and J. B. Trend and H. Loewe's *Isaac Abravanel, Six Lectures*.

Chapter Three. Abraham Zacuto

The primary source for the life and work of the Salamanca astronomer is Francisco Cantera Burgos' *Abraham Zacut*, in Spanish. We are not aware of an English translation. References to Zacuto are found in works on Spanish and Portuguese seafaring of the period, particularly the voyages of Columbus and da Gama, and the navigational instruments serving them.

A colleague has called to our attention a theater piece in Portuguese, *As Mãos de Abraão Zacuto* by Luis de Sttau Monteiro (1968).

Chapter Four. Luís de Santángel

The foremost source on the influential New Christian courtier is *Lluís de Santàngel y Su Época: Un Nuevo Hombre, un Mundo Nuevo*, the tastefully designed and illustrated folio edition published by the commission in Valencia, Spain that spearheaded the observance in 1992 of the Columbus quincentennial. This Spanish-language anthology, with articles by scholars, was published in a limited edition to accompany an exhibit and is not readily available. However, many of the scholars are included in *Lluís de Santàngel, Primer Financiero de América,* proceedings in Spanish and English of the International Symposium Santángel 98, recently published by the Generalitat Valenciana.

M. Kayserling, German historian in the early twentieth century, highlights Santángel in *Columbus and the Participation of the Jews in the Spanish and Portuguese Discoveries*.

This chapter pays attention to *judaizante*, observing Jewish ritual or customs in secret. Janet Liebman Jacobs' *Hidden Heritage: The Legacy of the Crypto-Jews* is particularly helpful in understanding this practice in New

Christian families. David M. Gitlitz' monumental work, *Secrecy and Deceit: The Legacy of the Crypto-Jews* is unequaled in presenting the phenomenon as it manifested among converts to Catholicism in inquisitional Spain.

Chapter Five. Doña Gracia Nasi

Three major sources stand out for in-depth exploration of *La Señora*'s life and times. Foremost is Cecil Roth's two-volume series, *The House of Nasi*. The English historian set out to write about Don Joseph Nasi, who became Duke of Naxos of the Ottoman Empire in the sixteenth century, then discovered that the achievements of Don Joseph owed much to the support and example given him by his aunt. So, *Doña Gracia Nasi* became the first volume of a series on the remarkable family, published in 1948.

One half century later, Andrée Aelion Brooks began amassing research to add to the literature on *La Señora*, resulting in 2002 in *The Woman Who Defied Kings*. Marianna D. Birnbaum's *The Long Journey of Gracia Mendes*, which followed in 2003, provides illuminating coverage of Doña Gracia's passage through Ragusa on her way to Constantinople, and the economic aspects of running the House of Nasi.

Martin A. Cohen's translation and introduction to *Samuel Usque's Consolation for the Tribulations of Israel* is the source for Usque, the writer whose epic poem was published with support from Doña Gracia.

Chapter Six. "Thou preparest a table before me"

In this section, we relied gratefully on the in-depth studies of pre-expulsion Spanish Jewish communities by scholars from the Hebrew University of Jerusalem, among them Yom Tov Assis, Haim Beinart, J. Doñate Sebastia, J. R. Magdalena Nom de Deu and José Hinojosa Montalvo.

We found Israel Abrahams' *Jewish Life in the Middle Ages* on a fortuitous hunt through used book store shelves in Santa Fe, New Mexico, and it proved to be as useful in 1996 as it must have been a century earlier, upon its publication in 1896. Also instructive was Jacob R. Marcus' sourcebook, *The Jew in the Medieval World* and Yitzhak Baer's detailed sections on Jewish life in Spain.

Chapter Seven. "In the presence of my enemies"

The works cited for Chapter Six were also of value here, as we continued our portrayal of everyday life in the days just before the edict of expulsion was to change it forever.

Chapter Eight. Resilience and Recovery

We call attention once again to Martin A. Cohen's translation of Samuel Usque's epic poem, cited above, and his introduction. This was the only work we found covering the life of one of five personages described in this chapter — Moses Hamon, Amatus Lusitanus, Samuel Usque, Saadiah Longo and Moses Almosnino. We secured our information on the others from references in works cited above, by authors such as Roth, Gerber, Baer and Brooks, and from essays in *Encyclopedia Judaica* and *The Jewish Encyclopedia*.

Internet sources were most valuable. On the website of The Society for Crypto-Judaic Studies, for example, an online issue of its publication, *HaLapid,* gave us David Hashavit's article "Amatus Lusitanus Discovered Valves in Veins and Arteries." Also found online was Norman Simms' "Being Crypto-Jewish in Colonial Brazil (1500–1822): Brushing History Against the Grain." We found continuing reference as well to the works of Anita Novinsky as foremost scholar of crypto Judaism in Brazil.

Chapter Nine. Endurance, Persistence and Identity

As much of this chapter is contemporary in focus, a considerable portion of the useful material on which it is grounded came from newspapers, magazines and websites. There were contributions from individuals, such as Kathleen Teltsch, offering theatre programs and newspaper articles acquired while covering events as a journalist, and Arthur Benveniste, passing along a relevant letter to the editor sent in response to one of his talks. And, there was the daily email in our inbox from forums such as saudades-sefarad@yahoogroups.com and anousim@yahoogroups.com.

As the issues presented on this most ancient yet contemporary subject continue to unfold, the reader is invited to join in the scholarly effort by staying alert to current events as they unfold in all varieties of media.

Glossary

aliyah Hebrew term signifying emigration to the Holy Land.
aljama from the Arabic *al yamaa,* or assembly, the semi-autonomous governing entity for a Jewish community in Christian Spain.
anus, anusim, anousim Hebrew for forced one or ones; refers to Jews converted by force to Catholicism.
auto-da-fé lit., act of faith; ceremony in which punishment was meted out by the state, after conviction of heresy by the Inquisition; usually death by fire.
baile general official representative of the Crown.
beit din rabbinical court, passing judgment on civil matters such as marriage, divorce and Jewish law, with jurisdiction in issues where both parties are Jews.
blood libel false accusation that Jews kidnap and murder Christians, usually children, on Good Friday to use their blood in religious rituals; also referred to as ritual murder.
caballero horseman, with or without arms; also signifies a gentleman, as distinguished from those of lesser means who might be traveling on foot (*de pie*).
call district or streets inhabited by Jews in pre-expulsion Aragón, Catalunya and Valencia; see *judería.*
contador mayor chief accountant; an office held by Luís de Santángel in the kingdom of Aragón.
converso/a individual who has converted to Catholicism.
Cristão Nuovo/a Portuguese for New Christian.
Cristiano/a Nuevo/a Spanish for New Christian.
crypto Jew New Christians who practiced Judaism in secret.
dama de la casa title given to wife in charge of the household; usually applied to those of wealth with servants and retainers.
dayenu repetitive litany chanted during the Passover seder, following enumeration of each of God's actions on behalf of the Hebrews during the exodus from Egypt; signifying "it would have been sufficient."
dhimmi Muslim term referring to unbeliever.
diaspora everywhere that Jews have lived following their expulsion from a region.

escribano de ración Chancellor of the Royal Household; title given Luís de Santángel by Fernando II.

gaon most learned one; Hebrew honorific title given to a scholar's scholar among rabbis.

Grand Porte the place where the sultan dwells, usually Constantinople, now called Istanbul; also known as Sublime Porte.

ha-Gaveret The Lady; Hebrew term of respect for a respected woman, applied to Doña Gracia Nasi; see *La Señora*.

Haggadah book containing ritual for annual *seder* or dinner at Passover, celebrating liberation of Jews from slavery in Egypt.

halakha Jewish law, as interpreted by the sages and rabbis.

Havdalah ritual performed at the close of the Sabbath, signifying passage into a new week.

judaizante term used by the Holy Office of the Inquisition, describing the actions of a former Jew who, despite conversion to Catholicism, practices Judaism in secret against state law.

judaizer one accused of *judaizante*.

judaría district or streets inhabited by Jews in pre-expulsion Castilla and León; see *call*.

ketubah written marriage contract, specifying legal and monetary agreements between parties.

kippah skullcap or head covering worn by observant Jewish males.

La Llorona The Crying Woman; popular legend of a woman who, having drowned herself and her children, seeks youngsters to replace her own; often used in the American southwest to frighten "naughty" children into approved behavior.

marrano pig or swine in Spanish and Portuguese; term of derision applied by Old Christians to New Christians or converts to Christianity, implying *judaizante* and distrust of sincerity of conversion; term used proudly today by some in Portugal, publicly accepting their former Jewish status and/or crypto Judaism.

messiah savior, promised in the Bible, who will come to lead Jews back to their homeland and create peace.

mestre Latin for master; term of respect preceding name of certain professionals, such as physicians and university professors.

mezuzah object of metal, wood or ceramic containing the *shemah* and placed on doorways; commemorates the passing over of Jewish homes by the Angel of Death, who claimed the first born of every Egyptian family as described in Exodus.

midrash from Hebrew for interpretation or exegesis; word has several usages: 1. a specific manner of studying and interpreting biblical sections; 2. a collection or book of teachings based on such study and interpretation; 3. a place where *midrash* takes place.

moysen term of status preceding name, conferring respect.

Nasi, *el nací* "prince" in Hebrew; title given to Jewish leaders who represented their communities before rulers.

Passover Annual observation of seven days in the Hebrew month of Nisan, observing the Jews' liberation from slavery in Egypt.

Pentateuch refers to the Five Books of Moses or first five books of the Bible.

Rambam name by which Moses ben Maimon, twelfth century philosopher, is referred to in Hebrew; in English, he is known as Maimonides.

Reconquista reconquest; period of eight centuries after Muslim conquest, signifying military efforts by Christian kingdoms to regain control of Iberian peninsula.

responsa rabbinical statement, usually in writing, on moral and theological issues.

Rosh Hashanah high holiday signifying the beginning of the Jewish New Year.

sanbenito yellow hooded garment with red crosses front and back, worn by those convicted by the Inquisition; symbolizes doing penance for *judaizante*.

Santa Hermandad Holy Brotherhood; religious order.

santero/a folk artist in New Mexico, reproducing biblical scenes and religious figures in Spanish colonial art forms; usually of Hispanic background.

seder Hebrew for "order"; used to refer to annual dinner to observe the holiday of Passover.

Sefarad name by which Sephardic Jews referred to Spain, derived from the biblical reference to "the captivity of Jerusalem that is in Sefarad."

La Señora The Lady; Spanish term of respect applied to Doña Gracia Nasi; see *ha-Gaveret*.

Sephardic Jews refers to Jews on the Iberian Peninsula during their period of settlement until 1492; plural is Sephardim.

shemah refers to statement made by Jews affirming belief in one God; *Shemah Yisrael Adonoy Elohenu Adonoy Echod,* Hear O Israel, the Lord is God, the Lord is One.

shohet ritual slaughterer, preparing meat according to Jewish law.

shtadlan defender.

tax farmer favored individual receiving lucrative appointment to collect taxes; paid a fee to the king for the right to collect taxes from a given area; expected to make loans to the ruler from wealth thus accrued.

Talmud commentaries by sages on Jewish law.

Talmud Torah school for teaching boys about Judaic law and observance.

Torah The Pentateuch; text of first five books of the Bible; refers to parchment scroll in synagogues; can also mean the body of Jewish law in print, electronic or digital form.

yahrzeit observance, with prayer and candle lighting, on annual date of family member's death.

yarmulka see *kippah*.

yeshiva school or academy for scholars of Judaic language, principles, foundations and rituals.

Yom Kippur The Day of Atonement, coming at the close of the annual observation of the Jewish New Year.

Index

Aaron, Jew of Valencia 139
Abayudaya: conversion of Gershom Sizomu and JJ Keki 191; Semei Kakungulu, leader 191; tribe 191–2, 198
Abec, Jafuda 147
Abenazar 64
Abrahams, Israel 141, 142, 155, 227
Abravanel, Allan R. 52
Abravanel, Benvenida (daughter-in-law of Isaac) 157; meets Gracia Nasi 115; with Samuel Usque 171, 172; tutor of Eleanora de Toledo 41; weds first cousin 105
Abravanel, Isaac ben Judah 15–20, 26–52, 226; contributions 48–52; student of Isaac Aboab 142; subject in book 9
Abravanel, Judah (father of Isaac) 26, 28, 29
Abravanel, Judah (son of Isaac) 39, 40, 41, 42, 43; as Leone Ebreo 44, 46; mourning for his son 201–7
Abravanel, Melamud (son-in-law of Isaac) 38
Abravanel, Samuel 41, 44, 157; with Samuel Usque 171, 172
Abravanel, Samuel (grandfather of Isaac) 28
Abravanel, Yaacov 152
Abravanel Family Newsletter 52, 211, 219
Abumasar 64
Abu Saud el Amadi 175
adelantado 135
adelantats 135
Affanso (Crown Prince of Portugal) 66
al-Andaluz 37
Alaxcar, Moises 71
Albo 48
Albulhosain 63
Alcalá de Guadaira 131
Alexy, Trudi vii; *The Marrano Legacy* 185; *The Mezuzah in the Madonna's Foot* 185
Alfonso (King of Naples) 42, 44, 52

Alfonso V (King of Aragón) 80
Alfonso V (King of Portugal) 16, 30–1
Alfonso X, *El Sabio,* the Wise (King of Aragón) 59, 63, 134
Alhambra Decree 159
aliyah 50, 229
aljama: all communities 22, 130, 135, 137, 139, 144, 145, 154; customs and practices in 155; manufacture of wine in 149; slaughter houses in 143; of Tortosa 152; of Trujillo 132, 133, 136
Almanach Perpetuum 53, 56, 63, 70; see also *Hajibbur Hagadol*
Almosnino, Abraham 173
Almosnino, Moses ben Baruch 9, 123, 166, 173–5, sources on 228
al yamaa 135
Amin, Idi 191
Amishav 190
Ancona: *Amatus Lusitanus* 169; boycott of 9, 101, 118–21, 143; Jewish and *converso* respite 163
Andalucía 7, 35, 131, 149
The Announcer of Salvation 46
Answers to Saul 48
anusim 98, 177, 192, 229
Aquinas, Thomas 33, 48, 158
Arbués, Pedro 19, 76–7, 91
Aristotle 28, 29, 64, 175
Arrobas, Yuce 152
Assyrians 189, 190
Astrolabe: Abraham Zacuto improves 21, 53, 85; Luís Vas de Camões in *Os Lucíadas* 67; use in Columbus voyage 73; use in da Gama voyage 66–7, 73, 85
Atereth Zekenim 29
Athias, Yomtob 114
Augustine 33
Averroes 63
Avichail, Eliyahu 190

233

Badajoz 147
Baer, Yitzhak 28, 163, 225, 227, 228
baile general 96, 135, 136, 139, 154
Barbastro 150
Barcelona: de Santángel on monument 98–99; Jehuda (Jafudá) Cresques 21, 55; Juana de Santángel 81; massacres of 1391 78, 130, 131; shipyards 5
Barchillon family: Schlomo 136; in Trujillo 133, 136
Bari 45
Bauza 88
b. Axer, Rabbi Judá 63
Bayazid II (Ottoman sultan) 20, 107, 163, 167
Beinart, Haim 128, 131, 150, 152, 227
beit din: conversions 191, 192, 193, 195; jurisdiction and roles 136, 143, 144, 154; regarding Gracia Nasi 117, 121
Belvedere 116, 124–5, 175
ben Axer, Rabbi Judá 63
Benedict XII (Pope) 77
ben Ezra, Abraham 63
ben Hanina Gaon, Sherira 71
ben Maimon, Rabbi Moses *see* Maimonides
ben Sheshet, Isaac 142
Benvenist, Vidal (jerkin maker of Tortosa) 149
Benveniste, Vidal (Jewish spokesman at Tortosa Disputation) 77
Benveniste family: Semah (later Mendes, Francisco; *q.v.*) and Meier (later Mendes, Diogo; *q.v.*) 22–4, 104; *see also* Nasi, Gracia
ben Verga 71
ben Yechiel, Rabbi Asher 156
ben Yehiel, Natan 72
Bernáldez, Andrés 14
Bershtel, Sara 194, 217, 218
Bessant, Brianda *see* de Santángel family
Bnei Menashe *see* India
Bomberg, Daniel 9, 106, 209n6
Bonnet, Honoré 60
Borgia, Lucrezia 102
Borja 150
Braganza (royal house of Portugal) 30–1, 34, 47
Brandeis, Madeline 6, 209
Brazil: as diaspora 161, 162, 163, 177–8, 180; sources on 228; survival of Judaism in 9
Briviesca 22
Burgos 131
Burgos, Bishop of *see* de Santa María, Pablo
Burma 190, 195
Burriana 135, 139

Cabral, Pedro Alvares 177
Cabrero, Juan 86, 94
Cabrit, Juceff Saltell 152
Caceres 128, 147
Cádiz 17, 37, 209
Canano, Giambattista 169
Canpanton, Isaac 59
Cantera Burgos, Francisco 66, 72, 226
Cantillana 131
Cão, Diogo 54
caps 154
Capsali, Eliahu/ Elija 39, 161, 210n17
Caro, Joseph 59
Castellón 139
Castellví, Mosén: 82; Castellví family 89; Jerónima 96
Catalán *Atlas* 56
Charles V (Holy Roman Emperor, also Phillip II of Spain) 109, 169
Charles VI (King of France) 54
Charles VIII (King of France) 42
chazzans 140
China: 1, 9, 84, 183; Kaifeng 190–1
Chinillo, Noah: 78, 88, 95–6; as surname 76, 88; *see also* de Santángel family
Chronicle of Jewish Historical Society of Southern Arizona 184
Cicero 33
clavario 135
clavarius 135
Cocumbriel, Isaac 173
Cohanim 189
Cohen, David 143
Cohen family (Trujillo) 129
Cole, Peter vii, xiii, xviii
Colonna, Vittoria 102
Columbus, Christopher: 1, 7–8, 17, 20–1; Luís de Santángel 84–7, 94–9, 226; support by Abraham Zacuto, appeal to Portugal 53, 57, 65, 70, 73, 82; support by Isaac Abravanel 36–37
Commentary 186
Condi, Jaffuda 147
Congregación Hebrea de Baja California *see* Salas, Carlos Samuel
Il Consiglio dei Dieci 47
Consolation for the Tribulations of Israel 115, 166, 171
contador mayor 17, 82, 83, 93
converso/a, conversos/as 7
convivencia, la convivencia 1, 2, 25, 63
Córdoba 7, 8, 131, 140, 142
Corfu: Isaac Abravanel in 44–7
Coría 131
Coronel, Francisco: 175; Catholic name Fernando Pérez Coronel 175; son Solomon 175

corregidor 136
Cortés at Toro 155
Cortés of Aragón 131
Cortés of Toledo 138
Cotel, Rabbi Moshe 195
councillors 135
counsellors 135
Crescas 48
Cresques, Abraham 21, 55–6
Cresques, Judah (Jehuda, Yehuda) 21, 65, 67, 72
Cresques family 8, 56
Os Cristãos Novos no Século XX 186
Cromwell, Oliver 177
Cromwell, Thomas 107
Crónica de la Orden de Alcántara 64
Crown of the Elders 29, 33, 42
Cuadran Judaicus 67
Cueta, Bishop of 85
Curationum Medicinallium Centuriae Septem 169, 170

da Gama, Gaspar 177
da Nóbrega, Manoel 177
Daroca: de Santángels in 74, 76, 78, 88, 96; inquisition testimony on de Santángels 80–1, 89, 93
David (King of Israel) 27, 50
The Days of the World 42
de Aragón, Jaime 139
de Arévalo, Zaadic 71
de Ayala, Hernando 96
de Centelles, Francina 96
de Chávez, Luis 152
de Coloma, Juan 83
de Córdoba, Gonsalvo 46
de Escobar, Alvaro 152
de Fenollet, Beatriz 96
de Fenollet, Luís 96
de la Caballería, Alfonso 38, 76–7, 81, 91, 93, 94
de la Ronha, Antonio 105
de Luna, Alvaro (father of Gracia Nasi) 24, 102; *see also* Nasi, Gracia
de Luna, Beatriz (later Nasi, Gracia; *q.v.*): 24, 102–113; daughter (Ana or Brianda, later Nasi, Reyna; *q.v.*) 106, 109–110, 112; niece Beatriz (later Gracia *la Chica*, daughter of sister Brianda and Diogo Mendes) 109; sister Brianda (later Mendes, Reyna; *q.v.*) 106–113–118, 124, 125, 126; *see also* Nasi, Gracia
de Medici, Cosimo 169
de' Medicis, Catherine 102
de Montesa, Jaime 76–77
de Oñate, Juan 7
de Paternoy, Sancho 76, 77, 88, 91

de Quintanilla, Alfonso 84
de Ribasaltas, Juan 78
de Santa Cruz, Antonio 78
de Santa Fé, Francisco 76
de Santa Fé, Gerónimo 76, 78
de Santa María, Pablo 33
de Santángel, Luís (*escribano de ración* of Aragón) 15–20, 74–100
de Santángel, Luís (judicial official of Zaragoza) 76–7
de Santángel, Luís, family of: brother Jaime 95; daughter Luisa 81, 88, 96; father Luís 80–1; grandfather Luís (formerly Chinillo, Noah; *q.v.*) 78–80, 81; maternal grandmother Gracia 89; mother Brianda 82, 89–94; son Alfonso 81; son Hernando or Fernando 81, 95; son Jerónimo 81; son of Jaime, Miguel Jerónimo 96; uncles and aunt of Luís, Berenguer, Pedro Martín, Constanza 78; wife Juana 18–20, 81, 95
de Sevilla, Juan Sánchez 28
de Sintra, Pedro 54
de Sousa, Tomé 177
Despés, Esperanza 96
d'Este, Isabel 102
de Talavera, Hernando 84
de Tarabau, Diego: 81; children (Alfonso, Hernando, Jerónimo, Luisa) 81
de Tavara, Manuel Alvares 72
de Toledo, Eleonora or Leonora 41
de Toledo, Fernán Díaz 132
de Toledo, Pedro 41
de Toledo, Sancho 83
de Torquemada, Tomás 1, 38
de Torres, Juan 36
de Torres y Tapia, Alonso 64
de Torrutiel, Abraham 71
de Ulloa, Rodrigo 83
de Vargas, Jerónimo *see* Athias, Yomtob
de Villanueva, Angel 88
de Vivero, Gonzalo 20, 59, 63
de Zúñiga y Pimental, Don Juan 20, 64
dhimmis 133
Dialoghi di Amore, Dialogues on Love 43, 46
Dias, Bartholomeu 54
Dioscorides, Index 169
Disputation at Tortosa 77, 78, 138
Disraeli, Benjamin xi, 2, 74, 98
DNA 25, 100, 189
Doña Juana (*La Enfanta*, Princess of Spain) 95, 96
"Dreams, Their Origin and True Nature" 175
Duarte (father of Alfonso V, King of Portugal) 30
Dueña La Morena 89
Dunash ben Labrat xiii

Eanes, Gil 54
Elizabeth (queen of England) 102
El Sabio see James I
El Tránsito 8, 142
En Salomon Nathan 135
Ericson, Leif 54, 84
Esdra, Jew of Valencia 139
Este, Duchy of 41, 213
Esther: biblical figure 123; Book of Esther 142; Feast of Esther 157; as saint 7
Eternal Justice 42
Extremos y Grandezas de Constantinopla 174

Fariza 150
Fernandes, Christopher 105
Fernando II (King of Aragón): with Abraham Zacuto 57, 65; capture of Granada 17; expulsion of Jews 13, 37; godfather of Abraham Seneor 175; with Isaac Abravanel 15, 33, 34, 35; with Luís de Santángel 15, 16, 77, 82, 86, 88, 91, 94; name in Spanish 10; plot to kidnap Abravanel grandchild 39, 201; Spain's golden age 2; sponsor of Columbus 1; Sultan Bayazid's statement 20, 116
Fernando III (King of Castilla) 128
Ferrante II (King of Naples) 40, 41, 42, 44
Ferrara: Amatus Lusitanus 168-9; Benvenida Abravanel 41; Gracia Nasi 107, 112-116, 118-9, 122, 124-6, 157, 163; open practice of Judaism 162; Samuel Usque 171, 172
Ferrer, Vicente 75, 77, 78, 94
The Forms of the Elements 29
France: Catherine de' Medicis 102; Columbus to petition for support 86, 97; path of Gracia Nasi 107, 110, 118; restrictions, expulsion of Jews 155, 159, 162; war with Naples 42, 44, 46-47, 171; Zacuto family origins 57
Francisco of Aragón 109
Freimann, Abraham Haim 57, 211, 220

Galen 171, 175
Gallano, Count of 96
Gaon, Rabbi Semaj 72
Garzon, Rabbi Benito 184
Gemetría 159
Genoa 1, 36, 40, 43, 44
Gerber, Jane 225, 228
Gerona 131, 142
Gitlitz, David: practices of *conversos* 103; *Secrecy and Deceit* 184, 227
Glenmary Research Center 193
Gomes, Diogo 54
Gorin, Howard 191
Granada 7, 8, 160; Columbus honored 97; Luís de Santángel 18, 98; Moses Hamon birthplace 167; Schmu'el Hanagid 74; siege and capture 1, 17, 24, 33-34, 36, 83-87, 130
Grand Mufti Abu Saud el Amadi 175
Graubard, Allen 194, 217, 218
Guadalajara: Isaac Aboab's *yeshiva* 36, 59, 142; Isaac Abravanel 16, 20, 35
Guimarães 30
Gutenberg, Johann 149

Haaretz 195
Haggadah 51, 230
Hajibbur Hagadol 53, 61, 63, 64
Hakhmei ha-Shir 172
HaLapid viii, 186, 188, 228
ha-Levi, Astruc 77
Halevi, Judah 144, 158
Hanagid, Schmu'el 74
Hamon, Joseph 175
Hamon, Moses 9, 112, 166-8, 228
Harper's 198
Hashavit 169, 228
havdalah 158, 230
Haviv 168, 169
Hebrew Union College 191
Henry VIII (King of England) 107, 108
Henry, the Navigator (Prince of Portugal) 54
Heyd, Uriel 168
Hidden Heritage: The Legacy of the Crypto-Jews 184; *see also* Janet Jacobs
"The Hidden Jews of New Mexico" 188
Hinojosa Montalvo, José: effect of usury doctrines 152; Jewish influence on economy 150; Jewish relations with Muslims 147; occupations of lower classes 149; as source 227; synagogues and Crown 135, 139
Hippocrates 64, 171
Hjosafot Hesefer ha-Àruk 72
Holy Leagues 157
Hordes, Stanley M. viii, 184
House of Mendes: 47, 102, 51; as creditor 107-8; Diogo Mendes 108; Francisco Mendes 104-5; João Miguez/Joseph Nasi 24, 118, 124; in Ottoman Empire 116; representative in Ancona 119; wealth 109
Hualngo, Yossi 190
Huesca 150, 173

I Am Jewish: Personal Reflections Inspired by the Last Words of Daniel Pearl 195
ibn David, Rabbi Abraham 71
ibn Regal, Alí 63
ibn Shoshan Synagogue *see* Santa María la Blanca
ibn Tibbon, Judah 145

ibn Yahya, Gedaliah 172
Il Consiglio dei Dieci 47
Index Dioscorides 169
India: Assam 189; Bnei Menashe 189–90; Columbus and da Gama 66, 84, 85, 106, 183, 195; Jewish communities 9; Mizoram and Manipur states 189; sea route to 47, 54, 56, 57
Inheritance of the Fathers 45
Innocent III (pope) 154
Institute for Jewish and Community Research 193
Isabel of Castilla 26, 39, 50; Columbus voyage 86, 87, 97; relations with Trujillo 132, 133

Jacobs, Janet 184, 226
James I (King of Aragón) 154
The Jew of Malta 125
João I (grandfather of Alfonso V, King of Portugal) 30
João II (King of Portugal): Columbus petition 84–5; courtier Joseph Vecinho 66; dies 22; opposes Braganzas 31–2; supports explorations 21, 54, 56, 61; threatens Isaac Abravanel 16, 34, 47; treatment of exiled Jews 20, 69
John I (King of Castilla) 155
John II (King of Castilla) 76, 96, 132
Juan (Prince of Aragón) 56
Juan II (King of Aragón) 78, 82
Juan Carlos (King of Spain) 188
Judah of Sevilla (grandfather of Isaac Abravanel) *see* Abravanel, Samuel
Judaism: Amatus Lusitanus 168–9; de Santángels 78–94, 98, 100; under Dutch in Brazil 177–8; endurance of 25, 180–200; Gracia Nasi family as *judaizante* 103, 109, 112; Gracia Nasi practices openly 113–22; observation 7, 9; influence of Isaac Abravanel 48–52; institutions 138–141; Isaac Abravanel on endurance of 38–40; Judah Abravanel 43; in Ottoman Empire 20; in Portugal 68–70, 129; women 141–42
judaizante 230
Judea 189
Juicio de los Eclipses 6
Julius III (pope) 169

Kahal Zur 178
Kerem, Yitzchak 88
ketubah 140, 144, 230
kupah 156-7

La Llorona 6, 230
La Lonja 79
La Opinión de Baja California 192

La Señora see Nasi, Gracia
Ladino 2
The Last Days of Shylock 125
"The Last *Marranos*" 186
Lateran Council in Rome 154
Law of Moses 9, 13, 75, 104
Lei, Shi 191
Lemba: 188–9, 190, 191, 198, 199; Lemba Cultural Association 189; Mozambique 189; South Africa 67, 189; Tanzania and Malawi 189; Zimbabwe 189
Leone Ebreo, Hebrew Lion *see* Abravanel, Judah
Lérida 131
Libro de ajuedrez, dados, y tablas (Book of Chess, Backgammon, and Dice) 134
limpieza de sangre 2, 95, 96
La Llorona 6, 230
Longo, Saadiah ben Abraham: biography 166, 171, 172–3; eulogy for Gracia Nasi 123, 171; sources on 228
La Lonja 79
Lopez Cardozo, David de Jahocob 176
López de Ayala, Diego 96, 138
Lord Redován of Orihuela 96
Los Angeles Times 3, 191, 193
Los Reyes Católicos 1, 13, 17, 33, 83
Lusitanus, Amatus 153, 166, 168–71, 228
Lusitanus, Zacutus 72

Machiavelli, Niccolò, 37, 91, 94
Madero, Francisco 192
Madrid 7, 16, 131, 174
Maimonides: Abraham Zacuto 61, 63, 71, 73; on Christianity and Islam 158; Isaac Abravanel 28–9, 33, 44, 46, 48; on tithing 156
Málaga 36, 39, 83
Mallorca 54, 55, 56
Maneti, Samuel 152
Manoel I (King of Portugal): Abraham Zacuto 57, 58, 66, 70, 73; Abravanel grandchild 201; called The Fortunate 70; marries Isabel 69; releases enslaved Jews 66–69; succeeds to throne 66; Vasco da Gama 58
Manoel II (King of Portugal) 73
Maria (Queen of Spain) 135
Marie (Regent of the Lowlands) 109–10
Marlowe, Christopher 125
Marques of Villena 133
Martinez, Ferrán 28
Mary (Queen of England) 102
Mary, Queen of Scots 102
Mathivha, Matshaya *see* Lemba
Mazzara 42
Melamud *see* Abravanel, Melamud

Menaleus 63, 64
The Merchant of Venice 125
Maximilian (Prince of Holy Roman Empire) 109
Memoría e Reencontro 188
Mendes, Beatriz (daughter of Brianda and Diogo Mendes; later Nasi, Gracia, *la Chica*): in Ferrara 114; inheritance 109, 112, 121
Mendes, Brianda (daughter of Beatriz de Luna, later Nasi, Reyna; *q.v.*): becomes Reyna Nasi 113; leaves Portugal 107; name 106; suitor 109; in Venice 112
Mendes, Brianda (sister of Beatriz de Luna): daughter's inheritance 112; leaves Portugal 107; reconciled with Gracia Nasi 113; weds Diogo Mendes 107–9
Mendes, Diogo: in Antwerp 104–110, 122; born Meir Benveniste 24, 104; House of Mendes 70
Mendes, Francisco: born Semah Benveniste 24; dies 106; buried in Holy Land 117, 123; House of Mendes 104–6
Mendoza, Cardinal 39
Messina 44
Miguez, Agostinho (later Nasi, Samuel; *q.v.*) 103–4, 106, 107
Miguez, João (later Nasi, Joseph; *q.v.*): arrives in Ottoman Empire 118; court favorite 109; House of Mendes 110, 118, 124; rescue of aunt 112–13; ward of Beatriz de Luna 104–108
Mishnah 71, 130, 155
Mivhar hashira ha'ivrit b'italya 201
Mora 6
Morvedre 131, 135, 139, 140
Moses, Portuguese court mathematician 85
Moya, Emma 184
Museo Luso-Hebraico 196–7
Myanmar 189

Nasi, Gracia (formerly de Luna, Beatriz; *q.v.*) viii, xi, 22–24; biography 101–26; called *La Señora* 22; defender of Jews 51; diaspora 163, 166, 172; House of Mendes 8–9, 47, 102, 109; patient of Amatus Lusitanus 169; patron of Samuel Usque 171, 173; philanthropy 157, 174; sources for 227
Nasi, Gracia, *la Chica* (formerly Mendes, Brianda) 114, 121
Nasi, Joseph (formerly Miguez, João; *q.v.*): Almosnino's tribute 173–4; Coronel family 175; death of child 126; defender of Jews 51, 110; governor of Tiberius 123; inspires *The Jew of Malta* 125; named Duke of Naxos 122; Ottoman Empire 124; returns to Judaism 118; sources for 227; weds Reyna 118, 168
Nasi, Reyna (formerly Mendes, Brianda; *q.v.*): charitable acts 124; children 125–6; lifestyle 124; Moses Hamon 168; name 106–113; as printer 124–5; weds João 118
Nasi, Samuel (formerly Miguez, Agostinho; *q.v.*) 121–2, 124
Nasi family *see* de Luna, Beatriz; Miguez, Agostinho; Miguez, João; Mendes, Beatriz; Mendes, Diogo; Mendes, Francisco
National Jewish Population Survey 193
Navarra 15, 40, 66, 163
Naxos, Duke of *see* Nasi, Joseph
Nayarit 192
Nehar Pishon 70
neo-Platonists 42
Netanyahu 28, 50, 88, 94, 226
Nevi'im Rishonim 49
New Heavens 46
New Holland 177–8
New Mexico vii, ix; crypto Jews 7, 185, 188; legends 6; old Spanish 184
New York Jewish Week 195
da Nóbrega, Manoel 177
Nom de Dieu, J. R. Magdelena 149
Novinsky, Anita vii, 177, 179, 186, 228
Nuñez, Hilda 191

Obadiah 5
La Opinión de Baja California 192
Ordinances of Cifuentes 158
Orthodox 194, 195
Os Cristãos Novos no Século XX 186
Osório, Jerónimo 69, 212
Ottoman Empire 47, 101; Abraham Zacuto and descendents 72, 175; Amatus Lusitanus 153, 168–71; crypto Judaism 183; destination and diaspora 14, 107, 109, 162, 163–175, 177, 180; Francisco Coronel 175; Gracia Nasi 9, 110–11, 112, 115–24; Isaac Abravanel 44, 56; Joseph Nasi as Duke of Naxos 51; Moses Almosnino 173–75; Moses Hamon 166–8; Saadiah Longo 172–3; Samuel Usque 171–2, 175; sources on 227; sultans 20, 40

Paolo, Amilcar 186
Padua 41, 48
Palermo 44
Palma 21, 131
Passover: Abravanel *Haggadah* 51; Luís de Santángel as boy 93; matzo/wine for poor 157; observance today 181–2; translation of Hebrew 141–2; wine 159
Passover Sacrifice 45

Paz, Octavio 97
Pedro IV (King of Aragón) 139
Pentateuch 29, 231
Pernumbuco 178
Perpignan 131, 149
Pesaro 118, 119,169
Petres 147
Philip of Habsburg (Archduke of Holy Roman Empire, later Charles I of Spain) 95
Pinel, Duarte *see* Usque, Abraham
Pinelo, Francisco 83
Poel, Jacob 63
Preto-Rodas 172
Principles of Faith 44, 48, 50
Ptolemy 63, 64
Purim 103, 142, 159
purity of blood laws 2, 95; see also *limpieza de sangre*

Quaestio de spiritualibus creatures 48

Ragusa: Amatus Lusitanus 169; diaspora of Gracia Nasi 107, 116, 227
Rambam *see* Maimonides
Rationalists 42
Recife 178
Reubeni, David 104
Los Reyes Católicos 1, 13, 17, 33, 83
Ribes, Jaume 21, 55
Riskin, Rabbi Shlomo 190
Rodrigo, court physician 85
Romero, Ysaque 143
Romi, Solomon 132
Ronda 7
Rosenblatt. Gary 195
Roth, Cecil: famous sixteenth century women 102; Gracia Nasi 104, 105, 108, 112, 113, 119, 125; Inquisition 2, 76; New Christians in Brazil 177; Saadiah Longo 172; as source 227, 228
Rueda 150

El Sabio see James I
Sagres 54, 55, 56, 67
Salamanca 20, 21, 226; Abraham Zacuto 56, 57, 59, 63, 65–6, 72; Amatus Lusitanus 169; Columbus 85–6;

Salas, Carlos Samuel: Congregación Hebrea de Baja California 191; rabbi 191–2
Salomo, Isaach 152
Salonika: Amatus Lusitanus 153, 166, 169; as diaspora 116, 163, 180; Gracia Nasi 116, 117, 119, 123; Saadiah Longo 173–4; Samuel Abravanel 44; Samuel Usque 171–2

The Salvation of His Anointed 46
Sánchez, Gabriel: courtier 88; Inquisition 76, 91; Luís de Santángel 83; Royal Treasurer 8; supporter of Columbus 86, 87
Sánchez, Pedro 88
Sánchez-Blanco 88, 97
Santa Hermandad 83, 231
Santa María la Blanca 75
Santángel, Luís de *see* de Santángel, Luís
Santángel, Luís de, of Zaragoza *see* de Santángel, Luís, of Zaragoza
Santángel family *see* de Santángel family
São Tomé 39, 169, 171
Saporta, Astruch 149
Saving Remnants, Feeling Jewish in America 194
Scheindlin, Raymond P. vii, 201
Schirmann, Hayim 201
Schwarz, Samuel 186, 188
The Scribe — Journal of Babylonian Jewry 189
Sebastia, J. Doñate 149, 215, 216
Seder Zemannim 173
Sedycias 178
Sefarad: origins of word 2, 5, 231
Sefer Yohassin (The Book of Lineage) 57, 71–73
Segovia 128, 131
Sela, Eliezer 189
Selayo, Juan 61, 63
Seneca 33
Seneor, Abraham: argues against expulsion 18, 37, 38, 175; Battle of Granada 36, 37, 65; chief tax farmer 34; conversion 39, 175; Coronel descendants 175; crown rabbi 136–7; Royal Counselor 8
La Señora see Nasi, Gracia
Sephardic Jews 231
Serrano 88
Sevilla: livelihood 149; massacres of 1391 28, 78, 131
Sforza, Caterina 102
Shakespeare 126
Shearith Israel 178
Shem Tov Ardutiel xviii
Shiloh 190
Shivrei Huhot 172
shohet 140
Sholal, Rabbi Isaac 72
Sicily 34, 42, 45, 88, 96, 152
Simms, Norman 177, 178, 228
Society for Crypto-Judaic Studies vii, 188
Soncino, Rabbi Joshua 101, 119, 121
Spanish Armada 162
Statutes of Valladolid 144, 145
Suleiman the Magnificent 107, 112, 168, 173
Synagogue Beth Eliahu 187

Tahuell, Homar 152
Tavys, Salomon 152
Teatro Nacional D. Maria II 188
Tenenbaum, Rabbi Edward M. 192
Tiberius 101, 117, 123, 124, 126, 143
Tijuana 191, 192, 195
Tikkun Olam 198
Tish Ba'av 15
Tobin, Gary 193
Toledo: center of Jewish scholarship 142; Ibn Shoshan Synagogue 75; Isaac Abravanel 34, 35; livelihood 149; massacres of 1391 78, 130, 131; restrictions on Jews 95, 138; *yeshiva* 59
Tomar 196–7
Tortosa: *aljama* officers 135; Disputation at 77, 78, 138; economy and livelihood 147, 149, 150, 152; massacres of 1391, 131; slaughterhouse 143
El Tránsito 8, 142
Tratado de las Influencias del Cielo 64, 72
Treatise on the Spheres 67
Trichardt, Louis 189
Tristão, Nuno 54
Trujillo: *aljama* 135; demographics and history 128–9; economy and livelihood 146–7, 150; hosting travelers 143; massacres of 1391 131; relations among Jews 136–7; relations with Crown 132–4; restrictions on Jews 138; theft and attacks 152
Turkey *see* Ottoman Empire
Twain, Mark 198, 199

Uganda 191
Usque, Abraham 114
Usque, Samuel: author of *Consolaçam as tribulaçoens de Israel* 114–5; biography 171–2; diaspora 166; praises Turkey 175; sources on 227, 228; tribute to Gracia Nasi 124

Valencia: Abravanels leave Spain 15–6, 37, 40; *aljama* officers 135; Columbus monument 98; de Santángel enterprises 79–81, 93; de Santángel home 82; de Santángel origins 77, 78; Jews trading with Muslims 147; *La Lonja* 79; loan for Columbus voyage 87; massacres of 1391 131, 142; money lending 154
Vatican 44, 163
Vaz Teixeira, Tristão 54
Vecinho, Joseph: converts to Catholicism 70; court mathematician and explorations 56, 67; opposes Columbus voyage 85; student of Abraham Zacuto 21; translates *Hajibbur Hagadol* 61, 63, 66
Venice: Gracia Nasi 107, 110–2, 115, 117; Isaac Abravanel 45–8; Judah Abravanel 43, 201; *The Merchant of Venice* 125; Portuguese *converso* escape route 106; spice trade 56, 70, 105
Vera Cruz 193
Viseu, Duke of 31, 47; *see also* Braganza

Wakin, Daniel J. 193
The Wall Street Journal 196
Weisel, Rabbi Mimi 192
Wells of Salvation 46

Yahrzeit 142, 231
Yemen 189
Yerro, Nuno 152
Yom Kippur: changing practice 180; release of *converso* oaths 98, 100, 103–4, 184

Zacuto, Abraham ben Samuel: as astronomer 20, 53; biography 53–73; Columbus 85, 175; diaspora 71–73, 163, 166; expulsion from Portugal 69–70; expulsion from Spain 65–66; *Hajibbur Hagadol* or *Almanach Perpetuum* 56, 61–63; Portuguese court astronomer and explorations 66–68; *Sefer Yohassin* 71–72; sources on 226; student of Isaac Aboab and Talmud 35, 59, 142; *Tratado de las Influencias del Cielo* 64–5; University of Salamanca 59–60
Zacuto, Rabbi Abraham, *el Viejo* 57
Zalmero, Salamo 147
Zaragoza 19, 65, 76, 88, 89, 142
Zarco, Gonçalvo 54
Zeyt, Abraham 147

www.ingramcontent.com/pod-product-compliance
Ingram Content Group UK Ltd.
Pitfield, Milton Keynes, MK11 3LW, UK
UKHW041938140426
5217IPUK00014B/543